WITHDRAWN

Theories
of Ethnicity

Recent Titles in Contributions in Sociology

THEORIES OF ETHNICITY

A CRITICAL APPRAISAL

Richard H. Thompson

CONTRIBUTIONS IN SOCIOLOGY, NUMBER 82

GREENWOOD PRESS
New York • Westport, Connecticut • London

Library of Congress Cataloging-in-Publication Data

Thompson, Richard H.
    Theories of ethnicity : a critical appraisal / Richard H. Thompson.
        p.   cm.—(Contributions in sociology, ISSN 0084–9278 ; no.
82)
    Bibliography: p.
    Includes index.
    ISBN 0–313–26636–0 (lib. bdg. : alk. paper)
    1. Ethnicity. 2. Race. 3. Ethnic relations—Economic aspects.
I. Title. II. Series.
GN495.6.T47   1989
305.8—dc20   89–2120

British Library Cataloguing in Publication Data is available.

Library of Congress Catalog Card Number: 89–2120
ISBN: 0–313–26636–0
ISSN: 0084–9278

First published in 1989

Greenwood Press, Inc.
88 Post Road West, Westport, Connecticut 06881

Printed in the United States of America

The paper used in this book complies with the
Permanent Paper Standard issued by the National
Information Standards Organization (Z39.48–1984).

10 9 8 7 6 5 4 3 2 1

Copyright Acknowledgments

Grateful acknowledgment is given for permission to use excerpts from the following
works:

The Ethnic Phenomenon by Pierre L. van den Berghe. Copyright 1981 by Elsevier Science
Publishing Co., Inc.

Assimilation in American Life by Milton Gordon. Copyright 1964 by Oxford University
Press, New York.

Ethnicity: Theory and Experience by Nathan Glazer and Daniel P. Moynihan, eds.
Copyright 1975 by Harvard University Press. Reprinted by permission.

Europe and the People Without History by Eric Wolf. Copyright 1984 by the University of
California Press. Permission granted on behalf of The Regents of the University of
California and the University of California Press.

Class, Caste and Race by Oliver C. Cox. Copyright © 1959 by Oliver C. Cox. Reprinted
by permission of Monthly Review Foundation, New York.

Old Societies and New States by Clifford Geertz, ed. Copyright © 1963 by The Free Press.
Reprinted with permission of The Free Press, a division of Macmillan, Inc.

For my mother, Irene, and my late father, Dale Thompson

Contents

Preface

This work may be considered an ethnography of theory; an attempt at what Clifford Geertz calls "thick description," an interpretation of the flow of, in this case, theoretical discourse within the domain of race and ethnic relations.[1] Much as people from different cultures talk past one another by virtue of the different worldviews (or "paradigms") that structure their understandings of life, so, too, it is my contention, do social theorists miscommunicate by virtue of their different theoretical presumptions. Such miscommunication does not stem, as is sometimes supposed, from different "languages" that talk about the same thing, but through mutually unintelligible vocabularies. The problem is more fundamental, and stems from underlying ontological and epistemological differences about human nature and society. That is, theorists disagree about how to *conceive* the problem of racial and ethnic inequality and discover the "facts" concerning it even as they agree that the issue is a problem of human existence that needs to be confronted.

This book is not, then, an exercise in translation, for that is inadequate, or an attempt at reconciliation, for that is impossible. It is a comparative *critical* study; critical in the sense of considering the merits and demerits of competing models so that readers might judge accordingly and thereby *choose*. The act of choosing is necessary, particularly for Americans, who these days are too quick to pat themselves on the back for the "progress" that has been made in dealing with their "race problem." Much of this progress is illusory, and sadly, W. E. B. Dubois' contention more than sixty years ago that "the problem of the twentieth century is the problem of the color-line" remains true today.[2] My own act of choosing is apparent in the pages that follow, but I have striven to provide readers with the rationale underpinning that choice and with the understanding that their choices may be every bit as informed, yet different. At the very least, I hope to have provided no room for neutrality.

Notes

1. Clifford Geertz, "Thick Description: Toward an Interpretive Theory of Culture," in Clifford Geertz, *The Interpretation of Cultures*. New York: Basic Books, 1973, pp. 3–30.

2. Quoted in *Eyes on the Prize: America's Civil Rights Years*, ed. Clayborne Carson, et al. New York: Penguin, 1987, p. 289.

Acknowledgments

Any work of criticism owes its greatest debt to those scholars whose writings have provided grist for the mill. Regardless of my appraisal of them, I am indebted to their contributions, which have made this study possible. In particular I thank Pierre L. van den Berghe, whose work figures prominently in Chapter 2 and elsewhere, and two anonymous reviewers who were kind enough to read an early draft and, despite some fundamental disagreements, provide criticisms and encouragement for the largely rewritten and, much improved version at hand. I also thank Professor Milton Fisk, my friend and former teacher, who will recognize his influence throughout, especially in the Introduction and the final chapter. I hope I have not disappointed him too much.

Several colleagues and friends at James Madison University—Bruce Busching, Steve Gibbons, John Sweigart, Robert Loube, Richard Lippke, and, especially, Vardaman R. Smith—read and commented on various portions of the manuscript and provided both encouragement and expertise. They should not be blamed for the remaining ineptitude, since they tried on numerous occasions to remove it, only to be confronted by my stubbornness. My wife, Ernestene, and my sons, Matthew and Andrew, as always provided unflinching support and love even though they suffered the brunt of the anxieties and terrible moods I heaped upon them. I thank them most of all.

Finally, this work was made possible by the generous fellowship support of the National Endowment for the Humanities, which enabled me to take a year's leave from teaching, and by a summer research grant from James Madison University. I am most appreciative to both.

Theories
of Ethnicity

1

Introduction

ETHNICITY AND HUMAN NATURE

This book is a critique of relatively recent theories purporting to explain humankind's "ethnic nature"—the propensity of individuals and groups to be organized and classified on the basis of race (i.e., physical or morphological characteristics) or ethnicity ("tribal," linguistic, national, religious, or other cultural characteristics). Manifestations of this ethnic nature everywhere surround us, from the almost-taken-for-granted symbols of dress, dialect, and other visible signs people use to indicate affiliation to the more serious and violent expressions of ethnicity that almost daily make headline news:

40 KILLED AS SECTARIAN FIGHTING INCREASES IN LEBANON

VIOLENCE AFTER SATURDAY KLAN RALLY

AREA PALESTINIANS WANT A HOMELAND

STUDY FINDS BLACK ECONOMIC GROWTH NOT ENOUGH

IRISH GUERRILLAS VOW REVENGE

Examples such as these, culled from a single week's issues of a major metropolitan newspaper, could be extended ad infinitum. This is hardly necessary, for in the 1980s neither scholar nor layperson doubts the ubiquity or importance of the ethnic factor in domestic and international affairs.

This almost universal acknowledgment of the ethnic factor is a recent phenomenon, however, and its historical genesis is quite easily traced. To those whose formal educations spanned, as did mine, the decades of the 1950s and 1960s, ethnicity (or, more popularly, "ethnic relations") was rarely mentioned, and then only to be denied or relegated to relative insignificance for the understanding of American life. Not only did the potential salience of ethnic factors conflict with our melting pot ideology, but sociologists of the period produced a considerable amount of good research that indicated that ethnic affiliation, while neither absent in the present nor historically unimportant, was nevertheless sufficiently malleable to be declining in significance in terms of its impact on the American social structure. The theoretical paradigm of this period was "assimilationism." Its appropriateness for understanding American ethnic relations was virtually unquestioned despite the fact that its validity as a scientific theory rested on a colossal misreading of Robert Park's pioneering work.[1]

To be sure, the "Negro question" remained a stubborn anomaly. But the fact that black Americans had not integrated into the melting pot could be passed over on the grounds that current discrimination represented a heinous survival from slavery. Blacks did suffer, it was admitted, but only because white attitudes had not yet sufficiently changed to permit blacks access to the dominant opportunity structure. Moreover, Afro-Americans, as a result of their collective slave and post-slave experiences, were "behind" other Americans in skills necessary to compete in a technologically complex society. They simply had more catching up to do, a matter that required, presumably, only time. A current notion that the nature of our capitalist system actually benefited from racism was never entertained—at least not in mainstream scientific or public consciousness.[2] The general optimism embodied in the assimilationism perspective called forth the following response: "Yes, the 'Negro situation' is not something we're proud of, but things are getting better."

Three concurrent events during the 1960s shook both our optimism and our naivete. The Civil Rights Movement, the Vietnam War, and a period of impressive economic prosperity combined in a way that revealed to many Americans the contradictory and oppressive aspects of their social system. The short-lived economic boom and the liberal policies of the Johnson administration provided the framework within which Afro-Americans especially could press their longstanding claims on the state. The struggles of Martin Luther King and his movement and, later, the violent urban ghetto riots pointed up the glaring contradictions between rich and poor, white and black. The Vietnam War became increasingly viewed as an unjust conflict, not only because we were not winning it, but also because its original legitimation—preserving democracy and preventing communist aggression—became an empty slogan amid 58,000 disproportionately poor and black American dead. In this context the minority view that the war was a brutal example of American imperialism gained more, though never widespread, acceptance.

The extension of our domestic malaise to world events in general was an easy step to accomplish. We took some solace in the fact that if race relations in the United States were bad, in South Africa they were much worse. We continued to apply salve to our wounds by noting that much of the conflict in the world appeared to have ethnic roots: the Protestant-Catholic conflict in Northern Ireland, the Arab-Jew struggles in the Middle East, Hindu-Muslim clashes in India, Pakistan and Bangladesh, and the multitude of "tribal wars" that still plague Africa. By the early 1970s scholars began asking new questions—the very opposite of those posed by assimilationists—"Why do ethnic and racial affiliations persist, seem particularly resistant to change, and appear to be particularly effective for organizing conflict? Why haven't ethnic ties disappeared, or at least become subordinated to other ties, such as class and occupation, as the assimilationists had predicted?"

This renewed concern with ethnic and racial issues, spurred by increased state attention and expenditures, represented a windfall for the social sciences. One commentator, during a speech in 1977, quite accurately noted that ethnicity is the social sciences' newest growth industry. New journals devoted to ethnicity proliferated, universities established ethnic studies programs by the score, and new textbooks on racial and ethnic studies spread as quickly and were received with as much enthusiasm as dandelions on a well-manicured lawn. Amid this scientific euphoria, we have been told that ethnicity is a cultural phenomenon, a political phenomenon, a psychological process, symbolic expression, social organization, and, most recently, a biological phenomenon. Ethnicity is most (though not all) of these things, a fact that accounts in part for the eclecticism and obscurantism so prevalent in the field of ethnic relations.

As a result of all this attention, theories of race and ethnicity have proliferated to the point where, to use Alan Garfinkel's expression, "we are surrounded by explanations."[3] Students are engulfed in what they view as a bewildering array of theories that claim to explain the "ethnic phenomenon," and the precocious among them have the temerity to ask some rather unsettling questions about their interrelationships. "Are these theories (sociobiology and assimilationism, for example) explaining the same phenomena? Are they compatible, or incompatible with one another? Is each asking the same questions as the other and arriving at different answers? Or are the differences between them the result of the different questions asked? What assumptions are implicit in these theories, and what is the quality of the evidence they offer in support of their positions?" Most unnerving is the most important question of all: "What difference does it make? What are the consequences of my (or perhaps the state) holding to one theory to the exclusion of others?"

In attempting to answer these questions (usually with a good deal of stammering) I have become acutely aware of how competing theories of ethnicity talk past one another for failure to agree not on that which needs to be explained, but on what an adequate explanation is. Most theories agree, for example, that what is in need of explanation is the continued persistence of racial and ethnic factors in human social relations. More particularly, they agree that racial and ethnic *inequalities*, particular forms of social inequality, are the root cause of the continued salience of racial and ethnic criteria. In short, there is a good deal of consensus on the "facts of the matter," but vociferous debate concerning how to best account for those "facts." Racial inequality can be (and is) explained as the result of differential, inherited potentials among the "races," the propensity for humans to maximize inclusive fitness, the dominance of the capitalist world-system, the tendency for governments to use race and ethnicity for the allocation of social rewards, a historical "leftover," or the expression of some primordial need for ethnic and racial affiliation.

To again quote Garfinkel, "now what do all these explanations have to do with one another?"[4] Some are clearly incompatible, while others perhaps seek explanations at different levels. What seems to be needed currently is not another new theory of ethnicity, but a critical appraisal of those that already exist. This book attempts to begin such an appraisal by considering the claims made by several of the more recent and important explanations of ethnicity in terms of their assumptions, methods, and substantive hypotheses. Beyond this I hope to at least indicate the ways in which these theories relate or do not relate to one another, as well as comment on the relative adequacy of each theory's explanation of racial and ethnic inequality.

Theories as Worldviews

Comparing the relative adequacy of competing social theories is among the thornier problems in contemporary social science. The reason for this is that different theoretical frameworks are much like "worldviews" in the traditional anthropological sense of that term. Social facts are interpreted through different visions and versions of the social world that are rooted in certain fundamental assumptions pertaining to human nature and society. Theoretical assumptions, much like basic cultural assumptions, tend to be so deeply held, so much a part of one's personal commitment, that not only are they resistant to refutation by the "facts," but instead tend to transform the nature and significance of those "facts" themselves.

What constitutes poverty, or unemployment, or racism at the conceptual level is as much a theoretical product as the purported causes of these phenomena. Thus people who hold widely divergent theoretical positions might agree that racial inequality "exists," but they have very different ideas about both the definition of inequality and its significance. Social theoreticians, despite their professed open-mindedness and value-free dedication to knowledge and the pursuit of truth, are not unlike a group of New Guinea gardeners who, having been told by an enterprising young anthropologist that their prescribed marriage rule of matrilateral cross-cousin marriage was not followed in 85 percent of all known marriages, proceeded to teach the young man how to do kinship charts the *right* way.[5]

Even when specialists agree that racial and ethnic inequality are the major issues, they vehemently disagree about why they exist, their causes, and potential remedies. These disagreements are not, at root, moral ones. The theorists discussed in this book generally abhor the various forms of racial and ethnic inequalities, and regard them as unjust and socially and personally disabling kinds of human relations. But even as they are abhorred, they are nevertheless regarded by some as natural expressions of a biologically based human nature, or a necessary or inevitable outcome of intergroup conflict and social development. Such an assessment argues that racial and ethnic inequalities are to be expected and, for some at least, to be lived with. Others see in racial and ethnic inequality the failure of social institutions to meet basic human needs and rights, and argue that such institutions have been humanly created and can thus be human(e)ly transformed. This tension between "accept it" versus "change it" theories is a central aspect of this book.

The issue in the field of race and ethnicity, as I see it, then, is the conflict among different theoretical versions that attempt to explain the same basic phenomena. This makes an appraisal of these theories a currently important task. But because works dealing with theory often evoke cries of "academic concern only" (or, worse, produce yawns), I can offer one further justification of why a theoretical appraisal is necessary. Just as cultural worldviews are blueprints for social understanding and social practice, so, too, are theoretical worldviews potential blueprints for social action. As Brian Fay has eloquently argued, there is "an intimate connection that exists between the ideas that we have and the sort of life we lead."[6] Every theory, as a set of ideas, necessarily implies particular ways that should be lived and that, under certain conditions, may in fact *be* lived. Although this work is not primarily concerned with this link between theory and practice, I have tried to indicate in my appraisal of each theory the kinds of social (and political) practices it leads to and the kind of social world it envisions.

The problem of *how* to analyze contending theories of race and ethnicity remains, however. Carrying the analogy between theoretical structures and worldviews further reveals the difficulty of this enterprise. Anthropology has, almost since its inception, grappled with the issue of how to compare different worldviews (or cultural systems) in such a way that we might choose some as "adequate and/or good" and discard others as "inadequate and/or bad." As an anthropologist myself, I am well aware of the disputes among the relativists, the absolutists, and the contextualists—well enough aware to maintain that it is not possible to develop a set of agreed-upon criteria against which to judge the worth of particular cultures. A culture can perhaps be judged internally (as opposed to comparison with other cultures)—that is, according to the particular standards and claims it makes for itself (this is the contextualist position)—but even this procedure requires the assumption that such internal standards and claims should be the basis for analysis and themselves beyond critique.

Philosophers of science have had a similarly difficult time establishing criteria by which to either compare or judge the adequacy of different theories. Positivist social science, the dominant metatheory in Western science, has, it seems, been sufficiently discredited so as not to permit the use of its basic principles of deductive-nomological accounts, a belief in a neutral observation language, and its value-free ideal of scientific knowledge for theoretical comparison.[7] Unfortunately no rival metatheory exists that permits valid comparison among rival theories. Thus the theories presented here are not so much compared as juxtaposed. My critique of each is primarily internal to them. I have attempted to lay bare the sometimes hidden assumptions and method of each theory and critique it according to its own stated assumptions. I have thus tried to assess the degree to which each theory is internally consistent, how it accounts for the "facts" pertaining to racial and ethnic relations, its comprehensiveness—that is, its ability to explain much rather than little, and the particular vision of the world it offers up. By means of this procedure certain of the theories discussed are more "adequate" than others, though by no means necessarily valid or true. I recognize that this procedure is only partially satisfactory.

I have used two principal guides in selecting the theories discussed here. First, I have chosen those approaches that currently serve as the basis of most of the work being written in the field of race and ethnic relations. Second, I have included works that have the status of theory, that is, works that are sufficiently general in their application and that propose an overall framework, based on a set of axioms or assumptions, by which to understand interethnic relations.

Using these criteria has produced a mix that, to some readers, may appear strange or, at least, narrow. The second chapter considers sociobiology, even though it clearly does not meet the first criterion above.

Only one major work has been published on the sociobiology of race and ethnicity, and it certainly represents a minority position within the field. Nevertheless, I have included it because it meets the second criterion better than most other theories and because its influence on both the scholarly community and the lay public appears to be increasing.

The third chapter considers what are often referred to as "primordialist" conceptions of ethnicity. To my knowledge, reference to ethnic or racial groups as primordial or basic to human self-definition and affiliation was first made by Edward Shils in 1957.[8] Since then primordialism has come to represent two quite different strains of theory, one of which I call the "natural" school, the other being the "social-historical" school represented by Clifford Geertz. These two varieties are discussed along with the general status of primordialism as a theory of race and ethnic relations.

Chapter 4 discusses assimilationism, which, as mentioned earlier, was the dominant paradigm in race and ethnic relations up through the middle of the 1970s. Although assimilationism primarily focuses on racial and ethnic change rather than persistence, its failure to explain the retarded rate of Afro-American assimilation in the United States spawned a new, yet related approach to explain ethnic persistence—what is usually called the "new ethnicity." Both assimilationism and the "new ethnicity" have been thoroughly critiqued by others, and my assessment of them relies heavily on these prior critiques. There is thus little that is new in this chapter. I have included it because assimilationist explanations remain important in any discussion of race and ethnicity, and because critiquing some of its implicit assumptions regarding the economy and the state provides clues to the development of later, more "radical" approaches.

Chapters 5 and 6 evaluate two of the most influential "radical" theories of race and ethnicity. Chapter 5 considers Immanuel Wallerstein's world-system theory and his application of it to racial and ethnic relations. Chapter 6 is devoted to historical materialist or Marxist approaches to race and ethnicity. In this chapter I attempt to develop a more open-ended Marxist theory in contradistinction to the functionalist varieties of Marxism that dominate theorizing on racial and ethnic social relations. Such an account must consider not only the functional aspects of racial stratification and racism, but also explain their structural underpinnings and transformational potentials. The final chapter summarizes my findings and concludes with brief remarks concerning theoretical choice.

Certain works have been omitted despite their continuing influence on students of race and ethnicity. The omission of the work of Fredrik Barth will no doubt strike many anthropologists as glaring.[9] Barth's *Ethnic Groups and Boundaries* has been required reading since its appearance in 1969, and has greatly influenced the current generation of anthropologists interested in ethnicity. His major contribution was to

reorient anthropological thinking away from the then dominant conception of "ethnic groups as cultural units" to the now prevailing view
of ethnicity as social organization. This was a much needed corrective
in anthropology, but this view was already accepted in the other social
sciences. Despite this important conceptualization, Barth's contribution
to ethnic theory has not been substantial.[10]

Another potentially important perspective neglected here is Michael
Banton's "rational choice theory" put forward in his recent book, *Racial
and Ethnic Competition* (1983). This book is currently receiving a good
deal of attention, especially in England, such that a brief summary of
Banton's position here seems in order, if only to justify its exclusion from
the chapters that follow.[11] Banton summarizes the main tenets of rational
choice theory as follows:

The theory that is now proposed shares with rational choice theories in other
fields two presuppositions: (a) that individuals act so as to maximize net advantage; and (b) that actions at one moment of time influence and restrict alternatives
between which individuals will have to choose on subsequent occasions....

The theory holds that:

1 Individuals utilize physical and cultural differences in order to create groups
and categories by the processes of inclusion and exclusion.

2 Ethnic processes result from inclusive and racial categories from exclusive
processes.

3 When groups interact, processes of change affect their boundaries in ways
determined by the form and intensity of competition; and, in particular, when
people compete as individuals this tends to dissolve the boundaries that define
the groups, whereas when they compete as groups this reinforces those boundaries.

According to the two presuppositions, individuals are pictured as optimizing:
they select the alternatives which give them the greatest benefits relative to costs,
and their choices have consequences for future actions by them and others. It
is assumed that people have wants or goals that cannot all be realized since they
live in a world of scarcity.[12]

As Banton recognizes, rational choice theory is rooted in what is usually
called "methodological individualism," an ontology that views humans
not primarily as social beings, but as individual cost-benefit maximizers
making rational choices from among whatever alternatives "society" provides. This view is basic to neo-classical economics and, as I discuss at
length in Chapter 2, sociobiology. In Chapter 2 I critique this ontology
and argue that its neglect of the structural dimension, that is, the social
milieu within which individual choices are made, leads to a weak and
incomplete theory of race and ethnicity. This critique thus applies, in
the main, to Banton's presuppositions.

It is to Banton's credit, however, that he recognizes the limitations of the rational choice position. As he says, "the theory recognizes that the alternatives [the ranges of choices permitted the individual] are part of structures inherited from the past which generate as well as regulate conflict. In applying the theory it may be more important to account for the particular range of alternatives available to individuals than to analyse choices between them."[13] As Banton admits, rational choice theory per se cannot account for these structures. The potential promise of this theory may be to provide an individualist model that is compatible with various structural accounts.

I also do not discuss the varieties of racist theories of either the nineteenth or twentieth century that argue that phenotypical differences among human populations are causally related to intellectual, psychological, or social abilities. These theories, especially those based on IQ studies that purport to explain inequalities among racial groups by alleged significant differences in mean group intelligence, remain powerful ideologies in a racially stratified society such as the United States.[14] But such theories have been sufficiently discredited scientifically and require no further elaboration.

I have not attempted to review the full range of literature applicable to the theories discussed. Such a task is beyond the purpose of this book and, to that extent only, unnecessary. Rather, I have stressed those influential works that best capture or illustrate the essentials of each theory. This approach does not deny the contributions that have been made to each theory by people who work within their particular traditions. But to the extent that these contributions are additions to or a fine-tuning of the basic theory and have not, therefore, involved a substantial reformulation, they have not been included.

Ethnicity and Human Nature

At the outset I contended that ethnicity is a particular aspect of human nature. That is, various human behaviors that are usually interpreted as ethnic behaviors are but a certain kind of human behavior we label "ethnic" rather than "class," "political," "psychological," or other names we might assign to those behaviors. In other words, there is the tendency (and to some extent the necessity) in science to break up the totality of human behaviors into various kinds, each kind being defined by some attribute the scientist chooses to emphasize. What is important to grasp is the degree to which this naming or labeling is both difficult and somewhat arbitrary. Let me give a specific example taken from my own research.

When I was conducting fieldwork in Toronto's Chinese community in 1977, immigrant Chinese parents launched a campaign directed to-

ward the City School Board to have incorporated into the regular curriculum a minimum amount of Chinese language instruction in two
elementary schools in which more than 90 percent of the students were
Chinese. Although the parents were pleased that their children were
quickly becoming literate in English, they were concerned about the
rapid deterioration of their children's Chinese language skills. They had
observed that by the fourth or fifth grade, children had developed negative feelings toward their Chinese heritage, feelings that led them to
refuse to speak Chinese to their monolingual parents (and ultimately to
lose the ability to speak Chinese) and to view their parents as poor,
uneducated, and backward people.

The parents believed that if Chinese language was taught as part of
the regular school curriculum, if only for a half hour a day, their children
would view their heritage in a more positive light and would perhaps
maintain their proficiency in spoken Chinese, thus leading to a better
relationship between them and their parents. The parents were respond-
ing to a very real threat. They understood through hard experience that
acculturation to the dominant Canadian Anglophone society, something
they sincerely wanted for their children, carried with it the dissolution
of the children's native skills and heritage. The parents believed, not
unrealistically, that acculturation could occur without sacrificing all of
Chinese culture, that their children might learn to be bicultural and
bilingual and, in the process, be spared the marginality often suffered
by others with Anglo-Canadian characteristics housed in Asian bodies.

By anyone's definition the campaign conducted by the Chinese parents
would be called "ethnic." The parents, members of an ethnic group—a
culturally distinct population set apart in various ways from the dominant
Canadian population—were asserting their "ethnic nature" by calling for
a program to institutionalize certain aspects of their Chinese heritage.
But a great deal more than just Chinese ethnicity was being expressed
through their behavior. Insofar as they were making a claim on the state,
the parents were expressing their political nature as well. At the same
time, as members of a minority group who are overwhelmingly confined
to low-paying proletarian positions in an ethnic economy, the Chinese
parents were exhibiting their "class nature" by attempting to have a
greater say regarding how institutions that dominate their lives are structured. What is more, the parents were motivated to act out of deeply
felt needs concerning the psychological well-being of the family and later
frustrations their children might experience.

It is appropriate to label this example "ethnic behavior." Had a similar
campaign been launched by parents in my own white, middle-class neighborhood concerning the establishment, let's say, of computer compe-
tency for children, we would not view this as an ethnic issue. This is
because the issue has nothing to do with cultural differences between

two or more groups who define themselves or are defined by others as culturally (or racially) distinct. We may thus define "ethnic behaviors" as those human behaviors that are, at a *minimum*, based on *cultural or physical criteria in a social context in which these criteria are relevant*. But as the example above illustrates, even those behaviors properly termed "ethnic" are not simply ethnic behaviors, or only ethnic behaviors, or even primarily ethnic behaviors. Rather, the view taken here requires us to interpret any human behavior as a complexity within an even more complex totality of human behavior in general.

This view has two important implications for theories of ethnicity. First, any theory that explains ethnicity by a simple, atomistic conception of human behavior is, at the very least, inadequate, inasmuch as it reduces complex behavior to a simple, and usually single, determinant. Second, inasmuch as ethnic behavior is only a kind of human behavior in general, theories of ethnicity must, at least implicitly, be based on an overall conception of human behavior in general, that is, be rooted in a general theory of human nature.

This brings us to the relation between ethnicity and human nature and to a consideration of what theories of ethnicity are supposed to do. Using the same example of the Chinese parents' efforts to institute Chinese language into the school system, we would ask "What explains the parents' behavior? What reason or reasons have led to or 'caused' the parents to assert their ethnicity?" These are theoretical questions, since theories are, at root, explanations of human behavior. A great number of explanations or theories might be offered, particularly if one were to ask the participants themselves (i.e., the parents, teachers, school board members, etc.). More likely than not, their explanations would correspond to some degree with those that have been offered by social scientists. These theories, though widely divergent in specifics, may be grouped into two general categories. On the one hand, people might argue that the Chinese were asserting their ethnicity because it is *natural* to do so. By "natural" I mean any explanation that regards our ethnic nature as an essential aspect of human nature. Just as needs for food, sex, sociability, and so on are biologically inherent, unalterable aspects of human existence, so, too, is the need for ethnic expression.

Two recent theories of ethnicity explain ethnic persistence in precisely this way. The more recent of these, the sociobiological theory, explains ethnicity as a natural expression of our genetic nature; a nature that is to be discovered ultimately in the structure of the gene itself. The second theory, which has been termed the "primordial sentiments" theory, asserts that expressions of ethnicity fulfill the human psychological need for identity, that human beings, by their nature, have a basic, primordial need for group affiliation that is best satisfied by the maintenance of an ethnic identity.

On the other hand, people might argue that there is nothing inherent about the Chinese parents' behavior. Instead, they were expressing their ethnic nature because the social situation or context in which they live has made their "Chineseness" a relevant aspect of their lives. The argument might go something like this. Before moving to Canada from Hong Kong or China, the Chinese parents did not exhibit their ethnic nature. They lived in a social system primarily based on Chinese language and culture, and, as a result, possessed the linguistic and cultural attributes necessary to full participation in their native societies. On immigration to Canada the parents found themselves in a society in which their inability to speak English had a forceful effect on their lives. They could only take jobs that employed a non-English-speaking or Chinese-speaking labor force. In Toronto these jobs consisted of work in the garment factories or in the Chinese ethnic economy of restaurants and tourist shops, where wages are low, job security is practically nonexistent, and the potential for exploitation is high. The Chinese, by virtue of their "Chineseness," became entrenched in a minority status in Canada, one that would be difficult to break out of unless they learned to be literate in English and acquired the cultural patterns of Canadian Anglophone society. For these reasons the Chinese parents were anxious for their children to acculturate—that is, learn the language and culture of Canada—so they would be able to avail themselves of opportunities outside the ethnic subsystem. But the parents also understood that Canada, like most pluralist states, uses racial classifications—systems of categorizing people according to physical characteristics such as skin color—and attaches social significance to them. The parents thus knew that their children, despite their acculturation to the dominant culture, would always be considered "Chinese" and expected to at least value, if not be proficient in, their cultural heritage. The actions of the parents were also determined, to some extent, by Canada's ethnic policy of bilingualism within a multicultural framework, a policy that at least pays lip service to the retention and "respect" of immigrant cultures. The parents believed that Canada had legitimated their ethnicity and was required to support their efforts to maintain or at least positively value Chinese language and culture.

This explanation emphasizes the particular social context in which the Chinese live and sees the assertion of Chinese ethnicity as complexly determined by economic, political, and cultural factors. Theories such as the one above may be called "social" theories of ethnicity because they explain ethnic behavior by social, rather than biological, forces. These theories differ from biological theories in that they regard human nature, at least those aspects of human nature such as ethnicity, not as largely fixed by evolution, but as changeable. Unlike biological theories, social theories argue that ethnic groups are made, not born, and thus view our ethnic nature as a socially determined nature.

Both types of theory are based on general conceptions of human nature itself. For this reason it is useful to examine more closely the major kinds of arguments that have been offered to explain human nature.

General Theories of Human Nature

Borrowing a framework developed by the social philosopher Milton Fisk, theories of human nature may be grouped into one of two basic kinds.[15] One class of theories can be called "universalist" because they assert a single, universal nature to all human beings regardless of social condition and kind of society in which they live. For example, a basic tenet of the Enlightenment philosophers, especially Locke, was that humans were, by nature, equally rational and free. This philosophy was an important instrument in undermining the old feudal system that saw different orders of human ranks and privileges as the creation of God. But the development of the new capitalist order soon posed a contradiction for Locke's philosophy. The new ruling class of capitalists appeared a great deal freer and more rational than did the poverty-stricken masses of the lower classes. In light of this new reality Locke could only respond that members of the working class were, "by the natural and unalterable state of things in the world, and the constitution of human affairs, unavoidably given over to invincible ignorance of those proofs on which others build."[16] Workers were, by nature, still free and rational, but their "invincible ignorance" prevented them from recognizing, not to mention asserting, their nature. Locke, when confronted by the multiplicity of human kinds, was ultimately led to view these different kinds as stemming from different natures, insofar as "rationality" and "invincible ignorance" are incompatible.

A type of universalist theory of human nature more relevant to ethnicity is the sociobiological theory, discussed in Chapter 2. This argument asserts that ethnic and racial sentiments are grounded in our genetic structure. Human (and indeed all animal) genes are predisposed to maximize their inclusive fitness, and ethnic and racial sentiments are but extensions of this maximizing nature. This view is universalist because it asserts a single, common nature held by all members of the species regardless of social or historical circumstance. (Most sociobiologists argue, somewhat contradictorily, that social and historical circumstances can profoundly affect the expression of this "ethnic nature," even to the point of its nonexistence. Chapter 2 deals with this issue in depth.)

Opposed to universalist theories are what may be called nonuniversalist theories of human nature. Theories of this type do not grant the existence of a single, universal human nature. Instead, they see multiple human kinds as these are expressed in the great variety of human societies and cultures. Nonuniversalists claim that there are many human natures that are produced by many different "causes." Thus nonuniversalists must, in order to uphold their view, define and classify these multiple human kinds and then discover what factors determine or produce these different kinds. As with universalist theories of human nature, it is possible to identify biological and social theories of a nonuniversalist sort.

Biological theories of multiple human natures argue that different human kinds are the product of different, unalterable biological natures. There are many varieties of theories that assert different biological natures for different groups within the species. In the field of race and ethnic relations, nonuniversalist biological theories are generally grouped under the rubric "scientific racism." These theories have been labeled "scientific" *not* because they have been validated by scientific procedures and are therefore "true" (in fact, they have yet to stand the test of scientific validation), but because they represent a century of effort on the part of philosophers, scientists, and other specialists to establish the veracity of important hereditary differences among human groups. These theories are termed "racist" because they argue that hereditary physical differences such as skin color and other morphological features determine important behaviors or capacities such as intelligence, emotional and psychological states, and social differences such as success and failure, power and powerlessness, and inequality. In other words, nonuniversalist biological theories pertaining to ethnicity argue that social relations among different ethnic and racial groups are the natural outcome of inborn, heritable, and essentially unalterable differences that are defined as characterizing the different "races" of humankind, such as Caucasians, Orientals, Negroes, and Indians. Such theories claim a natural, biological basis for the social fact that Afro-Americans are overrepresented in the lower classes of American society; that American Indians and other "inferior" races were savages and barbarians; that Europeans, by virtue of their "race superiority," are justified, by nature, to dominate the world; and a host of other specious arguments too numerous to list here. There clearly are multiple human natures, the racists maintain, owing to different biological potentialities among the species' multiple racial and ethnic groups.[17]

In opposition to racist theories are social theories of a nonuniversalist kind. Social theories accept the fact that phenotypic differences among human groups have not been shown to be linked to significant social or psychological behaviors, and reject the notion that social relations (relations among groups of people in a society; e.g., black-white relations in the United States) are the outcome of biological tendencies. Non-universalist social theories do stress the existence of multiple human kinds or "natures." However, they argue that significant human differences are the product of social, not biological, forces. For example, a white investment banker no doubt exhibits a different "nature" (the totality of his behavior) than a ghettoized, undereducated, and unemployed black man. But these different natures would be explained by a host of social factors such as family background, the social and psychological effects of racism, educational opportunities, and so on, and not in terms of inherited race differences. Such theories would draw on evidence that shows that black investment bankers tend to exhibit a "nature" much more similar to that of the white banker than to that of the unemployed black—an explanation that demonstrates the primacy of social roles in accounting for human nature.

Of the theories discussed in this book, sociobiology and the "naturalist strain" of primordialism are biologically based universalist theories, whereas the "social-historical strain" of primordialism, assimilationism, world-system theory, and Marxian approaches are socially based non-universalist theories. The degree to which these major types are compatible with or opposed to each other is discussed in the relevant chapters.

Another important criterion for comparing the theories discussed, be they social or biological, is their ontological basis. Theories of social behavior are, generally speaking, either "individualist" or "holistic" (i.e., "structural") in their ontology.[18] Individualist theories have at their basis explanations rooted in individual drives, motives, or characteristics of either a social or biological origin. Holistic theories, on the other hand, focus not on individuals per se, but on the structural interrelations among them, and assert these relations as necessary for adequate explanation. Sociobiology, primordialism, and assimilationism are individualist, whereas world-system theory and Marxian approaches are heavily structural. The importance of this distinction for understanding race and ethnicity is also discussed in the various chapters.

What Must Theories of Ethnicity Explain?

We have seen that those behaviors that are typically labeled "ethnic" are extremely complex and difficult to divorce from other kinds of behavior. For this reason I have maintained that theories of ethnicity are but subtheories of more general explanations of human action. But it is necessary to identify those aspects of human behavior to which theories of ethnicity specifically apply. The following list, though not exhaustive, embraces the major issues that surround the "ethnic phenomenon" and contains the basic questions any theory of ethnicity must address.

1. *Ethnic and racial classifications.* In all human societies people classify themselves and other people as belonging to certain categories. There are kin and nonkin, noblemen and commoners, chiefs and subjects, masters and servants, landlords and tenants, blacks and whites, Protestants and Jews, capitalists and workers, and so on. Some of these classifications are clearly restricted to certain kinds of society. In the United States, for example, we do not use classifications such as nobleman and commoner, nor is the master-slave category of antebellum times a socially significant classification today. Other categorizations are more universal, however. All societies distinguish kin from nonkin, although the particular criteria for determining kinship (degree of genetic relatedness, marriage, adoption, and so on) vary widely from society to society.

A major issue addressed by theories of ethnicity is the extent to which classifications of races and ethnic groups (e.g., blacks, whites, Orientals; or Protestants, Catholics, Jews) are relatively universal categorizations, and therefore found in most or all human societies, *and* whether or not such categorizations are the product of biological or social tendencies. For example, sociobiology argues that racial and ethnic categorizations are extensions of kinship classifications and, therefore, universal. Moreover, they argue that kinship classifications are the product of genetic processes and are thus "natural." If this is so, then ethnic and racial classifications are also genetic, insofar as they are extensions of kinship classifications. Social theories, on the other hand, claim that kinship systems are fundamentally social and that racial and ethnic classifications are not genetically programmed extensions of kinship.

2. *Ethnic and racial sentiments.* Human beings do not merely classify, but attach cultural significance or meaning to their classifications. In other words, classifications of people into kin and nonkin, nobleman and commoner, chief and subject carry with them constellations of feelings, beliefs, and sentiments that define and give meaning to these categories. Kin are *different* from nonkin and are to be interacted with differently than nonkin. Chiefs are different from subjects, and social behavior must reflect these putative differences. In the same way, the racial classification of blacks and whites in the United States has meaning and social significance only to the extent that blacks and whites are differentiated from each other on dimensions *other than* skin pigmentation. If people in the United States believed that blacks and whites are different only with respect to certain physical differences and that such physical differences have no social or cultural significance, then such a classification would soon go the way of other archaic classifications. But such is not the case. People *do believe* that there are socially meaningful differences between blacks and whites; that whites, by virtue of their being white, are better suited for this, and blacks, by virtue of their being black, are better suited for that. This is the classic definition of racism. Related to racism is

ethnocentrism, the belief that one's own group (be it an ethnic group or national group) is superior to other groups. At issue is whether such racial, ethnic, or national sentiments or beliefs are themselves natural, innate, or otherwise biologically derived, or whether they are socially derived.

3. *Ethnic and racial social organization.* A final issue that confronts theories of ethnicity is explaining systems of social relations that are based on racial and ethnic classifications. This means the degree to which certain social orders allocate social positions and roles on the basis of racial and/or ethnic criteria. For example, in the late 1800s in the United States, Chinese people resident in the country were prohibited from entering the universities and professions, from owning land, from becoming citizens, and from certain types of factory and other industrial employment. This caused the Chinese to gravitate to other forms of employment, particularly restaurant and laundry work, that did not place them in competition with non-Chinese labor and helped to shield them from anti-Chinese hostility. This in turn led to the development of "Chinatowns," enclaves of Chinese people working in jobs deemed suitable for the Chinese. This is a case of ethnic social pluralism, the existence of a separate, usually unequal social structure that exists side by side with the dominant social order and serves to maintain ethnic differences. What accounts for such ethnic subsystems—a biological tendency or "feeling" on the part of the Chinese to stick to themselves and maintain their separate identity? Or is it a complex interplay of social and historical circumstances that, had they been different, would have led to an altogether different form of ethnic organization, or perhaps none at all?

A particular kind of ethnic-racial social organization that is especially crucial for theories of ethnicity is ethnic and racial *stratification*. This refers to societies whose class hierarchies are based wholly or in part on racial and/or ethnic criteria. That is, people, by virtue of their racial or ethnic group membership, have less access or opportunity to the upper levels of a society's class structure or, conversely, are relegated to the lower levels of the class structure. The United States is, again, a useful illustration of ethnic and racial stratification. There exists in the United States an underclass of chronically underemployed and unemployed people—sometimes called the "subproletariat"—that is disproportionately composed of black and Hispanic Americans. Conversely, the upper class in America contains only a handful of members from either group. Thus "success" in the United States appears at least partially tied to ethnic and racial considerations. Theories of ethnicity must explain why this is so, and these explanations run the gamut from biological to social, universalist to nonuniversalist.

These three related phenomena—racial and ethnic classifications, sentiments, and social organization—constitute the totality that theories of ethnicity seek to explain. To add to the clarity of presentation, or at least to avoid possible confusion, I will try to make explicit the assumptions held by the various theories discussed and apply these views to certain "ethnic situations," such as slavery, ethnic stratification, and others, to facilitate comparison. I cannot claim that the reader will have found the answer to the "riddle of ethnicity" on finishing this book, for the search for an answer is only beginning. At the very least, though, I do hope to convince the reader that the answers recently proposed, especially those receiving so much attention in the popular and scholarly presses, are not only problematic, but also, in a few cases, a potential danger to our democratic tradition.

Notes

1. Park's famous "race relations cycle" has been misconstrued by later interpreters as a theory that saw assimilation as the inevitable end result of contact between two ethnic groups. Park did believe that long-term interethnic relations would produce social pressures leading to the assimilation of the weaker ethnic group into the dominant group. He recognized, however, that this assimilation process might be forestalled indefinitely, particularly in highly stratified accommodative systems such as slavery and apartheid.

2. Since the 1920s Communist party theorizing on the race question in the United States has consistently drawn a direct link between capitalism and racial inequality. Such theories, in addition to being ideologically self-serving, have not been very good, and have made little impact on the major theories of race relations advanced by U.S. scholars. A good review of communist theorizing on the race issue can be found in James Geschwender, *Racial Stratification in America*. Dubuque, Iowa: Wm. C. Brown, 1978.

3. Allan Garfinkel, *Forms of Explanation: Rethinking The Questions in Social Theory*. New Haven, Conn.: Yale University Press, 1981, p. 1.

4. Ibid., p. 2.

5. This practice is known as genealogical revision, and it is common to many kinship-based societies. When the empirical "facts" do not fit the model, the "facts" are transformed, not the model. Western culture and science practice similar revisions when confronted with discrepancies between fact and theory.

6. Brian Fay, *Social Theory and Political Practice*. London: Allen & Unwin, 1975, p. 11.

7. Ibid., pp. 44–49.

8. Edward Shils, "Primordial, Personal, Sacred and Civil Ties," *British Journal of Sociology*, 8, 1957, pp. 130–145.

9. Fredrik Barth, "Introduction," in Fredrik Barth, ed., *Ethnic Groups and Boundaries*. Boston: Little, Brown, 1969, pp. 9–38.

10. Although Barth defines his approach as theoretical, it is clear from his own description of his method that he is arguing for a new conceptual approach to the study of ethnic units, and not for an underlying theoretical framework

that seeks to explain the existence and persistence of ethnic units; "we need to investigate closely the empirical facts of a variety of cases, and fit our concepts to these empirical facts so that they elucidate them as simply and adequately as possible, and allow us to explore their implications" (ibid., p. 10).

11. *Ethnic and Racial Studies* 8(4), October, 1985, is devoted entirely to Banton's rational choice theory and is recommended to those who seek further discussion of his ideas.

12. Michael Banton, *Racial and Ethnic Competition*. Cambridge: Cambridge University Press, 1983, p. 104.

13. Ibid., p. 108.

14. See Richard Lewontin, Steven Rose, and Leo Kamin, "Bourgeois Ideology and the Origins of Biological Determinism," *Race & Class*, XXIV(1), 1982, pp. 1–16.

15. Milton Fisk, "The Human-Nature Argument," *Radical Philosophers' News-journal*, 9(Fall), l978, pp. 1–17.

16. Ibid., p. 7.

17. For relevant critiques of scientific racism consult Norman Daniels, "IQ, Heritability and Human Nature," *Proceedings of the Philosophy of Science Association*, 1975; Leo Kamin, *The Science and Politics of IQ*. New York: Halsted Press, 1974.

18. Garfinkel, *Forms of Explanation*, especially Ch. 3.

2 —————————————————————————

In Genes We Trust
THE SOCIOBIOLOGY OF RACE
AND ETHNICITY

> Sociobiology has two faces. One looks toward the social behavior of
> nonhuman animals. The eyes are carefully focused, the lips pursed
> judiciously. Utterances are made only with caution. The other face
> is almost hidden behind a megaphone. With great excitement,
> pronouncements about human nature blare forth.[1]

In his comprehensive and excellent critique of sociobiology, Philip
Kitcher distinguishes between two sociobiologies: one practiced by scientists primarily interested in the evolution of nonhuman animal behavior, the other mainly concerned with "appealing to recent ideas about
the evolution of animal behavior in order to advance grand claims about
human nature and human social institutions."[2] The latter brand he aptly
terms "pop sociobiology" (shortened from "popular sociobiology") because of its deliberate design to command popular attention and the
need to distinguish it from more cautious and rigorous studies within
the biological subdiscipline of evolutionary theory.

The pop sociobiology lineage is generally traced to the publication of
E. O. Wilson's *Sociobiology: The New Synthesis* (1975), in which Wilson alleged that certain behavioral dispositions observed in humans, such as
aggressiveness, selfishness, and xenophobia, were intrinsic aspects of
human nature. Additionally, certain human social institutions, such as
polygyny (males with multiple wives), incest tabus, and class and racial
hierarchies, were likely to rest on a biological basis, that is, to be determined in some significant manner by genetic causes.

Expectedly, Wilson's grand synthesis was greeted by enthusiasm from many (including many biologically illiterate social scientists) and vehement opposition from more (including many biologists and geneticists who specialize in animal social behavior). These critiques centered on the evidentiary basis of human sociobiology and the political implications of its pronouncements. Many biologists who understand the difficulties of formulating evolutionary hypotheses and generating the evidence to sustain them in a single nonhuman species were appalled by the readiness of Wilson to make little more than speculative and suggestive analogies linking biology with human social behavior.[3] Other critics, particularly social scientists and philosophers, interpreted Wilson's program as an ideology that justified continued racial, sexual, and class oppression; was "totemism masquerading as science"; and served as merely the latest version of a long trend in Western science dedicated to the "project of innateness"—explaining human behavior by instinctivist causes.[4]

In the decade since Wilson's early work, pop sociobiology has undergone several transformations and amendations, many of which have tried to answer the criticisms leveled against it. The pop sociobiology lineage has thus segmented into several rival versions containing important differences among them (see Kitcher, 1985, for an exhaustive analysis of these). What interests us here is the version that has been developed to explain racial and ethnic behaviors in humans, and the degree to which it succeeds on the basis of its assumptions and corresponding evidence.

That version was supplied by Pierre L. van den Berghe in his book *The Ethnic Phenomenon* (1981). Van den Berghe does not specifically relate his brand of pop sociobiology to the various rival versions alluded to above (he appears to select indiscriminately from all of them), but seems to be closest to the versions provided by Richard Alexander (1979), whom he does not reference, and R. Dawkins (1976), whose notion of the "selfish gene" he often invokes.[5]

Alexander's general theory of human social behavior is based on the presumption that all animals (including humans) are motivated to maximize their inclusive fitness. "It seems clear that *if we are to carry out any grand analysis of human social behavior, it will have to be in evolutionary terms and we shall have to focus our attention almost entirely upon the precise manner in which both nepotistic and reciprocal transactions are conducted in the usual environments in which humans have evolved their social patterns*" (original emphasis).[6] The principle of "inclusive fitness" and the notions of "nepotism" and "reciprocity" that are derived from it are the hypothetical constructs central to van den Berghe's pop sociobiology of race and ethnic relations:

Like other animal societies, human societies are held together by the self-interest of their individual members. This self-interest is best measured in terms of reproductive success, for it is through differential reproduction that biological evolution of all life forms takes place. Individuals, human or nonhuman, interact competitively or cooperatively to maximize their individual fitness. They do so in three basic ways: through kin selection [or nepotism], reciprocity and coercion. The human variations on these three basic mechanisms are much more complex than those observable in other species, but they are not *categorically* different.[7]

These central constructs will be discussed shortly, but it is necessary to distinguish van den Berghe's (and Alexander's) pop sociobiology from that of others, particularly Wilson's. All versions of pop sociobiology seek to apply constructs such as inclusive fitness derived from evolutionary theory to the explanation and understanding of human social behavior. But they differ considerably regarding the relative strength of biological causes to affect human behavior. Wilson's version tends to be "strong" to the extent that he suggests that human social behaviors that have successfully evolved over the species' history can only be abandoned at some risk or "cost" to the species' fitness. That is, those biological and social tendencies that have "proved" themselves successful in the evolutionary long run can only be abandoned at some expected fitness cost to ourselves.[8]

Van den Berghe's pop sociobiology, on the other hand, is a decidedly "weak" variety that claims that the reputed biological basis of human social behavior can be overridden or changed by the species' powerful cultural capacities—the ability to fashion our environments and adaptations to them by nonbiological means. Thus the importance of sociobiology for van den Berghe is to know our natural selves so that our cultural selves might liberate us from our very nature:

Sociobiology is a utilitarian model of behavior that sees organisms as blindly selected to maximize their reproductive success. Humans have been so spectacularly successful in this evolutionary game that they are now becoming the victims of their success: they are destroying through overreproduction and overconsumption, the habitat that supports them. . . . Unless we stop behaving naturally— that is, being our selfish, nepotistic, ethnocentric selves—we court collective extinction. . . . It is as an *anti-ethic* that sociobiology holds its greatest promise. We must know the nature of the beast within us to vanquish it. Unless we achieve both—and quickly—we are a doomed species.[9]

Such a weak version of pop sociobiology can be fairly construed as talking out of both sides of one's mouth. In *The Ethnic Phenomenon* van den Berghe goes to considerable lengths to suggest that the bases of human ethnic and race relations lie in the genetic predisposition for kin selection; that this force causes us to behave egocentrically and ethnocentrically; that society and culture are the mere sums of individually motivated actions; that social systems, as a result of these actions, are naturally hierarchical, coercive, and racist. In the same book we are also told that understanding the underlying biological basis of human ethnic and race relations tells us little about those relations because of the enormously complex environmental variables that affect human interaction. "Human ecology is peculiarly complex because, in addition to the physical and biotic (other plants and animals) features of the human habitat that importantly influence human adaptive behavior, humans have developed through culture an impressive capability to modify both the physical and biotic habitat and *the very forms of human sociality itself.*"[10]

The contradictory nature of weak versions of pop sociobiology has been criticized by philosopher Martin Barker: "[Human sociobiology] gives us a picture of genes as basic, solid and secure; and culture as ephemeral, changeable, dependent and fly-by-night.... When, therefore, we look to see how we are supposed, on these theories, to stand up to the genes with all their influence, we find it is on the backs of our culture.... The flea will rebel against the direction the cat is going!"[11] A more charitable interpretation of van den Berghe's version is to commend him for his caution in applying biological principles in any kind of direct cause-effect manner to human social institutions. Pop sociobiologists, be they biologists or social scientists, understand that there is no simple nature/nurture, genes/culture dichotomy, that both evolutionary theory and social theory recognize (though hardly understand) human behavior and institutions to be the outcome of complex interactions among biology, the environment (including human history), and social and cultural capacities. This recognition has led Wilson and colleague Charles Lumsden to formulate a theory of gene-culture coevolution in which they postulate certain "epigenetic mechanisms" (genetic tendencies or predispositions) that determine within a delimited range certain "culturgen" choices (human social and cultural behaviors) that presumably enhance inclusive fitness and that in turn lead to genetic change (evolution).[12] This model has been severely critiqued on numerous grounds (particularly its conceptualization of culture), but nevertheless remains a "strong" version of pop sociobiology relative to van den Berghe's.

Van den Berghe proposes that understanding the biological basis of human ethnic and race relations will merely *add to or supplement* our current historical and cultural understandings of these relations, rather than demonstrate genetic causes underlying cultural choices and institutions. He wants to argue that understanding the impact of the maximization of inclusive fitness (the biological principle) + human social and cultural history (the cultural principles) will add up to a more complete theory of ethnic and race relations than currently exists. Conceptualizing the biology-culture relation as an additive rather than a cause-effect relation enables van den Berghe to argue for a deeper level understanding that nevertheless retains a largely autonomous role for culture.

There are problems with this kind of weak sociobiology, however. On the one hand, there is the general claim that ethnic and race relations are rooted in the tendency for all animals (including humans) to maximize their inclusive fitness. Such a claim must, to some extent, be substantiated by evidence taken from human societies in varying environments, and not merely asserted or assumed because some studies have shown this principle to yield interesting explanations in some few other species. In other words, there must be some attempt to show that human racial and ethnic behaviors have, in fact, enhanced inclusive fitness, and some attempt to connect this to evolutionary pressures that historically affected the species. This is a tall order indeed, and one for which the data may be lacking. They are, nevertheless, necessary to confirm the hypothesis. On the other hand, there is also a claim that even though considerations of inclusive fitness are relevant, they tell us little and predict less about the content or course of race and ethnic relations owing to our species' capacity for culture. Thus independent of the claim concerning the validity of inclusive fitness as an underlying basis for race and ethnicity is the question of whether or not such an "addition" to our knowledge is but banal and wholly unnecessary. Both of these problems are evident in van den Berghe's pop sociobiology of the so-called "ethnic phenomenon."

Inclusive Fitness, Nepotism, and Reciprocity

The construct of inclusive fitness is central to all versions of pop sociobiology, and is the biological bedrock on which human social behaviors are seen to rest. The concept was introduced by W. D. Hamilton in a pair of papers published in 1964 titled "The Genetical Evolution of Social Behavior."[13] Hamilton made a valuable contribution to the classic Darwinian concept of fitness by suggesting that behaviors that contributed to an organism's reproductive success need to be understood not only in terms of the number of direct offspring produced by the organism, but also in terms of the inclusive effect of spreading one's genes indirectly by means of relatives with whom one shares a proportion of genes. Hamilton expressed this insight by means of a mathematical formula based on coefficients of relatedness, and suggested that where one could enhance the reproductive success of relatives with whom one shared genes such that the expected offspring would contain more of one's genes than by directly reproducing oneself, one might "sacrifice" one's own reproduction for that of one's relatives.

The notion of inclusive fitness served as a potential explanation for why some groups of social insects (such as worker and soldier "castes" in ants) seemed to sacrifice their own reproduction for the good of the group. The "good" being done need not be for the group, but could be conceived as an act of "selfishness" masquerading as altruism because the net inclusive effect of their behaviors favored the transmission of their own genes. By helping more of their relatives reproduce, they were transmitting more of their own genes, albeit indirectly, than they would by reproducing themselves. Through the notion of inclusive fitness biologists could preserve Darwin's notion of "survival of the fittest" and still explain behaviors that appeared to reduce personal fitness through sacrificial or altruistic behaviors.

The tendency to favor kin for the purpose of maximizing one's inclusive fitness has been called "nepotism" or "kin selection." This tendency is considered by pop sociobiologists to be the basic genetic motivation that propels animal social behavior. Van den Berghe illustrates the application of nepotism to human behavior thusly:

Why should parents sacrifice themselves for their children? Why do uncles employ nephews rather than strangers in their business? Why do inheritance laws provide for passing property along lines of kinship? Why, in short, do people, and indeed other animals as well, behave nepotistically.... We favor kin because they *are* kin. This is no answer of course, but a mere restatement of the problem. Besides, we do not *always* favor kin. Profligate sons are sometimes disinherited, incompetent nephews not hired and so on. Yet, on the whole we are nepotists, and when we are not, it is for some good reason. Nepotism, we intuitively feel, is the natural order of things. Where we feel nepotism would interfere with efficiency, equity or some other goals, we institute explicit safeguards against it and, even then, we expect it to creep in again surreptitiously.[14]

Despite van den Berghe's disclaimer that "we favor kin because they *are* kin is no answer," it should be his answer if kin selection in humans is presumed to maximize inclusive fitness. This answer does no damage to his claim that humans may nevertheless abandon or override nepotism when social or cultural circumstances dictate. But his explicit recognition of social circumstances in which humans do abandon nepotism points up the weakness of his "weak" sociobiology. Given the presence in humans of both nepotistic and antinepotistic behaviors, and the absence of any data or claim beyond "intuition" that antinepotism might reduce fitness, it can be argued with equal force (and more evidence) that we are naturally nonnepotistic, save for circumstances that force us to act nepotistically. Why, for example, do I favor my children over other children? Because I live in a social system that legally and morally obligates me to care for them and imposes severe penalties when I do not. Moreover, if I don't care for them, no one else is likely to. There is abundant evidence that many parents treat their children badly despite social pressures not to such that in the absence of these pressures the situation might be a great deal worse than it now is.

Van den Berghe gives us no argument to the effect that nepotism is the "natural order of things" that, given the potentially rich set of social and historical arguments that explain nepotism independent of nature, makes his hypothesis unnecessary. His claim that the principle of kin selection adds to our understanding of nepotistic behaviors (and later, ethnic relations) is not demonstrated. Nothing has been gained or, for that matter, lost.

The principle of inclusive fitness does not require people to always favor kin, that is, be nepotistic. Maximizing inclusive fitness might entail, under certain conditions, favoring less related or unrelated people over more closely related kin. Cooperation among distantly related or unrelated people is called "reciprocity." If, for example, a person lives in a social system in which he and his relatives are stigmatized and given less access to socially valued or required resources, he may maximize his fitness by abandoning his association with relatives and associating instead with unrelated people. The concept of reciprocity is neither a descriptive statement nor biological prediction about how humans will behave. It is a hypothetical corollary of inclusive fitness that states that under conditions in which favoring kin might lead to a loss of inclusive fitness, cooperation with unrelated people might enhance it. The costs of favoring kin might be sufficiently heavy so that the benefits of favoring nonkin over kin are greater.

Van den Berghe recognizes the widespread forms of cooperation that exist among human groups, and tends to indiscriminately apply "reciprocity" as their explanation. But he regards systems of reciprocity, though widespread among humans, as inherently unstable strategies that are ultimately based on coercion.[15] Systems of reciprocity seldom work in the absence of coercion because they are open to "cheating." That is, person A is not likely to cooperate with unrelated person B unless A can be assured that B will reciprocate the cooperation. B is motivated both to gain favor from A and to not reciprocate. In van den Berghe's words, "there is, however, a catch to reciprocity, especially to self-conscious reciprocity of the human type: it is open to cheating or free-loading. The temptation not to return a favor is irresistible. Therefore, systems of self-conscious reciprocity have to detect and control cheating, excluding cheaters from subsequent interactions."[16] What van den Berghe suggests is that the Golden Rule of "do unto others" is not a strategy that would be favored by natural selection, since "taking from all and giving to none" would be the fitness-maximizing strategy. (As Kitcher details, it is possible for the Golden Rule, or what he terms the "TIT for TAT" strategy, to become evolutionarily stable under conditions in which the interacting individuals have the ability to keep track of their past behaviors—an ability humans possess in abundance.[17]) Because of this, van den Berghe argues that underlying what appear to be systems of reciprocity in humans are systems of coercion whereby one group dominates another group often by means of ideologies that mask the domination in terms of cooperative or reciprocal arrangements. The most obvious examples are complex state societies in which a ruling group or class uses ideologies of "democracy" or "socialism" to coerce minority groups or classes into serving the ruling group's interests at the expense of the minority's interests. In practice, then, reciprocity usually becomes transformed into coercion of a weaker group by a stronger one.

The concepts of nepotism (kin selection) and reciprocity derived from the notion of inclusive fitness are the additions that van den Berghe attempts to tack on to our understandings of race and ethnic relations. In the sections that follow I will outline his reasoning and assess the degree to which he has, in fact, enhanced our understanding. Before doing so, however, a brief comment on the concept of "fitness" itself is needed. In evolutionary terms "fitness" refers to reproductive success. An individual or population is fit to the extent of its transmission of genes to succeeding generations. Pop sociobiologists such as van den Berghe tend to forget this and assume, without warrant, that behaviors or characteristics that lead to social fitness (for example, wealth and high levels of education in American society) either are expressions of or conveniently translate into reproductive fitness.[18] This cannot be assumed. What pop sociobiologists must show is how certain social behaviors, be they nepotistic or reciprocal, enhance the inclusive fitness of the organisms under study. This is an admittedly monumental task that requires detailed reproductive histories of the organisms, knowledge of long-term and complex environmental pressures on them, and how the social and cultural responses to these pressures maximized biological fitness. Nowhere in *The Ethnic Phenomenon* is such an analysis even attempted. Instead, we are treated to cases of racial and ethnic behavior that appear to fit the logic of inclusive fitness, and are urged to accept the possibility that they might have something to do with inclusive fitness. Such a possibility no doubt exists, as does the possibility that God created heaven and earth. But a high degree of faith is needed to sustain both. With this in mind, I can summarize the articles of this new faith as they apply to race and ethnic relations.

Ethnicity as Kin Selection

As I noted in Chapter 1, theories of ethnicity seek to account for three phenomena: ethnic classifications, ethnic sentiments, and forms of ethnic social organization. Addressing himself to these phenomena, van den

Berghe argues that ethnic classifications and sentiments can be under-stood as extensions of kin selection or nepotism. Forms of ethnic social organization, on the other hand, although they probably rest on a ne-potistic basis, are extremely variable and complex, and mainly the prod-uct of cultural developments. Van den Berghe gives the following summary of his central claims:

Let me summarize the argument so far. Humans, like other social animals are biologically selected to be nepotistic because, by favoring kin, they maximize their inclusive fitness. Until the last few thousand years, hominids interacted in relatively small groups of a few score to a couple of hundred individuals who tended to mate with each other and, therefore, to form rather tightly knit groups of close and distant kinsmen. Physical boundaries of territory and social bound-aries of inbreeding separated these small human societies from each other. Within the group, there was a large measure of peace and cooperation between kinsmen and in-laws (frequently both kinds of relationship overlapped). Rela-tions between groups were characterized by mistrust and avoidance—but fre-quently by open conflict over scarce resources. These solidary groups were, in fact, primordial ethnies [ethnic groups].

Such was the evolutionary origin of ethnicity: an extended kin group. With the progressive growth in the size of human societies, the boundaries of the ethny became wider; the bonds of kinship were correspondingly diluted, and indeed sometimes became fictive, and ethnicity became increasingly manipulated and perverted to other ends, including domination and exploitation. The urge, however, to continue to define a collectivity larger than the immediate circle of kinsmen on the basis of biological descent continues to be present even in the most industrialized mass societies of today. A wide variety of ethnic markers are used to define such collectivities of descent, but their choice is not capricious. Those markers will be stressed that are, in fact, objectively reliable predictors of common descent, given the environment in which the discriminating group finds itself. Sometimes, but rather rarely, race is the paramount criterion; more commonly, cultural characteristics, especially language, do a much better job of defining ethnic boundaries.

So far, we have suggested the *raison d'etre* of ethnicity—the reason for its persistence and for its seeming imperviousness to rationality. Ethnic (and racial) sentiments often seem irrational because they have an underlying driving force of their own, which is ultimately the blunt, purposeless natural selection of genes that are reproductively successful. Genes favoring nepotistic behavior have a selective advantage. It does not matter whether their carrying organisms are aware of being nepotistic or even that they consciously know their relatives. Organisms must only behave *as if they knew*. It happens that, in humans, they often know in a conscious way, though they are sometimes mistaken.[19]

Van den Berghe's assertions contain the following steps:

1. Ethnic and racial classifications are extensions of kinship classifications. Kin-ship classifications are groupings of men and women into categories of kin and nonkin based on "objectively reliable predictors" of common descent.

2. Ethnic and racial sentiments are extensions of kinship sentiments, the tendency to favor kin over nonkin. Racism and ethnism are thus extensions of nepotism.

3. Ethnic and racial classifications and sentiments are the product of an underlying, perhaps unconscious, force or drive whereby genes engage in the "blunt, purposeless" reproduction of themselves.

Each of these assertions is undemonstrated and, as is often the case with many pop sociobiology pronouncements, quite unrelated to considerations of inclusive fitness. Arguments 1 and 2 consist of two related assertions, each of which is suspect: (1) that human systems of kinship classification are based on the degree of biological relatedness among kin and (2) that ethnic and racial classifications are extensions of kinship classifications.

Human kinship classifications clearly have something to do with biology, although the precise relation to biology is not so clear. All classification systems recognize a broad category of consanguineal kin—those related to ego by blood. The American kinship terminology system (which is often called the "Eskimo type" because of its prevalence among Eskimo groups and which is found among numerous other groups as well) is noted for its close correspondence between certain kinship terms and degree of biological relatedness. That is, particularly close biological kin are called by kinship terms that are used only for those kin and not extended to other, less closely related kin. "Father," "mother," "son," "daughter," "brother," "grandmother," and so on are restricted to those kin with whom we share a high degree of heredity. Less closely related kin—cousins, for example—are not differentiated terminologically, and remotely related kin (third cousins and beyond) are scarcely recognized. There is, then, some explicit recognition in our kinship classification system of biological descent and degree of relatedness. Biological kin are also viewed as "closer, more important" kin than relatives by marriage or adoption.

The matter of kin classification and its correspondence to biological relatedness is much more complicated, however. Certain categories of kin—"uncles" and "aunts" in our system, for example—do not distinguish rather close biological kin from biologically remote kin through marriage. The situation is even further complicated when we examine other common types of kin terminology systems, such as those characteristic of societies organized into unilineal (patrilineal or matrilineal) descent groups. In unilineal societies fully one-half of one's biological relatives (either father's or mother's relatives) are relegated to "inferior" status vis-à-vis the other, favored half. Van den Berghe is well aware of such systems and provides the following forthright explanation for their existence:

Either one follows kin selection pure and simple and opts for bilateral descent, but then the scale on which stable groups of kinsmen can collectively organize and cooperate is effectively limited to sets of full siblings; alternatively, one has to jettison most of one's kin in order to organize into larger groups with some of one's kin, if necessary, against other kinsmen. Unilineal descent is a trade-off between kin selection and reciprocity. It still utilizes the principle of kinship to organize society. Indeed unilineal descent is the simplest and the most common device for organizing large collectivities on the basis of kinship. But unilineal descent increases the scope of reciprocity in human interaction. Unilineal descent is, in fact, *a social contract* between a particular category of relatives to gang up against all others, including, if necessary, other relatives. Unilineal descent, then, is an adaptive response to societies that were under great pressure to increase the size of their cooperative groups (as indeed most humans must have been for thousands of years) without abandoning kin selection altogether.[20]

Aside from the unnecessary and undemonstrated claims that kin selection and reciprocity are the underlying genetic motivations for unilineal descent groups, this reasoned explanation is likely to meet with acceptance from most social anthropologists. That is because the explanation stresses the capacity of human groups to culturally transform their modes of social organization to meet the "great pressure" of the environment—an environment that is as much "man-made" as physically given.

What anthropologists and others readily agree to is that which van den Berghe implies: human beings do have a powerful genetic capacity to adapt, but that capacity is the ability to both create and respond to a human and physical environment by nongenetic means—the capacity for culture. Throughout his writings and on occasions too numerous to list, van den Berghe makes similar pronouncements: "The issue ... is not whether genes are more important than culture, for both are inextricably intertwined. Culture itself grew out of a process of biological evolution, but it gained sufficient autonomy from specific genotypes to become not only an array of behavioral phenotypes, but also a man-made part of the environment."[21] Again, we are led to ask that if culture is "sufficiently autonomous" (i.e., independent) from biology, what is added to our understanding of human behavior by asserting genetic causes for which the evidence is lacking? If kin selection and reciprocity do become potent explanations of human social behavior, it will be *because* their relation to certain cultural and social forms has been specified more concretely. They are currently merely two additional riders on the already overcrowded bus of social explanations.

The point, however, is even more basic. Human kinship classifications bear little correspondence to biological relatedness, and do not constitute "objectively reliable predictors" of common descent. Even more distant from such reliable predictors are racial and ethnic classifications that

encompass literally millions of people. Van den Berghe again makes our
point:

> Descent, I asserted, is the central feature of ethnicity. Yet, it is clear that, in
> many cases, the common descent ascribed to an ethny is fictive. In fact, in *most*
> cases, it is at least *partly* fictive.... If kinship in the most restricted circle of the
> nuclear family is sometimes a biological fiction, it is little wonder that the greatly
> extended kind of kinship implicit in ethnicity should often be putative. The
> larger the ethny, the more likely this is. Clearly, for 50 million Frenchmen or
> 100 million Japanese, any common kinship that they may share is highly diluted,
> and known to be so.... Yet—and this is what begs explanation—the fiction of
> kinship, even in modern industrial societies, has to be sufficiently credible for
> ethnic solidarity to be effective. One cannot create an instant ethny by creating
> a myth. The myth has to be rooted in historical reality to be accepted. Ethnicity
> can be *manipulated* but *not manufactured*. Unless ethnicity is rooted in generations
> of shared historical experience, it cannot be created *ex nihilo*.[22]

Aside from the mistaken assertion that ethnicity cannot be manufactured (it is manufactured all the time, particularly in those societies that
legitimate ethnic identities), van den Berghe admits that there is little
correspondence between biological relatedness and ethnic group membership. Moreover, he provides a quite adequate explanation for his own
begged question concerning ethnic (and racial) solidarity: "generations
of shared historical experience."

Why, then, all this talk about inclusive fitness, kin selection, and so
forth? We do not know to what extent our ethnic and racial behaviors
have maximized inclusive fitness, and whether they have or have not
can only be known by tracing the complexities of generations of shared
historical experience. The issue is not, as van den Berghe suggests, that
ethnic solidarity is the expression or outcome of some drive to maximize
fitness, but rather the extent to which ethnic solidarity, as a complex
social and historical phenomenon, has or has not maximized inclusive
fitness.

The same can be said for the existence of racial and ethnic sentiments—racism, ethnocentrism, and all other forms of "in-group–out-
group," "we-they" dichotomies. Such invidious distinctions are so prevalent in human history that the temptation to view them as basic and
"natural" is nigh overwhelming (particularly in European societies,
whose main legacy to the world since the origins of capitalism is not the
machine, but the economic exploitation of the nonwhite, non-European
world). Van den Berghe proposes that racism and ethnism are the cultural expressions of the underlying tendency for nepotism—the biological disposition to favor kin over nonkin—and that they do, in fact, rest
on a genetic basis.

The evidence does not point in that direction, however. Both the existence and intensity of racial and ethnic sentiments are clearly tied to the degree of racial and ethnic inequality within and between societies. Racism and ethnism are particularly virulent in those societies that have long histories of often brutally enforced racial and ethnic stratification. Conversely, racial and ethnic sentiments tend to decline as racial and ethnic equality increase. Thus all we know about racial and ethnic sentiments indicates a strong, dependent relation on the forms of ethnic social organization in which they exist. As with ethnic classifications and solidarity, there is no reason to assume a priori some unconscious instinctual mechanism that blindly drives us to associate with our fellow ethnics so as to maximize fitness. This does not constitute an evolutionary explanation for either the origin or the persistence of ethnic sentiments. The truly important evolutionary questions are those that try to determine the biological outcomes (of which fitness maximization might be one) of our often racist human social practices.[23]

Sociobiology and Ethnic Social Organization

The greater part of *The Ethnic Phenomenon* is devoted to the discussion of those forms of interethnic relations that have characterized human existence for the past several thousand years. There are separate chapters on colonialism (including imperialism), slavery, caste societies, middleman minorities, consociationalism, and assimilation, as well as a chapter devoted to "stages of ethnic relations." These chapters are wide-ranging in their scope, ethnographic repertoire, and historical span. They are useful summaries of much that has been written on these topics, and generally reflect the current wisdom as adopted from various social scientific sources. There is little that is new, however, save the sociobiological perspective by which van den Berghe seeks to reinterpret certain well-known social practices pertaining to intergroup behavior. There is even precious little of that, since he explicitly recognizes that the forms of ethnic and racial organization he discusses are the product of "overwhelmingly *cultural*, not genetic evolution,"[24] and that sociobiology so underspecifies their complexity as to be virtually useless:

Merely to give an evolutionary explanation for ethnic solidarity, however, says little about what is generally called ethnic (and race) relations. To say that kin relation is the underlying biological basis of ethnic solidarity allows only the grossest of predictions, because social relationships take place, not in the abstract, but in an environment in which organisms compete with each other for scarce resources.... The sociobiological model, therefore, does not predict that fellow ethnics will always stick together, or that enmity or conflict will always prevail between ethnies. Behavioral outcomes are always mediated through a vast number of environmental variables.[25]

Van den Berghe's discussion of race and ethnic relations focuses almost entirely on the specific social, cultural, and historical forces (that "vast number of environmental variables") that have produced the various forms of interethnic relations listed above. In these chapters his references to sociobiology are little more than restatements of well-known situations couched in the pseudobiological language of kin selection and reciprocity. As the following examples indicate, the same mistake of introducing evolutionary considerations in the wrong place and cluttering up descriptive history with biological constructs typify van den Berghe's treatment of ethnic social organization.

Van den Berghe's discussion of assimilation is particularly revealing, inasmuch as he proposes a new model of assimilation based on sociobiological premises. Assimilation refers to the process whereby individuals from an ethnic or racial minority enter into the social positions occupied by members of the dominant ethny, or, as van den Berghe puts it, "the group that was originally distinct has lost its subjective identity and has become *absorbed in the social structure* of another group."[25] Assimilation generally requires acculturation, in which members of the culturally distinct subordinate ethny or race adopt the language and culture of the dominant group and, in the process, often lose their native culture. Acculturation and assimilation are, therefore, cultural and social behaviors that lead to or at least attempt a change in ethnic affiliation. Acculturation and assimilation occur in multiethnic states characterized by ethnic inequality such that one ethny is dominant, and thus controls the resources (political, social, and cultural, as well as economic) necessary for full social participation. Given these circumstances, individual members of subordinate ethnies generally seek to acculturate, and are quite successful in doing so despite attempts by the dominant group to prevent it. Assimilation, on the other hand, is determined more by the policies and "openness" of the dominant group to permit minority access to the dominant institutions. The presence of strong racial and ethnic barriers may retard assimilation for generations despite acculturation (witness the experience of Afro-Americans).

This story is familiar, known by anyone who is acquainted with the sociology of race relations, and repeated at length by van den Berghe. The story is merely retold in terms of his newly discovered jargon:

Contrary to what the American experience might seem to suggest, assimilation is not to be taken for granted. Ethnic sentiment being, as I suggested earlier, an extension of kin selection, it is deeply ingrained and, barring countervailing forces, tends to endure. Its disappearance is problematic, not its persistence....

A realistic model of assimilation, therefore, must bring in a powerful force to motivate people to behave otherwise, that is, in this case, to want to assimilate strangers or to be assimilated by them. That powerful force, I suggest, is the maximization of individual fitness. Fitness is generally maximized by behaving nepotistically (and, therefore, ethnocentrically), but, under some conditions presently to be specified, kin selection may be superseded by other considerations that in turn lead to assimilation. . . .

Desire for assimilation is the outcome of two countervailing forces, the ethnically centripetal force of kin selection and the ethnically centrifugal force of fitness maximization through other means. The balance must favor the centrifugal force for assimilation to take place.[26]

The propositions "generated" by this model are as follows:

1. The greater the phenotypic resemblance between groups, the more likely assimilation is to take place.
2. The greater the cultural similarity between groups, the more likely assimilation becomes.
3. The smaller a group is in relation to the rest of the population, the more likely assimilation is.
4. Lower-status groups are more likely to assimilate than high-status groups.
5. The more territorially dispersed a group is, the more likely it is to assimilate.
6. Immigrant groups are more likely to assimilate than native groups.[27]

On closer inspection it turns out that there are numerous and important exceptions to each of these propositions. The degree of assimilation based on phenotypical similarity or dissimilarity (no. 1 above), for example, is a dependent variable determined by the social structures of the societies in question, not an independent variable based on biology that determines that structure: "Physically undistinguishable groups (e.g., Koreans in Japan) can also be rejected and remain unassimilated, so looking alike is not sufficient condition for assimilation, but it seems to be close to a necessary condition *in a number of racist countries.* Phenotype seems much more salient a criterion of acceptance in some countries than others (the Japanese, for instance, seem much more racist than the Chinese, though both are about equally ethnocentric)" (my emphasis).[28]

Each of the other propositions is similarly dependent on the nature of the society in question (consider no. 3 and American Indians, for example). These propositions, labeled "conditions favoring assimilation" by van den Berghe, are not conditions at all, but low-level empirical outcomes that hold up some of the time in certain social situations. If this is indeed that "grossest" level of prediction provided by sociobiology, then I surrender to having been "grossed out." Unless van den Berghe can establish that the structure of society itself is, to an important degree, the outcome of biological propensities (this would be a strong version of sociobiology), we have no basis for accepting his claims that assimilation is unnatural, and thus "problematic" except for strong countervailing forces, or that the desire to assimilate rests on some calculation of the fitness costs between the centripetal force of kin selection and the centrifugal pull of assimilation.

One final example of the poverty of pop sociobiology to explain complex social relations leads us to an examination of some general problems of van den Berghe's theoretical stance. This example concerns one of the most important and most written about aspects of interethnic relations, the relation between ethnicity and class.

Van den Berghe correctly states that forms of social organization based on ethnicity or race can be viewed as opposite to class-based forms of organization. People grouped on the basis of their shared ethnic or racial characteristics—common language or skin color, for example—are lumped together irrespective of whatever other characteristics they possess that might be used to differentiate them. One's membership in the social category of "Afro-American" in the United States or "non-Jew" in Israel is based solely on racial and ethnic criteria, and not on such characteristics as level of education, occupational status, and economic resources. Class membership, on the other hand, relegates ethnic and racial considerations to the background, and emphasizes the bonds among people with respect to their similar positions in the social hierarchy. Miners or secretaries or schoolteachers group together on the basis of common interests stemming from their social roles, and deemphasize potentially differentiating factors such as race, ethnicity, and gender.

In practice, of course, the relation between ethnicity and class is often confounded, particularly in those societies in which social roles are allocated, partially or wholly, on the basis of race or ethnicity or gender. The very notions of "women's work" and "nigger labor" exist in those societies in which racial and sexual stratification are most entrenched and in which one's class position is often viewed as the unfortunate result of being a member of the "inferior" sex or race or ethnic group.

Van den Berghe neither condones ethically nor attempts to justify scientifically the existence of racial and ethnic inequalities as they exist in various societies. He is an avowed antiracist and liberal who vigorously denies that sociobiology lends any support to racist claims or to social inequalities based on race, ethnicity, or sex:

There is no denying the reality of genetic differences in frequencies of alleles between human groups. None of these differences, however, has yet been shown to bear any functional relationship with the *social* attribution of racial characteristics in any human society nor with the relative positions of dominance and subordination of racial groups in any society. There is nothing, either in the study of human genetics or in sociobiological theory, to support any social order or ideology, to vindicate or challenge the position of any group or to buttress or attack any ethical premise or philosophical system. Human genetics and the presence or absence of racial distinctions in human societies are two almost totally discrete orders of phenomena.[29]

This is a statement of van den Berghe's universalist stance. He denies the racists' claim that there are significant biological differences between groups that translate into important social differences, and thus washes his hands of any presumed complicity in support of racist and inegalitarian social orders. It is true that sociobiology is not racist in this classic sense, and that it does not lend support to any *particular* social arrangement. Van den Berghe's pop sociobiology nevertheless makes a *general* argument to the effect that racism, ethnism, and inequality are expected outcomes of our biological nature, and that attempts to modify both through, for example, self-conscious class organization are fraught with difficulty. His argument takes the following form.

Van den Berghe argues that social organization based on ethnic or racial ties is biologically based, and therefore more basic and "primordial" than social groups organized on the basis of class: "Clearly, then, ethnicity is more primordial than class. Blood runs thicker than money." Class, on the other hand, "is dependent on a community of interests, which must be convincingly demonstrated before class solidarity can become effectively mobilized.... Class is therefore an alliance of convenience, based on selfish opportunism. It is vulnerable to changes in circumstances and can quickly disintegrate, because class is not a preexisting solidary community."[30] On this view, ethnic and racial ties are deep-seated, genetically based, and thus strong, whereas class ties are ephemeral, socially based, and correspondingly weak.[31]

This explanation has appeal, particularly in the United States, for several reasons. First, it seems to account for the current low level of class organization and class consciousness. Union membership has steadily declined in the past two decades, and the American labor movement has seldom attempted, with some notable exceptions to be sure, to build a class-conscious movement on which socialism or some other strong anticapitalist position was the centerpiece. Instead, unions have manifested the racism present in the society at large and sought increased wage levels and job security to the practical exclusion of other, equally fundamental issues. Given this history of class formation in the United States, van den Berghe's assertion that class is "an alliance of convenience, based on selfish opportunism" finds ready popular acceptance.

Second, the degree to which class issues are often defined in terms of and, in fact, made to appear as ethnic or racial matters seems to reinforce the pseudobiological wisdom that blood runs thicker than money. To treat problems of poverty, unemployment, crime, and other social ills as stemming from anomalies in the "black family" or some other racial "cause," or to view substandard housing and exploitative work in China-towns as a "Chinese" issue obscures the class antagonisms underpinning these problems and absolves the unequal and racist social structure of blame.

Van den Berghe understands these issues and is well aware, for ex-ample, of how class issues get translated into ethnic ones. He even de-velops a typology of different societies based on their degrees of class and ethnic mobility, a typology that shows how such mobility varies, depending on the social order in question. What, then, is wrong with his basic position that ethnic ties are genetically based and primordial, whereas class ties are merely utilitarian, and thus difficult to form and maintain? Practically everything. Up front there is the very conceptual-ization of the issue as one of blood versus money. I have shown earlier how little race and ethnicity have to do with blood, and to reduce class relations to money does violence to what is a similarly complex issue. The "blood versus money" metaphor is not just a simple euphemism that van den Berghe uses to cutely describe a complex question. It is, ipso facto, his position, or at least the sociobiological aspect of his position.

Beyond the question of adequate conceptualization, there is—again—the matter of evidence. Genetic science has begun to isolate various genetic causes for a range of human traits and problems, particularly in the area of disease. Some of these are quite complex in terms of the interaction among genetic and nongenetic factors. There is a disease called phenylketonuria (PKU), for example, which is caused by a genetic defect that prevents the metabolization of the protein phenylalanine. But the actual symptoms of PKU develop only among those whose diets contain phenylalanine. If a baby is placed on a diet free of this protein, the effects of the disease can be effectively blunted. Here is a good example of how a genetic tendency, once known and clearly specified, can be modified by nongenetic manipulation. Fitness maximization, the presumed genetic tendency underlying racial and ethnic behaviors, can-not be so neatly described. No one has isolated a genetic trait for fitness maximization, nor, given the unlikely presence of alleles for such a trait, does anybody seem to be looking. Sociobiologists are thus faced with trying to design studies in which a genetic tendency for fitness maxim-ization might (sometimes) be a reasonable inference. A few such studies exist, but they are confined to nonhuman animal species in which evo-lutionary and reproductive histories can be traced over generations and *in which there is the reasonable presumption that biology, and not culture*, is the root cause of their behaviors. Pop sociobiology of the van den Berghe variety does not even purport to be such a study applied to humans, nor does he seem to recognize the need for one. Simple assertion on the grounds that humans, too, have biology seems to be enough, despite his own admission that the predictive power of that assertion approaches zero.

Pop sociobiology's appeal does not rest on the scientific credibility of its central claim that important human social and cultural practices are the expressions of an underlying tendency for fitness maximization. The very notion of fitness maximization as it might be inferred from human behavior requires a case-by-case examination of properly designed studies, and there is no reason to assume a priori that humans behave in ways that maximize fitness. Sometimes they may and sometimes they may not. There is nothing in the general theory of evolution, the holy writ to which pop sociobiology claims to pay homage, that requires either humans or nonhumans to always behave in fitness-maximizing ways. Pop sociobiology is not just bad sociology; it is also bad biology.

The appeal of van den Berghe's sociobiology derives from its correspondence with certain American cultural values—ideas propagated by the dominant culture and embraced by many of us. Americans (and other bearers of European culture) believe that humans are, on the whole, selfish, individualistic, racist, and "out for themselves." We mistrust any call to altruism or collective behavior, save for the national defense. Much of our behavior reinforces our beliefs. We are often selfish, racist, competitive, and absorbed with "number 1." We are, in effect, what our culture requires us to be.

It is pop sociobiology's very consistency with our cultural reason that should make us suspicious of its claims. Every culture is a self-validating, self-confirming justification of its own morality. Basic to this justification is the claim that culture is an expression of nature—a mere outlet for what we really (that is, *biologically*) are. Unlike the magician who delights us by showing a reality that is unreal, culture is the trickster whose illusions are presented as real. Pop sociobiology is merely the latest trick. It says that we are by nature what we appear to be by culture. Such a trick, if successful, leads us to accept that which is, not necessarily because it ought to be, but because it must be or, in the absence of superhuman effort, will be. If sociobiology does not support a particular social order, its general effect is to anesthetize us to the contradictions of the current social order. We are told that class formation is difficult because it is unnatural and not primarily due to the long-term and often brutal attempts of a privileged class (which, contrary to the sociobiological prediction, seems quite well organized) to maintain its privilege and power. We are asked to believe that class issues are often expressed in ethnic or racial terms because these are natural, preexisting solidary communities rooted in blood. The fact that the state, often self-consciously, actively promotes the belief that problems of unemployment, crime, and other social ills are racial issues, and thus obscures their class origins, is of little consequence. If I may be permitted a culturally appropriate retort, "buyer beware!"[32]

Reductionism and Individualism in Sociobiological Thought

I have tried to show that van den Berghe's pop sociobiology of race and ethnicity fails on several levels: its inadequate conceptualization of the phenomena to be explained, an improper use of "fitness maximization" as well as a misunderstanding of the kinds of studies necessary for its proper application, and a general theoretical stance that leads to an ideological understanding and acceptance of the cultural (and social) status quo. Beyond these substantive considerations is the additional question of the kind of explanation, in a methodological sense, that pop sociobiology is. This issue concerns the adequacy of pop sociobiology, viewed as a model or structure of explanation, to account for the social and cultural behaviors it claims to address. This is an important issue because van den Berghe, who seems to recognize some of the substantive weaknesses in his argument, ultimately justifies pop sociobiology on general methodological grounds. He argues that sociobiology is a superior way of looking at the world because it is reductionistic and explains complex social relations by means of a simple "individual choice" model of behavior:

In the last analysis, a scientific paradigm is a way of looking at the world. It is not true or false in an absolute sense. It is merely a more or less useful, parsimonious and elegant way of reducing the enormous complexity of the world to a manageable number of normative and predictive statements. The more that is accounted for with the fewest number of principles, the better the theory.[33]

Van den Berghe asks us to accept the superiority of his theory on the grounds that it is reductionistic, that ethnic and race relations are somehow "accounted for" by the single principle of fitness maximization that presumably underlies human behavior. On various occasions throughout his book he extols reductionism and individualism as virtues by which to gauge the adequacy of a scientific theory. Referring to his model of assimilation, he writes:

The reductionist model of assimilation we have just presented purports to predict empirical outcomes on the basis of individuals making selfish cost/benefit calculations of alternative strategies of ethnic nepotism versus assimilation.... Crude and simple though the model is, it generates propositions that seem in fact to be borne out by empirical evidence.[34]

I have already discussed the propositions generated by this crude and simple model, and suggested that they are not predictive statements, but already known empirical outcomes that hold up some of the time in certain societies. Furthermore, whatever predictions might be made with regard to assimilation or nonassimilation do not flow from the crude and simple model of fitness maximization, but from knowledge of the social structures of the societies in question. The model predicts nothing, and thus fails in terms of its own stated criterion of predictiveness. We can reasonably ask, then, of what value is the reduction of assimilation to concerns about fitness maximization.

Reductionist statements are those that claim that a given state of affairs is "just the expression of x" or is "really the outcome of x." A reductionist statement thus specifies a fundamental or basic underlying cause of something that supercedes or "envelops" other proposed causes. As Garfinkel suggests, we evaluate a reductionist theory in terms of whether it "gives us all the explanatory power of the theory [or theories] being reduced."[35] What van den Berghe proposes to add to our understanding of race and ethnic relations is just such a reductionist theory rooted in the notion of fitness maximization. The following list of recurrent ethnic/racial situations discussed in *The Ethnic Phenomenon* exemplifies his reductionist program.

Explaining acculturation and assimilation, colonialism and imperialism, slavery, apartheid, and reservation systems is the task of theories of race and ethnicity. But to say that the basic cause underlying each of them is either nepotism or reciprocity is an improper reduction. We have learned nothing about the various forms of racial and ethnic relations by positing the existence of a generalized drive to maximize fitness, whatever the circumstances. Even if such a drive exists, it tells us little of what we want to know about systems of ethnic and racial organization. It is akin to explaining the variety of sexual practices and their social regulation by appeal to the sex drive. Both explanations so radically underdetermine the form and content of the complex behaviors they are designed to explain as to be virtually useless for explaining them. Reducing ethnic and race relations to considerations of fitness maximization neither supercedes nor envelops nor modifies *nor adds* to the various theories, either social or biological, that have been proposed to account for race and ethnicity. Van den Berghe, on occasions already alluded to, seems to recognize the inadequacy of his reduction but nevertheless insists that it adds to a more complete picture or account of ethnic phenomena.

What his addition amounts to is a statement to the effect that fitness maximization is a genetically (and thus individually) based drive or tendency that underlies all human behavior, and that independent of social or cultural circumstances that dictate otherwise, humans are essentially

Van den Berghe's Reductionist Explanations

Racial/Ethnic Situation	Definition	Basic Cause
Racial or Ethnic Solidarity	Groups of "related" humans organize for the pursuit of selfish (though common) interests	Nepotism—fitness is maximized by organizing with relatives
Class Solidarity	Groups of "unrelated" individuals organize along economic lines for the pursuit of selfish interests	Reciprocity—fitness is maximized by organizing nonkin
Racial or Ethnic Stratification	Any situation in which a dominant ethny establishes a class hierarchy and allocates class positions on the basis of race or ethnicity	Nepotism—leads to coercive social institutions based on race/ethnicity

Types of Racial or Ethnic Stratification

Imperialism	The domination of one or more ethnies over others	Nepotism
Colonialism	Long-distance imperialism over culturally unrelated ethnies	Nepotism
Slavery	Domination over foreign, involuntary immigrants who are "torn out of" their network of kin	Nepotism

Common Behaviors in the Context of Racial or Ethnic Stratification

Acculturation	Subordinate ethnies adopt the language and culture of the dominant ethny and generally give up or "hide" their former ethnic affiliation	Reciprocity
Assimilation	Subordinate ethnies attempt to enter the social positions occupied by dominant ethny	Reciprocity

racist, egocentric, nepotistic, and selfish. The problem with this "addition" is that we cannot even conceive of humans independent of social and cultural circumstances. It is these circumstances that make us human, in all our variety, and there exists no essentialist biological makeup that would reveal itself if only we could strip away our social and cultural selves. Unless van den Berghe wants to argue that fitness maximization causes, in a more or less direct manner, the particular forms of racial and ethnic organization observed (a strong claim he neither wants to nor can sustain), we can echo Kitcher's refrain regarding some of the other anthropological misuses of fitness maximization—"we have no need of that hypothesis."[36]

Van den Berghe also extols pop sociobiology as superior to other worldviews because it is based on what he calls an "individual-choice" model.[37] By this he means a scientific model that sees human institutions and society itself as resulting from the choices that individuals make concerning their behaviors. These choices are based on a cost-benefit calculus such that behavior A is chosen because the "costs" of choosing A are less than those for choosing B, or the benefits of choosing A outweigh the benefits of option B. Another way of stating this principle is that humans behave so as to maximize benefits and minimize costs. This generalized model of human behavior follows from the sociobiological axiom that humans, like other animals, are "blindly selected to maximize their individual fitness" and make individual choices based on the calculation of the cost-benefit ratio.

Those of us in Western societies are accustomed to thinking about behavior in individual, cost-benefit terms. We live in societies in which the notion of "choice," in both the economic and political arenas, is the ultimate justification of capitalist democracies. Individual choice among a range of alternatives, be they commodities or political candidates, is necessary to a "just" system, since individuals, and not groups, are to be served and such service must permit individuals to seek gain for their own self-interest. Such individual choice is basic to our cultural morality, and thus we often view individual entitlements, from what kind of job or how much money one has to who becomes president, as the outcome of self-interested individuals making choices. Conversely, people who fail to achieve what they desire in life are seen as making bad choices, or as not choosing alternatives, however difficult these might be, that would lead to the desired ends. Failure, as well as success, is an individual matter, and the kind of society, including its negative as well as positive aspects, in which we live is but the sum total of millions of individual social, economic, and political transactions.

The idea of isolated individuals making self-interested cost-benefit choices is a powerful one, both because it fits Western conceptions of human nature and because, when we examine any individual transaction, we often behave according to some cost-benefit calculation. The computer on which I am typing this manuscript resulted from a rather lengthy cost-benefit analysis of the microcomputing alternatives available to me. Similarly, when purchasing a new car, voting for president, writing a critical memo to my employer, or shopping in the grocery store, I make hundreds of conscious and unconscious decisions, weighing the advantages and disadvantages of my choices. These choices do make a difference, provided enough others make the same ones. If millions of car purchasers decide not to purchase Chevrolets, their decisions will no doubt impact on General Motors. What the individual-choice model confirms is that human beings are decision-makers who often make decisions to maximize some benefit.

What the individual-choice model does not enlighten us about is the nature of those "costs" and "benefits" that individuals have to choose among and what Garfinkel calls the "structural presuppositions" that underpin individual choices.[38] For example, my "choosing" to become a college professor rested, quite unconsciously at the time, on a prior decision that I work at all. This decision was no doubt based on a cost-benefit analysis of the following design: if I don't work, I don't live, or to use Marx's famous dictum, I work in order to live. I find it difficult to view such a decision as a "choice" among alternatives. The decision to work was dictated to me by my social standing in a particular kind of society. I was born into a family of modest means who owned nothing that would enable me to live without working. Others, luckier perhaps than I, were born into families who did own resources that would enable them not to work or, more usually, live off the work of others. For them the decision to work or not work was an entirely different kind of choice. My second-order decision to become a college professor was a choice among alternatives, but alternatives provided by the society in which I live. I did not choose, nor did the thought occur to me, to become a mule-team driver or a peasant farmer. Such roles do not exist in my society, are in fact incompatible with my society, and the idea that such roles would exist if only thousands of individuals "chose" them strains even the most vivid imagination.

This seemingly trivial example illustrates a couple of very nontrivial matters. First, my decision to work or not work is hardly an individual matter, but one that is shared by the overwhelming majority of Americans. It is a group phenomenon common to a *class* of individuals who, lacking ownership of the means necessary for life, and thus dependent on selling their labor power to sustain that life, are, in a very sense, coerced into their decision. Furthermore, it cannot be argued that this class of individuals, despite these "accidents" of birth, could have chosen to become owners of capital rather than sellers of labor power, since the structure of capitalism, which at a minimum requires the relation between owners of capital and owners of labor power for its very existence, makes such a choice impossible. Capital, viewed not as an attribute held by certain individuals, but as a social relation among individuals, is the structural presupposition that governs my (and millions of others') individual choices. Second, because capitalism and all other modes of production are systems of social relations, the choices made by seemingly independent individuals impact in both known and unknown ways on other individuals whose own choices become circumscribed, proscribed, or otherwise dictated by their relations to other individuals. Thus there is no meaningful sense in which the notion of individual choice is a choice by an individual (who is, at minimum, a thoroughly formed *social* individual) independent of preexisting social circumstances and predetermined social relations. Individual choices that do exist do so within and sometimes against these relations, but do not add up to those relations.

It is a problematic methodological stance, then, to argue that social institutions result from the conscious or unconscious choices of atomistic individuals seeking self-interested gain. Furthermore, when we analyze racial and ethnic social situations, we are mainly interested in explaining the structural features of those relations and are not primarily concerned with how a particular person, John Doe, is affected by those relations (although that may be exactly what John Doe himself is interested in). For example, we know that the poverty and unemployment rates for blacks are approximately three times as high as those for whites in the United States. We also know that this has been a relatively stable proportion since World War II and seems to change little despite government programs designed to alter this inequality. It could be argued (and, as we will see in Chapter 4, often *is* argued) that poor blacks, having been dealt a cruel hand by American society, simply have to work harder to make it out of poverty. They will have to adopt new (white middle-class) values, work hard in school, and take advantage of the many programs provided for them by various arms of state and federal governments. Such an argument will then proceed by citing specific examples of successful blacks who followed all of this advice and became famous doctors, businessmen, and ball players. The moral of the story will not be lost on the perceptive listener—there are few obstacles that cannot be overcome through hard work, and it is up to the individual person to succeed.

It turns out, however, that many obstacles are quite difficult to overcome. One of these seems to be a certain level of unemployment generated by the society at large, irrespective of individual choice or hard work. The fact of the matter is that all blacks cannot become successful lawyers, doctors, or ball players, or even ordinary workers, because the social system both creates and requires a certain structural level of failure, such as unemployment, for its continued functioning. Capital must have the freedom to close down plants, lay off workers, move from North to South or even overseas in order to serve its interest of profit maximization. Such freedom for capital entails the loss of freedom for those dependent on it. In the face of black resistance, both the state and capital have made accommodations to ensure that blacks who attain educational qualifications are permitted into the corporate and state institutions such that we have witnessed a burgeoning of the black middle class since the mid–1960s. But none of this has impacted much on the black underclass, which remains poor and undereducated and lacks decent job opportunities. This structural level of unemployment cannot be explained by reference to individual behaviors. It must be explained by the historical dynamics of the capitalist system itself and the system of race relations that has been part of that history.[39] The kind of reductionistic and individualistic explanation that pop sociobiology is casts doubt on its ability to serve as an adequate explanation of complex racial and ethnic social relations. This is so irrespective of whether or not humans behave (seldom, sometimes, often, always?) according to some fitness maximization calculus. Human beings inherit more than heredity. They inherit a system of institutions, values, their own place in the system, and the social and cultural history of generations past. Under certain conditions this cultural inheritance can be revolutionized and another one put in its place. It might be interesting to know how this social and cultural diversity has affected our biology, how our fitness has or has not been enhanced by our practices. But this is not the kind of sociobiology currently being practiced. Pop sociobiology insists on appealing to the genetic nature of the beast within us, not that we might change it, but to absolve us of responsibility for it. Those seeking absolution should take little consolation from the evidence or the promise of pop sociobiology.

Notes

1. Philip Kitcher, *Vaulting Ambition: Sociobiology and the Quest for Human Nature.* Cambridge, Mass.: MIT Press, 1985, p. 435.

2. Ibid., pp. 14–15.

3. J. Maynard Smith, "Introduction," in P. Bateson, ed., *Current Problems in Sociobiology.* Cambridge: Cambridge University Press, 1982, pp. 1–3.

4. For these critiques consult Richard Lewontin, Steven Rose, and Leo Kamin, "Bourgeois Ideology and the Origins of Biological Determinism," *Race & Class*, 24(1), 1982; Marshall Sahlins, *The Use and Abuse of Biology.* Ann Arbor: University of Michigan Press, 1976; Martin Barker, *The New Racism: Conservatives and the Ideology of the Tribe.* Frederick, Md.: University Publications of America, 1981.

5. R. Alexander, *Darwinism and Human Affairs.* Seattle: University of Washington Press, 1979; R. Dawkins, *The Selfish Gene.* Oxford: Oxford University Press, 1976.

6. Alexander, *Darwinism and Human Affairs*, p. 56.

7. Pierre L. van den Berghe, *The Ethnic Phenomenon*. New York: Elsevier, 1981, p. 11.

8. Kitcher, *Vaulting Ambition*, p. 283.

9. Van den Berghe, *Ethnic Phenomenon*, p. xii.

10. Ibid., p. 37 (emphasis added).

11. Barker, *New Racism*, p. 159.

12. C. Lumsden and E. O. Wilson, *Genes, Mind and Culture*. Cambridge, Mass.: Harvard University Press, 1981. For a critique of this more recent position see Kitcher, *Vaulting Ambition*, Chapter 10. In a recent article van den Berghe adopts the gene-culture coevolution theory as proposed by Lumsden and Wilson to explain preferences for lighter skin color (Pierre L. van den Berghe and Peter Frost, "Skin Color Preference, Sexual Dimorphism and Sexual Selection: A Case of Gene Culture Co-evolution?" *Ethnic and Racial Studies* 9[1], January 1986, pp. 87–113). He does not address the compatibility of the Lumsden and Wilson view with the pop sociobiology he proposes in *The Ethnic Phenomenon*.

13. W. D. Hamilton, "The Genetical Evolution of Social Behavior I" (1964), pp. 23–43, and "The Genetical Evolution of Social Behavior II" (1964), pp. 44–89, in G. C. Williams, ed., *Group Selection*. Chicago: Aldine, 1971. For a brief discussion of Hamilton's contribution see Kitcher, *Vaulting Ambition*, pp. 77–84.

14. Van den Berghe, *Ethnic Phenomenon*, p. 19.

15. Ibid., pp. 8–11.

16. Ibid., p. 9.

17. Kitcher, *Vaulting Ambition*, pp. 99–104.

18. A particularly good example of van den Berghe's misuse of the biological notion of fitness is contained in an earlier work on sociobiology titled *Human Family Systems: An Evolutionary View* (New York: Elsevier, 1979), p. 179. In this passage he implies that considerations of "social" fitness ultimately pay off in increased biological fitness:

Better to have only two children who are university graduates with good jobs, a secure income and a good home to raise four highly viable grandchildren in, than eight badly educated, underfed children who are likely to become juvenile delinquents, to be shot by the police or locked up under conditions of compulsory celibacy in the state penitentiary, so that, in the end, they may end up producing few or no grandchildren. We know the cost of raising a child in an industrial society at a level of health and education that will secure him or her a good, steady middle-class job is staggering and ever escalating. Most parents are aware of this and very few can afford to carry more than two or three of the "capital-intensive" offspring through college (p. 179)

Van den Berghe does not supply us with the data that demonstrate that middle-class parents with many children produce fewer grandchildren than middle-class parents with two or fewer children. Rightly so, for it seems that our jails, penitentiaries, and morgues are not filled with middle-class kids from large families who, in addition to being underfed, were later arrested or shot by the police. Instead, our jails, penitentiaries, and morgues are filled with the children of lower-class, disproportionately minority children who have been arrested or shot by the police. If anybody should heed van den Berghe's advice for limiting their reproductive behavior, it is these poor souls. But alas, as van den Berghe says, "parents who can least afford children tend to have the most. Clearly, factors other than kin selection are at work" (p. 178). On the contrary, it could be argued here that kin selection is at work if reproductive success and not social success is the "fitness" being maximized.

19. Van den Berghe, *Ethnic Phenomenon*, p. 35.

20. Van den Berghe, *Human Family Systems*, p. 91.

21. Van den Berghe, *Ethnic Phenomenon*, p. 220.

22. Ibid., p. 27.

23. In effect, van den Berghe introduces evolutionary considerations in the wrong place in his analysis. This point is nicely demonstrated by Kitcher in his critique of anthropological discussions of alliance formation and infanticide that invoke inclusive fitness as the underlying cause of these practices (Kitcher, *Vaulting Ambition*, pp. 307–329).

24. Van den Berghe, *Ethnic Phenomenon*, p. 40.

25. Ibid., p. 216.

26. Ibid., pp. 216–217.

27. Ibid., p. 218.

28. Ibid., p. 219.

29. Ibid., p. 31.

30. Ibid., pp. 243–244.

31. As van den Berghe later states, "class ties, being openly utilitarian, do not commit one emotionally as do ethnic ties. One can resign from a trade union or a professional association in a way in which one cannot resign from a family, an ethny or a caste" (*Ethnic Phenomenon*, p. 257). It is unlikely that van den Berghe himself is emotionally committed to a trade union, but my experience with coal miners affiliated with the United Mine Workers of America in southwest Virginia provides abundant evidence not only for a strong emotional commitment, but also one that often transcends commitments to families and ethnic groups.

32. Critiques that focus on the correspondence between European culture and sociobiology's view of human nature are found in Sahlins, *Use and Abuse of Biology*, and Barker, *New Racism*.

33. Van den Berghe, *Ethnic Phenomenon*, p. xi.

34. Ibid., p. 217.

35. Allan Garfinkel, *Forms of Explanation: Rethinking the Questions in Social Theory.* New Haven, Conn.: Yale University Press, 1981, p. 50.

36. Kitcher, *Vaulting Ambition*, p. 329. Consult ch. 9 for his analysis of other anthropological varieties of pop sociobiology.

37. Van den Berghe, *Ethnic Phenomenon*, pp. 254–256.

38. Garfinkel, *Forms of Explanation*, especially ch. 4.

39. William J. Wilson, *The Declining Significance of Race.* 2d ed. Chicago: University of Chicago Press, 1978, especially chs. 4–7.

3

Primordial Sentiments Versus Civil Ties

THE DIALECTIC BETWEEN ETHNICITY AND THE STATE

Sociobiology is merely the latest theory to suggest that ethnic and racial ties and sentiments are deeply rooted aspects of human nature. At least since Ferdinand Tönnies' famous distinction between Gemeinschaft (or "primary" community) and Gesellschaft (associational or "secondary" community), social theorists have grappled with the issue of how large-scale, complex, heterogeneous societies, such as the United States, the Soviet Union, and Canada, can maintain order and solidarity in the absence of a common body of tradition and despite the superficial social relations that characterize them. Underlying this issue was the assumption that "primitive" or tribal societies were "natural" human communities based on intimate association with one's own kind—people who shared the same origin and ancestry, adhered to the same body of beliefs and values, adhered to and played by the same set of social rules that governed everyday interaction. Such communities were "natural" be-cause they were based on what have been termed "primordial affinities," feelings of belongingness or "we-ness" that are rooted in a common origin or source. No attempt was made to examine or explain the human necessity for such primordial atttachments.[1] It was taken for granted that human beings are, by nature, social beings who require intimate, affective, and deeply personal associations with other human beings for their proper development.

Classic studies of psychological development, particularly those by Cooley and G. H. Mead, demonstrated the crucial role played by "sig-nificant others"—parents, peers, and other intimate associates—in the development of a person's self-concept. Even today there is widespread consensus that a person's self-identity and self-esteem, both of which may be considered universal, unalterable human needs, are the products of a complex social psychological process dependent, for the most part, on the nature or quality of a person's intimate associations with family and close friends.

It was generally taken for granted that in kin-based societies, self-development was unproblematic. A person was born into an immediate family that was in turn a member of a lineage and clan that, in combination with other related lineages and clans, made up a "tribe" or a "people." Any person born into the group was securely connected to his community by a series of overlapping kinship and residential ties. One's identity was fastened to a set of predetermined or ascribed group identities—I am Hopi, a member of the Cottonwood clan, of my great grandmother's lineage—each of which carried with it a set of rights and obligations to one's family members, one's clan brothers and sisters, one's tribe. As a member of the community, the person was guaranteed a place to live, access to the means necessary to secure a productive livelihood, education into his community's customs and religion, and, in return for a properly lived life, the respect and admiration of his people. Despite this somewhat idealized and romanticized notion of the "noble savage," it is certainly true that the modern refrain "Who am I?" was seldom heard in kinship societies.

With the advent of large-scale or "mass" society, the individual and social security that was embedded in small-scale, face-to-face communities was swept away. The development of the state, a form of political organization based on the effective (at root, military) control of a territory and the people residing in it, produced social orders that ultimately rested on coercion. The natural or "folk" community based on ethnic homogeneity, cultural consensus, and a large measure of autonomy became incorporated into polities in which a dominant ethny—now a ruling class or elite—exercised political and, to some extent, ideological control over one or more subordinate groups. In this context a person's identity and his rights and obligations stemmed as much from his (and his group's) position in the new state order as from his membership in a natal or "home" community. In addition to whatever primordial attachments remained, a person's social identity was now partially shaped by his classification as a nobleman or as a commoner, freeman or serf.

In the agrarian feudal states of preindustrial Europe and Asia the divorce of the individual from his natural community ties was only partial and incomplete. The great mass of people still were born, grew up, and died in their home communities, where kin, neighbors, and the land formed the basis of one's significant attachments and served as the locus of everyday interaction. The state remained a distant, usually foreign institution, both materially and symbolically, a fact of life that need not be confronted, provided one feigned obeisance, paid tribute or taxes, and did not seek to overthrow it. Even in the preindustrial state, then, one's primordial affinities and attachments remained tied to the local community, which, in most cases, embodied centuries of common tradition, language, and people. A strong sense of personal and group identity could still be forged and maintained even among peasants or serfs, who, despite their subordinate political status, derived a sense of honor and personal esteem from the primary ties that still bound them. Serfdom was not slavery, which, as Orlando Patterson has eloquently argued, "is the permanent, violent domination of *natally alienated* and generally dishonored persons" (emphasis added).[2]

It was the rise of the new industrial order in eighteenth-century Europe that augured the dismantling of the primordial bonds of kinship and community. The peasant's displacement from his land; his reluctant, but forced relocation to the squalid manufacturing towns of London, Birmingham, and Manchester; his very living now determined by his ability to sell his and his family's labor power to someone who, for his own very different reasons, needed to buy it; the breakdown of traditional privileges and duties, however insidious, that were guaranteed by the feudal order; the necessity of a maturing capitalist system to expand beyond its borders of origin to first conquer and then administer the still primordial worlds of Africa, Asia, and America—these are the general processes unleashed against primordial ties in the names of "development and freedom," and that ironically spawned the modern refrains of "nationhood" and self-determination.[3]

For those at the center of this development—the propertied and monied classes of England, France, and Holland—the new economic order meant the opportunity to accumulate both wealth and power on a scale that was not possible under the feudal system of inherited ranks and privileges. For the great mass of their nonpropertied countrymen, however, this new freedom based on private property and hyperindividualism meant freedom *from* the security of the family, the community, and the land, and the freedom *to* toil tortuous hours in unhealthy factories or, perhaps even less worse, to become the first "clients" of a newly created and ever-expanding poor relief system. It is in this context that the two great social theorists of their (and even our) time, Marx and Durkheim, each diagnosed in a single word the social *and* personal sickness created by the new order: alienation and anomie.

For the millions of non-European, nonwhite people living in the colonized peripheries of capitalist development, mere alienation or anomie would have been, had they foreseen their fates, almost welcome pathogens. Instead, they were confronted with more direct and more effective threats to their traditional existence: smallpox, measles, and the barrel of a gun. Those who survived the genocide still suffered the ensuing "ethnocide"—the transformation and, in many cases, extinction of their traditional way of life. Hundreds of thousands of indigenes were forcibly uprooted from their families and communities and sent to labor in the mines, construction gangs, and plantations of the conquering Europeans. Many among these were transported across the Atlantic to face the greatest ignominy of all—slavery.

I do not mean to suggest that this historical process was even, uniform, or monolithic. Different colonial regimes administered native peoples in substantially different ways with substantially different outcomes, much of it dependent on the amount of resistance encountered from the native peoples themselves.[4] But from the viewpoint of the conquered nations, this process was thoroughly systematic in its effects. Nor do I mean to suggest that this process *ended* with the dismemberment of the European colonial empires after World War II. The political and economic repercussions of capitalist development are still being felt—even in the anticapitalist world—and one does not have to go back to prior centuries to document either ethnocide (the case of Amazonian Indians comes to mind) or colonialism (the formation of the state of Israel and the subsequent incorporation and displacement of Palestinians is, from the Palestinian perspective, just such a case).[5]

In the context of this broadly sketched, but nevertheless accurate, historical landscape it is not an overstatement to claim that the great majority of the ethnic and racial conflicts both in the past and in the contemporary world are the products of this historical process. The situation of Afro-Americans in the United States, apartheid in South Africa, ethnic factionalism in the new African states, the Middle East and northern Ireland crises—all can be traced in a rather direct, but by no means simple, manner to the development of the Euro-capitalist world. This development as an institutional process is examined in later chapters. Here I want to critique theories that have explored the psychodynamics of this process, that is, the effects of this global movement on the personal and group *identities* of those who have had the fortune or, in most cases, the misfortune of being labeled "ethnics" in the modern world. This involves an examination of what ethnicity means to people and groups for whom an ethnic identity is a powerful symbolic aspect of their self-concepts, their self-esteem, their collective identity. Put another way, it is an attempt to uncover the social psychological dimensions of ethnic pride.

With the renewed interest in ethnic persistence, ethnic "revivalism," ethnic conflict, the search for one's "roots," and a host of other ethnically or racially based phenomena, there has arisen in the social sciences a body of writings that suggests that this ethnic renewal represents a turning away from what are seen as the false, superficial, nonaffective, alienating ties of one's state, class, occupation—one's civil ties—and a turning back to the "natural," deep-rooted, affective ties of family, community, and *ethnic group*.[6] Collectively, these writings represent an emergent position that argues that ethnic identity is a primordial tie, since an ethnic attachment represents a feeling of "we-ness" or community that is rooted in a common origin or ancestry.

There is no coherent set of statements by a single author, or even by several authors, that permits me to straightforwardly list the basic tenets or assumptions that underpin what is known as the "primordialist" theory of ethnicity. This is due in large part to the *absence* of a theory or explanation of why we should regard ethnicity as a natural, primordial sentiment. Pierre van den Berghe is quite right when he suggests that the

primordialist position on ethnicity [is] vulnerable on two scores: 1. It generally stopped at asserting the fundamental nature of ethnic sentiment without suggesting any explanation of why that should be the case.... What kind of mysterious and suspicious force was this "voice of blood" that moved people to tribalism, racism and ethnic intolerance? 2. If ethnicity was primordial, then was it not also ineluctable and immutable? Yet, patently, ethnic sentiments waxed and waned according to circumstances. How is all this circumstantial fluidity reconcilable with the primordialist position?[7]

Van den Berghe's intention is to demonstrate that the primordialist position is correct, but that it requires sociobiological theory in order to be compelling. As I tried to show in Chapter 2, sociobiology cannot adequately rescue the primordialist position by means of its alleged biological constructs of nepotism (which would explain proposition 1 above) and reciprocity (which would explain proposition 2). If this is so, then the primordialist position is still vulnerable insofar as it cannot establish the causes of ethnicity in natural, biological terms.

Despite this shortcoming, the primordialist view cannot be so easily dismissed. Many writers who have, rightly or wrongly, been identified with the primordialist position have produced some of the best work on the dynamics of ethnicity in the contemporary world and greatly advanced our understanding of both the personal and social dimensions of the ethnic factor. Two scholars to be discussed later in this chapter come to mind: sociologist Edward Shils and anthropologist Clifford Geertz. Both have been repeatedly linked to the primordialist theory of ethnicity. Shils is generally cited as the founding ancestor of the primordialist position. Geertz, on the other hand, has clearly defined ethnicity as a primordial sentiment, *not* because ethnicity is a natural, biologically based identity, but because ethnicity is a historically important cultural identity that, in certain parts of the world, has become particularly crucial or salient politically.

Inasmuch as the primordialist position on ethnicity is characterized by the absence of an explicit theoretical framework, there is a good deal of confusion about the causes of ethnic classification, sentiments, and social organization within the primordialist tradition. The very use of the term "primordial" to define this view adds to, rather than clarifies, the confusion. My standard college dictionary lists three usages of "primordial": first, "constituting a beginning or source"; second, a definition used in biology meaning "primitive, initial, first formed"; third, "pertaining to or existing at or from the very beginning."[8] If ethnicity is primordial in the senses implied above, then we are placed in the rather difficult position of trying to explain a phenomenon that, like God, "always was, always is, and always will be." Yet, as I will argue later, ethnicity is not primordial in this sense; it is a phenomenon whose origins can be traced and whose expression waxes and wanes regularly (though not always predictably) according to definite sociohistorical conditions.

Amid this atheoretical confusion, it is nevertheless possible to identify two quite different strains of primordialist writings. One strain implies that ethnicity is a primordial sentiment in a sense that leads one to search for a natural, genetically based origin for ethnic group sentiments. Thus the attempt of van den Berghe to provide just such a biological basis for these sentiments is fully compatible with this approach. A second strain, most evident in the writings of Clifford Geertz, implies a theoretical basis for ethnic sentiments that is located in the dialectical interplay between deeply rooted historical ties based on assumed kinship, custom, language, and race and the recent demands placed on such primordial ties by the requirements for effective statehood. This approach is most compatible with a social theory of human nature, especially one that stresses the historically evolved changes in modes of social organization. By briefly outlining and critiquing each position, I hope to demonstrate that although neither view is a sufficient explanation for ethnicity, the second view is far superior to the first and, combined with an adequate social theory, can advance our understanding of the ethnic factor in the modern world.

Ethnicity as a "Natural" Primordial Tie: Basic Assumptions

The following assumptions represent my appraisal of the biological "school" of primordial sentiments. I stress the words "my appraisal" because it is not possible to find the list produced below in any single work or combination of works. This is because the scholarly writings within this tradition are sufficiently unclear regarding the theoretical underpinnings of ethnicity to preclude an explicit and perhaps defensible list of theoretical assumptions. For this reason some of the writers discussed below in connection with these assumptions may object to my characterization of their position. This caveat notwithstanding, the notion that ethnicity is a "natural" primordial tie seems tied to the following assumptions.

1. *A group identity is an indispensable aspect of a person's personal identity.* Because human beings are, by nature, social beings, every individual human defines himself or herself largely in terms of those other humans and groups who have had a significant impact on the person's lifelong development. In other words, a person's *individual* identity is a complex composite formed by the quantity and quality of that person's social experiences, especially those interpersonal relationships (both positive and negative) that are long-lasting and intimate—what sociologists have called "primary group" ties. This is true even in complex, heterogeneous, industrial societies where the locus of everyday life is still to be found in the personal attachments among family members, intimate peer groups, and other deeply binding relationships. It is this fact that Edward Shils was trying to impress on his colleagues in his elegant and justly famous speech, "Primordial, Personal, Sacred, and Civil Ties":

As I see it, modern society is no lonely crowd, no horde of refugees fleeing from freedom. It is no Gesellschaft, soulless, egotistical, loveless, faithless, utterly impersonal, and lacking any integrative forces other than interest or coercion. It is held together by an infinity of personal attachments, moral obligations in concrete contexts, professional and creative pride, individual ambition, *primordial affinities*, and a civil sense which is low in many, high in some and moderate in most persons. (Emphasis added.)[9]

Shils' own research on soldiers' behavior during World War II had convinced him that combat effectiveness and morale had less to do with a soldier's patriotic zeal or attachment to the symbols of the state or party than his personal attachments to his comrades, family, and "outfit." This was as true for Soviet and German soldiers as for Americans. This led Shils to the view that social life even in atomized, individualized, complex societies still revolved in the main around various kinds of primary group relationships: "Man is much more concerned with what is near at hand, with what is present and concrete than with what is remote and abstract. He is more responsive to whole persons, to the status of those who surround him and the justice which he sees in his own situation than he is with the symbols of remote persons, with the total status system in the society and with the global system of justice."[10] Shils was particularly impressed by what he called "significant relational" qualities among family members "which could only be described as primordial": "The attachment to another member of one's kinship group is not just a function of interaction as Professor Homans would have it. It is because a certain ineffable significance is attributed to the tie of blood."[11]

Shils later extended this notion of "primordial" to the processes of ethnic and racial identification: "The need for connections or relationships of a primordial character will be endemic in human existence as long as biological existence has a value to the individual organism. Ethnic identification, of which color identification is a particular variant, is a manifestation of this need."[12] Shils was claiming that there exists an unalterable biological need for deep-seated, affective, primordial relationships, a need that, under certain sociohistorical circumstances, can be satisfied by ethnic or racial identities. He was not claiming that either race or ethnicity was the only form of identification that could fill this need, although I do interpret his writings as suggesting that other forms of personal identification with groups such as classes, occupations, and political parties would not as effectively meet this primordial need because they are not rooted "in ties of blood." Shils, then, interpreted ethnicity and race as more primordial than other personal ties to the extent that they were extensions of family and other kinship connections. This view produced the second assumption that characterizes the naturalist school of primordialist theory.

2. *Ethnic attachments are a natural kind of group affiliation.* Ethnic or racial ties are "natural" insofar as they possess "ineffable" significance rooted in ties of blood. A useful illustration of this assumption is Harold Isaacs' concept of "basic group identity":

This is the identity derived from belonging to what is generally and loosely called an "ethnic group." It is composed of what have been called "primordial affinities and attachments." It is the identity made up of what a person is born with or acquires at birth. It is distinct from all the other multiple and secondary identities people acquire because unlike all the others, its elements are what make a group, in Clifford Geertz' phrase, a "candidate for nationhood."[13]

In another definitional passage Isaacs writes, "To begin with, then, basic group identity consists of the readymade set of endowments and identifications which every individual shares with others from the moment of birth by the chance of the family into which he is born at that given time in that given place."[14] Isaacs goes on to specify and perceptively discuss the various elements that together constitute a person's "BGI" (basic group identity): (1) a person's body (including its size, shape, skin color, etc.), (2) a person's name (individual and family), (3) the history and origins of one's group, (4) nationality or other group or tribal affiliation, (5) language, (6) religion, (7) culture, (8) geography and topography of one's birthplace.[15]

At one level there is nothing in Isaacs' characterization of BGI with which to quarrel. All human beings are born into a particular sociohistorical context that serves to define any person in relation to all other people. At another level, however, the notion of BGI contains several disturbing and incorrect implications. First, there is the synonymous use of BGI and ethnic group identity. This implies that all people have an ethnic group identity when, in reality, an ethnic identity may or *may not be* a part of a person's BGI.[16] Second, there is the implication that an ethnic identity is *more basic* than what Isaacs calls "secondary identities," such as occupational and class identities. This is presumably because one is born into an ethnic group and is socialized into its culture early in life, whereas occupational identities are acquired later in life or, in the case of class identities (which can also be ascribed at birth), do not have the "force of blood" behind them.

One encounters this idea repeatedly in primordialist writings on ethnicity. One representative example has appeared in a recent book titled *Ethnic Identity*, by A. P. Royce: "One has a more distinct, more-individual identity as a member of an ethnic group than as a member of a social class, and the satisfaction of participating in an ethnic festival is missing from events connected with one's social class."[17] This view, one that is asserted and not explained, has led to the implication that an ethnic identity is a *necessary* aspect of one's personal identity, that people who possess an ethnic identity have a more complete, fulfilling, and satisfying identity than those who do not have an ethnic identity. The back of the jacket of Royce's book expresses this sentiment clearly, as does Royce herself:

Attitudes toward ethnicity have changed dramatically over the years to the point when to be lacking in an ethnic background is to be perceived as culturally disadvantaged.... Today, ethnic identity is not a shameful thing; in fact its absence is. Ethnic pride is not limited to the group itself; it is the heritage of each and every member. It is the savor and remembrance of the past. More important, it is the promise of the future.[18]

It is precisely Royce's future that troubles me, for it envisions, nay, *values* a human community that is organized on the sectarian biases of ethnic background, be they real or putative, on the grounds that such affiliations are affectively fulfilling and natural. Moreover, there is clearly enough of this envisioned future in the current world to make us all skeptical of such a future's promise. The message of this brand of primordialism is not merely conservative, but reactionary, for it suggests that the way out of our current malaise is to retribalize according to our various ancestral myths. Forget one's current affective ties to friends of different colors, religions, and origins. Dispense with one's deeply felt occupational and class identities. These are all false gods.

This kind of theorizing not only makes it difficult to understand ethnic processes, but it also positively obscures them. It asserts that the cause of alienation, anomie, interethnic hostility, and conflict is due to some mysterious loss of a basic, necessary, and affectively fulfilling identity that is rooted in a primordial ancestral tie. It thus argues that the way out of the modern dilemma is to *find* or otherwise recapture what has been lost, even though we are given no theory that explains how our ethnic identity was lost in the first place. If ethnicity is so basic and positive to a healthy personal identity, why have parents, schools, and other formative agencies failed to properly socialize the young into the wonderful bliss of the ethnic womb? Or, if they have tried to do just this (as immigrant parents no doubt attempted to foster a sense of ethnic identity in their American-born children), why have they failed so miserably? Any view that asserts ethnicity to be necessary and "good" cannot answer these questions.

This brand of primordialism also obscures the nature of ethnicity by failing to recognize those ethnic and racial processes that contradict its basic tenets. In an excellent critique of primordialism, Edna Bonacich discusses three reasons for questioning the tenets of this approach. First, there is the fact that the pervasive tendency among humans to interbreed makes it nearly impossible to define ethnic group boundaries according to ancestral ties of blood. Moreover, ethnic groups that formerly did not exist (Asian-Americans, for example) are constructed out of formerly distinctive and sometimes hostile national elements. Second, there tends to be as much conflict *within* ethnic groups as between them, particularly when ethnic groups are beset by class divisions. As my own work on the class structure of the Chinese in North America has shown, shared ethnicity does not necessarily lead to ethnic solidarity or harmony.[19] Third, conflicts based on ethnic and racial differences are quite variable. In some places they are fierce, while in others they are moderate or even nonexistent. A full range of interethnic relations has been encountered in the world—from assimilation to genocide to pluralism. As Bonacich concludes:

For all these reasons, and there are probably others, we cannot simply accept communalistic groups as natural or primordial units. Ethnic, national, and racial solidarity and antagonism are all socially created phenomena. True, they are social phenomena which call upon primordial sentiments and bonds based on common ancestry. But these sentiments and bonds are not just naturally there. They must be constructed and activated. It is thus incumbent upon us not to take ethnic phenomena for granted, but to try to explain them.[20]

Several writers who are generally considered to be "primordialists" in their theoretical outlook have called attention to the social and historical bases of ethnic attachments. Isaacs, for example, recognizes that both the content and significance of basic group identity is ultimately dependent on "the group's position relative to other groups in its environment—all the political-social-economic circumstances that impinge on the family and the group."[21] In an even more straightforward continuation of this passage he writes:

Of this [political-social-economic circumstances] most decisive are the political conditions in which the group identity is held, the measure of power or powerlessness that is attached to it. How dominant or dominated is the group to which this individual belongs? . . . This is the cardinal question and it is essentially the question of the governing politics, the push and pull of power among the groups who share the scene.[22]

This statement would seem to compel Isaacs to closely examine the various political-economic-social conditions in which BGI (and ethnic identity) is held, and develop a theory that helps us to explain both the existence and impact of these conditions on ethnic group relations. But Isaacs retreats from this admittedly large and difficult task by focusing on a discussion of how a BGI can fulfill human needs for belongingness and self-esteem without discussing why such needs are not effectively met under certain political arrangements. He fails to address that "most decisive" factor that he identifies—the structures of political domination in the contemporary world.

What needs to be addressed, then, are the social, political, and historical circumstances that cause ethnic or racial identities—identities based on real or assumed ancestry or "ties of blood"—to become symbolically, emotionally, and politically forceful. One primordialist scholar, Clifford Geertz, has located the meaning of ethnicity within the context of world historical circumstances and sought to understand the cultural and political significance of ethnicity as both a product and a determinant of the changing and still fluid social structures that characterize much of the developing world. His writings constitute that strain of primordialism that is consistent with, dependent upon, *and* contributory to a social theory of ethnicity. This must be stressed, for Geertz has been both associated with and criticized for holding the view that ethnic attachments are primordial in a natural, biological sense.[23] This stems from his somewhat careless definition (borrowed from Shils) of primordial attachments that does imply a mysterious, if not biological, basis for ethnic sentiments:

By a primordial attachment is meant one that stems from the "givens"—or, more precisely, as culture is inevitably involved in such matters, the assumed "givens"— of social existence: immediate contiguity and kin connection mainly, but beyond them the givenness that stems from being born into a particular religious community, speaking a particular language, or even a dialect of a language, and following particular social practices. These congruities of blood, speech, custom, and so on, are seen to *have an ineffable, and at times overpowering, coerciveness in and of themselves.* One is bound to one's kinsman, one's neighbor, one's fellow believer, ipso facto; . . . in great part by virtue of some unaccountable absolute import attributed to the very tie itself. . . . But for virtually every person, in every society, at almost all times, some attachments seem to flow more from a sense of *natural*—some would say *spiritual*— affinity than from social interaction. (Emphasis added.)[24]

Like other primordialists, Geertz does seem caught up in the atheoretical, almost mystical, vagaries that surround the nature of ethnic sentiments. And on one occasion, at least, he appears guilty of attributing a primacy and constancy to ethnic attachments vis-à-vis social attachments of other kinds:

There are many competing loyalties in the new states, as in any state—ties to class, party, business, union, profession, or whatever. But groups formed of such ties are virtually never considered as possible self-standing, maximal social units, as candidates for nationhood. . . . Economic or class or intellectual disaffection threatens revolution, but disaffection based on race, language, or culture threatens partition, irredentism, or merger, a redrawing of the very limits of the state, a new definition of its domain.[25]

These and other isolated statements regarding primordial ties do indicate a weakness ("incompleteness" is a fairer criticism) in Geertz's theoretical underpinnings, a weakness that stems from the philosophical incompleteness of Geertz's interpretive anthropology. But to use such isolated statements to argue that he regards the primordial nature of ethnicity to be a biologically rooted nature violates both the intent and the overall content of his work. For example, the quote immediately above is certainly true in one sense: ethnic disaffection does represent a challenge to authority that is *different* from class or intellectual disaffection. But only under certain circumstances (to be specified below) is ethnic disaffection the primary challenge, a fact Geertz is well aware of. As the foremost proponent of interpretive anthropology, Geertz rightfully insists that a proper understanding of social practices requires their examination in the total context of their symbolic and material aspects— an admonition we must heed to arrive at an understanding of his work.

Ethnicity as a Socially and Historically Produced Primordial Tie: Basic Tenets

Using Geertz's work, then, it is possible to identify a series of factors that links the significance of primordial ties to particular socio/historical conditions and, by extension, argues for a socially determined view of ethnic sentiments. The following principles are consistent with this view:

1. *Ethnic bonds and sentiments become politically significant when formerly autonomous, prestate societies are forced to reorganize into state-level social systems.* This constitutes the "definition of the problem" that I was addressing in the title of this chapter—the "Dialectic Between Ethnicity and the State." This dialectic, or contradiction, between primordial ties (to tribe, language, culture) and civil ties (to state or party) is, on the one hand, *social* because it involves a transformation of social organization, a transformation of the institutional structure of society that can only be called revolutionary. It is also a concrete and continuing *historical* process, one that is occurring predominantly in the "new states"—former colonial territories in Africa, Asia, and the Middle East—that, having been thrust into independence since 1945 (or later), are still struggling to forge a civil identity from among the multitude of primordial communities of which they are made.

It is in locating the issue of primordialism within this sociohistorical process that Geertz has made a lasting and eloquent contribution; one that deserves to be quoted at length:

The peoples of the new states are simultaneously animated by two powerful, thoroughly interdependent, yet distinct and often actually opposed motives—the desire to be recognized as responsible agents whose wishes, acts, hopes, and opinions "matter," and the desire to build an efficient, dynamic modern state. The one aim is to be noticed: it is a search for an identity, and a demand that the identity be publicly acknowledged as having import, a social assertion of the self as "being somebody in the world." The other aim is practical: it is a demand for progress, for a rising standard of living, more effective political order, greater social justice, and beyond that of "playing a part in the larger arena of world politics," of "exercising influence among the nations." The two motives are, again, most intimately related, because citizenship in a truly modern state has more and more become the most broadly negotiable claim to personal significance, and because what Mazzini called the demand to exist and have a name is to such a great extent fired by a humiliating sense of exclusion from the important center of power in world society. But they are not the same thing. They stem from different sources and respond to different pressures. *It is, in fact, the tension between them that is one of the central driving forces in the national evolution of new states; as it is, at the same time, one of the greatest obstacles to such evolution.*

This tension takes a peculiarly severe and chronic form in the new states, both because of the great extent to which their peoples' sense of self remains bound up in the gross actualities of blood, race, language, locality, religion, or tradition, and because of the steadily accelerating importance in this century of the sovereign state as a positive instrument for the realization of collective aims. Multiethnic, usually multilinguistic, and sometimes multiracial, the populations of the new states tend to regard the immediate, concrete, and to them inherently meaningful sorting implicit in such "natural" diversity as the substantial content of their individuality. *To subordinate these specific and familiar identifications in favor of a generalized commitment to an overarching and somewhat alien civil order is to risk a loss of definition as an autonomous person, either through absorption into a culturally undifferentiated mass or, what is even worse, through a domination by some other rival ethnic, racial, or linguistic community that is able to imbue that order with the temper of its own personality.* (Emphases added)[26]

From this passage we can derive a corollary to our first proposition concerning the significance of primordial sentiments:

2. *When an individual's personal or a group's collective identities have been forged in the context of primordial communities, and when these communities' autonomy is threatened by the present-day necessity of forging a new and as yet unstable state order, then primordial sentiments may serve to define politically significant social movements.* Viewed in this context, ethnically and racially based conflicts are not reactionary, genetically determined attempts to "hold on to a remembrance of things past," but a forceful attempt to maintain or, in many instances, *gain* the freedom to be self-determining in an emerging world-order that threatens to deny such freedom. I can scarcely think of an ethnic conflict in the new states that is not fundamentally a conflict over "autonomy," "self-determination," or, to use an equally ambiguous concept, "equality." The Kurdish conflict in Iran, Malays versus Chinese in Malaya, Muslims versus Christians in Lebanon, Sinhalese versus Tamil in Sri Lanka, Ibos versus Biafrans in Nigeria, the Palestinian "question"—all are struggles that can be *defined* in terms of primordial affinities and ethnic attachments, but *they are not about* primordial affinities and ethnic attachments. If such conflicts were merely the result of trying to maintain a tribal or ethnic identity, then any reasonably astute politician could solve the conflict by simply recognizing or otherwise legitimating this claim (a tactic that has been tried literally hundreds of times and failed almost as often).

The current Palestinian-Israeli crisis demonstrates that much more than "identity," ethnic or otherwise, is at stake. A steadfast principle of Israeli policy toward Palestinians has been to deny their existence as a separate "people." Palestinians who live in Israel are officially classified as "non-Jews," whereas those Palestinians who are scattered throughout the rest of the world are simply "Arabs." Would not the crisis be ameliorated, if not solved, by the Israeli recognition of the Palestinians as a people who have a history and culture distinct and autonomous from other Arab people? From the Israeli point of view, the answer is no, for they understand that to recognize the Palestinian name is to legitimate the Palestinian cause.[27] It would mean recognizing that Israel, with the complicity of the Western powers, has been established on the soil of Palestinians, resulting in the mass exodus of its native people, and constructed a sectarian state that discriminates against Palestinians who have remained on the basis of religion and ancestry. The Palestinian quest for recognition of their existence is important to the extent that it will further their struggle to establish an independent state, which they think is necessary to undo their current domination by Israel and, to some extent, by other Arab states. In a world in which membership in a modern state "has more and more become the most broadly negotiable claim to personal significance," the aims of "being noticed" and playing a part in the new political order are conjoined. Geertz is technically correct when he says that these two aims "are not the same thing." But each *is* an indispensable, though differentiable, aspect of the same process, a process in which realization of the second aim—to have political rights and powers—is dependent on achieving the aim "to be noticed."

If primordial sentiments display both a persistence and a power to command the emotions and loyalties of human beings, it is not because they possess an ineffable and unaccountable "coerciveness in and of themselves." It is because millions of the world's people still live in archaic primordial social structures defined by kinship, language, custom, or "race." And inasmuch as these primordial communities are forced by twentieth-century circumstances to forge a new civil authority—an authority that is not only "up for grabs," but in many cases has already resulted in the subordination and extinction of formerly autonomous groups—it is little wonder that people caught in this transformation strenuously attempt to maintain and even institute aspects of their prior existence into the new. Thus the need of human beings to have an identity—an answer to the question of "who am I" as both individuals and social beings—is only an "ethnic" question or answer under certain circumstances. In the new states and, as we shall see, in modern states characterized by ethnic or racial stratification, ethnic identities are particularly efficacious. In other social formations, identities to class or party or occupation serve the same needs for "belongingness" and "self-esteem." But regardless of which identity defines the issue, the issue itself lies much deeper than mere belongingness or self-esteem. It is the human need for some measure of security, some measure of autonomy, some measure of freedom, some right to develop one's potential that is at stake. "Ethnic pride," "class pride," or "occupational pride" are, in different times and different places, important manifestations of the struggle to achieve these needs, but should not be confused with them. For these more basic needs are not met simply by forging and embracing a name, be it "Palestinian" or "proletariat." This is but the initial and necessary task for establishing an effective framework of human action, action that must ultimately build an institutional structure that both nourishes and permits these human needs to flourish.

This insight, too, we owe to Geertz who, in characteristic fashion, expresses it better than most:

The interplay of [primordial and civil ties] is not, therefore, a kind of cultural dialectic, a logistic of abstract ideas, but a historical process as concrete as industrialization and as tangible as war. The issues are being fought out not simply at the doctrine and argument level—though there is a great deal of both—but much more importantly in the material transformations that the social structures of all the new states are undergoing.[28]

Thus, the dialectic between ethnicity and the state—between primordial and civil ties—must be seen, at root, as a struggle over the institutional forms that the new society will embrace. What form of economy, what political process, what educational system, what language(s) will structure the new polity, and how will these structures integrate the multitude of primordial communities out of which they must be built? The answers are many and varied, not to mention provisional, both because of the diversity of still extant primordial institutional forms within the new states *and* because of the relative dependence of the new states on the advanced, powerful states that dominate the entire world-order.

Despite the complexity and difficulty of forging an autonomous civil order, however, the process is taking place, and enough of this process *has* taken place to enable us to describe its general outlines. In sketching these outlines it is remarkable to observe not the persistence of primordial attachments, but the degree to which such attachments have been put aside—not completely, but nevertheless significantly—in favor of civil ties. Moreover, this movement from primordial ties to civil ties and back and forth again follows a definite pattern, one that is discernible only by viewing it as part of the larger pattern of colonization—independence-postindependence. Nowhere is this pattern more clear than in Africa.

Ethnic versus State Claims: The Question of Self-Determination

Before its full-scale colonization by European states during the nineteenth century, Africa south of the Sahara consisted of literally hundreds of primordial societies, societies whose social organizations were rooted in principles of kinship and common territory. These societies varied widely from small-scale bands based on hunting and gathering to large pastoral tribes organized into nonhierarchical, complementary arrangements of lineages and clans to equally large-scale agricultural communities, some of which had developed centralized political structures based on chiefs and kings. Despite this diversity several features were common to the precolonial African landscape. First, each society identified with a "homeland," a specific territory defined not in the legalistic sense of a modern state boundary, but in the equally forceful sense of the "common land" occupied since the beginnings of "the people" themselves. "Nuerland," "Iboland," or "Bambutiland" could not be conveyed by mere lines on a map or viewed as a mere habitat or "environment" containing the basic resources that sustained a livelihood. Each place was imbued with an emotional and cultural significance that could only be regarded as sacred.

Second, each society maintained a high degree of autonomy economically, politically, and culturally. This autonomy was not maintained, as is often assumed, by virtue of isolation. Rather, contiguous African societies developed relatively stable forms of intergroup relations that, depending on time and place, varied from benign to hostile. At one pole were relations characterized by what Barth has termed "complementarity" or "symbiotic interdependence"—exchange relations between adjacent groups.[29] The classic case of Bambuti Pygmies trading their products of the forest for agricultural goods produced by their Bantu-speaking neighbors is a good example of such complementarity.[30] At the other pole were intergroup relations that resembled a near perpetual state of war. The famous example of the regular skirmishes between the Nuer and the Dinka, two great pastoral tribes of the Sudan, demonstrates how even hostile relations were patterned or regularized in a way that did not result in the wholesale conquest and incorporation of entire societies. The Nuer, who were usually victorious in such skirmishes, had a means for incorporating captured Dinka into a separate and subordinate status within Nuer society, and forms of slavery were practiced in other parts of precolonial Africa.[31] But even among these more hostile relations that often resulted in the displacement and alienation of *individuals* from their native society, the *group boundaries* of these societies remained intact. Despite the conflict between the Nuer and the Dinka, the Nuer and the Dinka remained discrete and independent entities.

European colonization of Africa was a conflict of altogether different proportions and results. The overwhelming military power possessed by the Europeans made the establishment of the new colonial boundaries a relatively quick matter. These new boundaries bore little resemblance to the primordial ones, a well-known fact that has produced serious consequences for present-day African statism. But with these new boundaries came new forms of rule that produced a new African reality. In some places European settlers displaced Africans, "developed" their land, and established their own states based on European hegemony and African subordination. In other places the domination was less complete. For millions of Africans life remained largely "traditional" save for the specter of smallpox and other diseases that seriously affected life in even remote villages. Hundreds of thousands of others, however, were conscripted into the new armies and labor corps overseen by colonial authorities, and several thousands of others were recruited into the new colonial bureaucracies. Given the largely extractive aims of Europe, the forms of colonization they produced in Africa produced a situation with

an interesting contradiction. On one level primordial communities retained some local autonomy, and everyday life proceeded much as it
had in the past. On another level, though, an entire class of Europeanized
Africans who had been instructed in the ideals of "modernity" and the
tactics of modern politics was created.

It is the African *response* to European colonization that is most interesting in light of primordialist theory. It was a response that was decidedly *anti*primordial in its content, one that stressed the necessity of
defeating colonialism within the framework of the new boundaries that
colonialism had created—a national strategy. As Geertz has stated it:

The first, formative stage of nationalism consisted essentially of confronting
the dense assemblage of cultural, racial, local, and linguistic categories of self-
identification and social loyalty that centuries of uninstructed history had produced with a simple, abstract, deliberately constructed, and almost painfully self-
conscious concept of political ethnicity—a proper "nationality" in the modern
manner.... The men who raised this challenge, the nationalist intellectuals, were
thus launching a revolution as much cultural, even epistemological, as it was
political.[32]

As Crawford Young has skillfully shown, the principle of territorial
(and not primordial) integrity was the master principle on which African
nationalism was based, one that remains the cornerstone of the Organization of African Unity. This was a remarkable event, given the still
significant strength of primordial ties within the colonial framework and
the fact that international jurisprudence has legitimated the right of
primordial entities based on common language, culture, history, and so
on to political independence. In other words, the multitude of tribal
African units could have claimed the right to self-determination. But as
Young states,

With a small number of exceptions, however, anticolonial nationalism found
inconvenient the notion that cultural affinities were a necessary basis for exercise
of this right. A shared condition of oppression and alien rule was the essential
cause of revolt. This could be remedied only by the pooled efforts of all who
participated in a given framework of subordination. Thus, the particular colonial
territory was the necessary framework for challenging foreign hegemony. Na-
tionalists, in seeking united support of all inhabitants of a given territory to
sanction the independence demand, embraced the colonial entity itself as the
defining basis for the "people" to whom self-determination should apply.[33]

Primordial challenges to territorial integrity have been a phenomenon
of the postindependence era. The great nationalist leaders produced by
the colonial period who led their states through the early years of independence have died, leaving behind the new institutional legacy they

helped to form. In some cases these new institutional structures have been relatively stable, consisting of viable political parties and strong, if not efficient, bureaucracies. In other cases weak institutional forms have created a vacuum in which old primordial loyalties have surfaced.

There have been several serious secessionary movements based on tribal, linguistic, and religious affinities not only in Africa, but in the new states of Asia as well. But the emergence of these primordially based political movements and their significant strength are neither surprising nor inexplicable. What is surprising is the degree to which such movements have not appeared or, where they have, have failed. The "failures" are particularly instructive, at least in Africa, for they have failed not only as a result of overwhelming opposition force, the lack of international recognition or support, and other material circumstances (in some cases these factors "favored" the primordial forces). They failed in great part because the strength of the primordial ties on which they were based was not sufficient to overcome the strong national ties that colonialism and independence had forged. In his analysis of three great primordial struggles in Africa—the Ibo, Katangan, and Eritrean secessionary movements—Crawford Young concludes that "were it not for the power of the doctrine that self-determination could apply to the territorial states of the decolonization settlement, there is good reason to believe that all three of the entities in question would today be independent."[34]

The Status of Primordialism as a Theory of Ethnicity

I have attempted to show in this chapter the degree to which the primordialist position on ethnic and racial sentiments is both a bewildering and conflicting set of propositions. On the one hand, it is possible to identify a primordialist view that must ultimately be grounded in a universalist and biological theory of human nature. So far, no such theory (e.g., sociobiology) has proved adequate to sustain such a view of human nature that, for the time being at least, casts doubt on the validity of this kind of primordialism. On the other hand, there exists an altogether different primordialist position, one that, despite its ambiguous references to the nature of primordial sentiments, ties the strength and efficacy of such sentiments to definite sociohistorical conditions (e.g., colonialism). Such a view is much easier to sustain insofar as it is possible to demonstrate the waxing and waning of primordial sentiments according to definite sociohistorical changes, and to thus argue that only under some circumstances do human beings exhibit a primordial nature based on ethnic or racial identifications.

Even this latter, more acceptable brand of primordialism contains deficiencies that make it difficult to embrace as a sufficient theory of

ethnicity, however. A major deficiency is in viewing primordial sentiments as mysterious, ineffable, and immutable, as having a certain coerciveness "in and of themselves" that commands the loyalties of men.
What I have tried to show is that they are none of these things. Instead,
primordial sentiments derive their strength from two quite nonmyster-
ious forces: one, where people still live in "primordial communities"—
societies in which the great bulk of economic, political, and cultural needs
are still met through social arrangements based on kinship. Primordial
sentiments have efficacy in primordial social structures (e.g., kinship
societies, precapitalist societies, prestate societies). Two, primordial sentiments tend to command people's loyalties under circumstances that
threaten the existence, autonomy, and independence of their communities, and even then they must often compete with other sentiments
such as a nationalism, which is not exclusively defined in terms of prior
ethnic identities. Thus the expression of ethnic, racial, cultural, or other
forms of primordialism reflects deeper, increasingly unmet human
needs.

Aside from the ambiguities that surround the concept of "primordial,"
there remains a theoretical void even in Geertz's profound and complex
analysis. Although he has led us to see in the dialectic between primordial
and civil ties the need for a historical and comparative theory of intergroup relations, such a theory is not provided. It is not enough to suggest
that ethnicity is a function of historical events such as colonialism, the
emergence of the modern state, and so on. Geertz takes these historical
movements for granted and then proceeds to the *very necessary* task of
interpreting the impacts of these movements on the symbolic construc-
tions of those affected by them. But history itself must be explained if
we are ever to exercise some measure of control over our future. We
still need a theory that suggests the causes of colonialism and other
exploitative social relations that continue to produce ethnic, racial, linguistic, and other forms of antagonism and resistance. The search for
such a theory occupies our attention in Chapters 5 and 6. But there
remains to be discussed another theory of ethnicity, one developed to
explain ethnic and racial movements not in the new states, but in the
most "modern" and advanced of all states—the United States.

In the United States the primordial expression of ethnicity is altogether different in its origins and political character than in the new
states. It has emerged from a different set of social, political, and economic circumstances, and thus cannot be understood in terms of the
historical processes that occur in the peripheries of capitalist development.

The primordialist conception of ethnicity in America is usually called
the "new ethnicity," and refers to the revival of ethnic consciousness and
political activism among largely assimilated white ethnic groups such as

Italians, Germans, Poles, Irish, and, to some extent, Jews. The ideological and political characteristics of this white ethnic movement have been thoroughly critiqued by several scholars.[35] The theoretical underpinnings of this movement have not been adequately discussed, however. What I want to show is that the emergence of the "new ethnicity" as a *social theory* developed out of a crisis in assimilationism, the dominant social theory designed to explain interethnic and interracial relations in modern states. It is to this that I now turn.

Notes

1. Sociobiology claims to have located the source of the human need for primordial sentiments in the genetic tendency for nepotism. Cf. Pierre L. van den Berghe, *The Ethnic Phenomenon*. New York: Elsevier, 1981, pp. 17–18.

2. Orlando Patterson, *Slavery and Social Death*. Cambridge, Mass.: Harvard Univerisity Press, 1982, p. 13.

3. A brilliant exposition of the view I am espousing here is found in Ernest Gellner, *Nations and Nationalism*. Ithaca, N.Y.: Cornell University Press, 1983. Gellner argues, rightly I think, that most of the racial and ethnic conflict in the world results from the dominance of industrialism as a way of life, and the impact of industrialism on prestate and agrarian state structures.

4. A more thorough examination of the impact of capitalist development on ethnicity is presented in Chapter 5, "Ethnicity and the Capitalist World-System."

5. An excellent treatment of the Palestinian question is Edward Said, *The Question of Palestine*. New York: Vintage Books, 1980.

6. What has been termed the "new ethnicity" in the United States is, at root, a revitalization movement—the attempt by "white ethnics" to construct, symbolically and politically, a new ethnic identity from the idealized remnants of a past and largely forgotten immigrant ethnicity. An excellent analysis of the White Ethnic Movement in the United States is Howard F. Stein and Robert F. Hill, *The Ethnic Imperative: Examining the New White Ethnic Movement*. University Park, Pa.: The Pennsylvania State University Press, 1977. This study focuses on the psychosocial aspects of the movement. In Chapter 4 I discuss the theoretical underpinnings of this movement.

7. Van den Berghe, *Ethnic Phenomenon*, pp. 17–18.

8. *The Random House College Dictionary*. Rev. ed. New York: Random House, 1982, p. 1052.

9. Edward Shils, "Primordial, Personal, Sacred, and Civil Ties," *British Journal of Sociology*, 8, 1957, p. 131.

10. Ibid., p. 130.

11. Ibid., p. 142.

12. Edward Shils, "Color, the Universal Intellectual Community, and the Afro-Asian Intellectual," in John Hope Franklin, ed., *Color and Race*. Boston: Houghton Mifflin Co., 1968, p. 4.

13. Harold R. Isaacs, "Basic Group Identity: The Idols of the Tribe," in Nathan Glazer and Daniel P. Moynihan, eds., *Ethnicity: Theory and Experience*. Cambridge, Mass.: Harvard University Press, 1975, pp. 29–30.

14. Ibid., p. 31.

15. Ibid., p. 32.

16. For example, I have a basic group identity that is composed of several group identities. I am an American, an anthropologist, a member of the "professional" class, a white male, a father, a husband, and so on. Only a few of these identities are personally significant to my own self-definition and self-esteem. I identify most strongly with my occupational and family identities. I do not identify with the religion in which I was reared, nor with my ancestral connection to Italian immigrant grandparents. Other people might stress those identities that I could but don't claim (e.g., Italian-American and Catholic) and not stress others. Those identities that are personally significant and meaningful to a person and that constitute a person's Basic Group Identity can only be discovered and understood within a social and cultural framework. There is no "biological" content to the notion of basic group identity.

17. Anya Peterson Royce, *Ethnic Identity: Strategies of Diversity*. Bloomington: Indiana University Press, 1982, p. 231.

18. Ibid., p. 232.

19. Richard H. Thompson, "Ethnicity vs. Class: An Analysis of Conflict in a North American Chinese Community," *Ethnicity*, 6, 1979, pp. 306–326; and "From Kinship to Class: A New Model of Urban Overseas Chinese Social Organization," *Urban Anthropology*, 9(3), 1980, pp. 265–292.

20. Edna Bonacich, "Class Approaches to Ethnicity and Race," *The Insurgent Sociologist*, 10(2), 1980, p. 11.

21. Isaacs, "Basic Group Identity," p. 33.

22. Ibid.

23. Both Royce, *Ethnic Identity*, p. 98, and Bonacich, "Class Approaches," p. 10, misinterpet Geertz in this respect.

24. Clifford Geertz, "The Integrative Revolution: Primordial Sentiments and Civil Politics in the New States," in Clifford Geertz, *The Interpretation of Cultures*. New York: Basic Books, 1973, pp. 259–260.

25. Ibid., p. 261.

26. Ibid., pp. 258–259.

27. The Israeli denial of Palestinian ethnicity is mainly based on the following claims: the area known as Palestine has never been populated solely by either Arabs or Palestinian Arabs; Palestine has never been an independent state, but instead ruled by a series of colonial regimes; a distinct Palestinian identity is a relatively recent historical development; the Old Testament legitimates Palestine as the ancestral home of the Jews. Applying all but the last criterion makes it relatively easy to dispute Jewish ethnicity as well.

28. Clifford Geertz, "After the Revolution: The Fate of Nationalism in the New States," in Geertz, *Interpretation of Cultures*, p. 243.

29. Fredrik Barth, "Introduction," in Fredrik Barth, ed., *Ethnic Groups and Boundaries*. Boston: Little, Brown, 1969, pp. 18–19.

30. Colin Turnbull, *The Forest People*. New York: Simon & Schuster, 1962.

31. See Patterson, *Slavery and Social Death*, for a discussion of precapitalist slave systems in Africa.

32. Geertz, "After the Revolution," p. 239.

33. Crawford Young, "Comparative Claims to Political Sovereignty: Biafra,

Katanga, Eritrea," in Donald Rothchild and Victor A. Olorunsola, eds., *State vs. Ethnic Claims: African Policy Dilemmas*. Boulder, Co.: Westview Press, 1983, p. 200.

34. Ibid., pp. 200–201.

35. Cf. Stein and Hill, *Ethnic Imperative*; Orlando Patterson, *Ethnic Chauvinism: The Reactionary Impulse*. New York: Stein & Day, 1977; Stephen Steinberg, *The Ethnic Myth: Race, Ethnicity and Class in America*. Boston: Beacon Press, 1981.

4

Assimilationism and Its Discontents

RACE, CLASS, AND THE NEW ETHNICITY

The idea that ethnic and racial ties and sentiments are natural or basic features of personal identification and social organization is quite recent. As late as 1964 the most prominent and still highly respected treatise on race and ethnicity in the United States, Milton Gordon's *Assimilation in American Life*, was published. This book reflected the continued dominance of assimilation theory, first articulated in the 1920s by Robert Park, as the basic paradigm by which to understand ethnic processes in industrial countries. Assimilationism rested on precisely the *opposite* assumption from that of sociobiology or the naturalist brand of primordialism—that racial and ethnic forms of identification and social organization, though historically important, were *unnatural* and represented archaic or premodern forms of social organization. In a modern industrial society (of which the United States was the supreme example) in which social positions are allocated on the basis of achieved criteria such as education, learned skills, and personal qualities, racial and ethnic criteria were both inappropriate and a hindrance to social functioning. Racial and ethnic criteria were thus incompatible with a modern form of society that required meritocracy for its proper development and could be expected, over time, to disappear.[1]

The actual U.S. experience, however, posed a serious dilemma for the assimilationist assumption. It was clear that race had always been used as a criterion for the allocation of social roles, not only in the obvious case of slavery (which could be explained away as an archaic, preindustrial social formation), but also in the modern industrial urban economy that had emerged during the twentieth century. Events of the 1960s, particularly the Civil Rights Movement and the urban ghetto riots, forced an acute awareness of this chronic dilemma and made it clear that for black Americans, assimilation into the dominant society was still more fiction than fact. These events in turn provoked a series of responses by the state designed to redress the imbalance between white and black Americans. The Civil and Voting Rights Acts, desegregation of public schools, employment training programs, equal opportunity legislation, affirmative action programs, and a greatly expanded social welfare system had two related aims: one, to *remove* all illegal and unconstitutional barriers to integration (Jim Crow laws in the South and segregated school districts, for example); two, to *positively promote* and accelerate black assimilation by instituting programs that required "race" to be taken into consideration in employment practices, admission to universities, and government granting activities to states and businesses.

The "assimilationists," for the most part white liberal social scientists (some of the most important of whom in the mid–1960s included Pierre van den Berghe, Daniel Moynihan, and Milton Gordon), unanimously hailed the removal of all legal barriers to assimilation and generally supported the idea of "equal opportunity" in employment, education, housing, and so on regardless of race, creed, and national origin. This was consistent with their staunch antiracist view that the historical inequality between the black and white populations stemmed in the main from long-term discrimination and prejudice against blacks, and that once the legal barriers to black participation were removed, blacks would not only begin to achieve parity with whites, but racism itself—beliefs that blacks are inferior to whites—would slowly wane. On the basis of their own research they argued quite persuasively that other ethnic groups, including other racially defined groups such as the Chinese and Japanese, had, within a generation or two after their arrival in the United States, successfully assimilated into the American mainstream. They did not see the historical relationship between blacks and the dominant society as a special or substantially different case, and thus felt that black Americans, like millions of immigrants and other strangers before them, would "naturally" and over time assimilate into the American mainstream and achieve equality with whites.

Following the logic of their theory, the assimilationists were generally *opposed* to the second aim of government policy—the institution of programs designed to quickly reverse the effects of past discrimination by using racial criteria for admission to jobs programs, schools, government posts, and the like. Milton Gordon stated the case forcefully in *Assimilation in American Life*:

It is neither the responsibility nor the prerogative of the government to use racial criteria positively in order to impose desegregation upon public facilities in an institutional area where such segregation is not a function of racial discrimination directly but results from discrimination operating in another institutional area, or from other causes.... The obvious case in point is the operation of the public school system. The attempt by well-meaning "race liberals" in a number of northern communities to desegregate public schools by overturning the principle of neighborhood assignment—that is, to positively promote Negro-white intermixture by means of racial assignment across neighborhood lines—is, in my opinion misguided.... It puts the government in the business of using race as a criterion for operating one of its facilities.[2]

In one sense Gordon was right on the mark. If school segregation was a function of neighborhood segregation, then the government's role should be to end practices that created segregated neighborhoods. But it is quite clear from Gordon's last sentence above that he would have been as much opposed to government intervention into neighborhood assignment to the extent that race would have had to be used as a criterion for neighborhood integration. On the matter of affirmative action, Gordon followed a similar line of argument:

It is unwise and unjustifiable for the government to create programs labeled and reserved for the benefit of any special racial group, or to set up quotas in any area of activity such as employment, as is currently demanded by some civil rights proponents. It is undeniable that the burden of unemployment bears most heavily on Negroes, as a result of the cumulation of past discriminatory events. ... Present wrongs do not solve the problems created by past injustices and only assure that the underlying social evil will further plague us in the future. We do not want "see-saw discrimination" in American life; we want the dismantling of the discriminatory apparatus.

In sum, the proper role of government is to deal equitably with all persons under its jurisdiction without taking into consideration their racial background for any purpose.[3]

Gordon and the other assimilationists who shared his views were making policy statements that were consistent with the basic assumptions of assimilationism. They were eschewing any "quick fix" to the race problem on the grounds that it would solve itself over time (to some extent because of their firm belief that blacks were every bit as capable of achievement as whites), and that for the government to use racial criteria would produce a heightened race consciousness and no diminution of racism. To a large extent their second prediction has been borne out. Racism remains a powerful ideology in this country and, to the extent that one can measure it, may have actually increased in the form of a white backlash against government programs designed, in the main, for black Americans.[4]

Assimilationists also objected to any government programs that moved away from acceptable "equal opportunity" provisions to enforced statistical representations based on racial or ethnic categories. The main target here was affirmative action, which, as a result of various court interpretations, became a program based on racial quotas rather than ensuring equal opportunity. Such programs were wrongheaded not only because they wouldn't work and would tend to promote racial backlash, but also because they violated basic American principles, particularly the "individual rights" provisions underlying the Constitution. Nathan Glazer, one of the most important and eloquent spokesmen among the assimilationists, stated the case forcefully in his excellent book *Affirmative Discrimination*:

A new course in dealing with the issues of equality that arise in the American multiethnic society has been set since the early 1970s. It is demonstrated that there is discrimination or at least some condition of inequality through the comparison of statistical patterns, and then racial and ethnic quotas and statistical requirements for employment and school assignment are imposed. This course is not demanded by legislation—indeed, it is specifically forbidden by national legislation—or by any reasonable interpretation of the Constitution. Nor is it justified, I have argued, by any presumed failure of the policies of nondiscrimination and of affirmative action that prevailed until the early 1970s. Until then, affirmative action meant to seek out and prepare members of minority groups for better jobs and educational opportunities.... But in the early 1970s affirmative action came to mean ... the setting of statistical requirements based on race, color and national origin for employers and educational institutions. This new course threatens the abandonment for individual claims to consideration on the basis of justice and equity, now to be replaced with a concern for rights for publicly determined and delimited racial and ethnic groups.[5]

The assimilationists believed that Afro-American assimilation would eventually occur, but their beliefs were constructed out of a conservative analysis of how American society works, especially their analysis of the two basic sectors of institutional life—the economy and the state, and the nature of the relation between them. What Gordon, Glazer, and others failed to recognize is that "the dismantling of the discriminatory apparatus" they so much hoped for might require the dismantling of the major institutions of American society—something they clearly did not hope for.

In the beginning, government programs did not use racial categories for the promotion of desegregation or affirmative action. All of the programs were designed for *minority* citizens regardless of race, that is, people of the lower classes of American society who tended to be chronically underemployed or unemployed and, as a result, exhibited high and persistent rates of poverty (the War on Poverty, for example, was fought with much vigor and money, but little success in the overwhelmingly white region defined as Appalachia). But because government programs had been instituted largely in response to black protest, the early emphasis on "minority" was quickly replaced by an emphasis on "black." The government's emphasis on "race" instead of "class" as a way of "solving" the race problem has had several important consequences. One consequence has been to shift the focus of the problem away from its fundamental *economic* causes (persistent unemployment) and toward an emphasis on race alone. This shift is not mysterious, and can be traced to the state's inability to contradict the "rationality" of the capitalist economic system that underpins it. In short, the government is severely restricted in its capacity to attack the fundamental causes of poverty, be it black or white poverty.[6]

Another consequence of this shift has been its considerable impact on the black population itself. On the one hand, those blacks who have achieved high levels of education and experience by reason of their class backgrounds, location in particular regions of the country, and/or individual talent and perserverance have been given access to secure and relatively high-paying positions in education, government, and big business. Chronically poor, ghettoized blacks, on the other hand, have not been granted access to either secure or well-paying positions or to the kind of education or job training that might help them get such jobs. Instead, they have been provided with government assistance programs—food stamps and Aid to Families with Dependent Children, particularly—that have increased their dependency on the government, maintained them in a state of poverty, and, for the most part, secured their quiescence. The combined effect of governmental actions has been to bifurcate the black population into a relatively advantaged and largely professional black middle class (there are still few blacks in the upper class) and an increasingly destitute and impoverished black lower class.[7] In sum, the "gains" experienced by black Americans as a result of their protest movements and the state's responses to them have accrued largely to a minority of the black population—the college-educated professional class—whereas the black underclass, after experiencing some income gains during the years 1964 through 1969, have become relatively worse off since 1970.[8]

A final important consequence of the emphasis on race instead of class has been the heightened race consciousness and increased racism that Gordon feared, racism that has been felt as much by upwardly mobile blacks as by the black underclass. One of the major reasons for this is because certain government programs, particularly school desegregation and increased welfare payments, have impacted most on working-class whites, many of European ethnic background, who remain concentrated in the deteriorating cities of the North, where desegregation and welfare programs have been most vigorously pressed. Affluent whites have moved to the suburbs, taking with them the resources necessary to build communities consisting of shopping malls, neat and expensive housing subdivisions, and first-rate, all-white schools.

Moreover, as the urban white working classes have experienced deterioration in their economic position during the 1970s and 1980s, they have vented their anxieties and fears against their black urban counterparts, whom they perceive as having benefited by government action at their expense. This is understandable in light of the government's emphasis on race (and, by implication, its blaming of whites in general for the black situation) and the fact that white working-class neighborhoods have borne the brunt of increased welfare payments, neighborhood housing projects, and school desegregation. They thus link their own economic deterioration to governmental programs aimed at "improving" the situation of blacks.[9]

The response of white workers to the economic crises of the past decade has taken an additional turn. In cities in which whites still live in ethnic neighborhoods, second- and third-generation white ethnics of European ancestry have organized themselves into ethnic associations as a means of pressing their interests on the state. They have observed the degree to which black organization has influenced state action and the readiness of the state to deal with ethnic rather than class claims. For its part, the state has legitimated these ethnic associations through passage of the Ethnic Heritages Act (1973), which, while hardly alleviating the conditions of white workers, has paid lip service to the "rights" of white ethnics to foster a new sense of ethnic identity and organization by providing grants for the sponsorship of ethnic festivals, ethnic history projects, and the recognition of ethnic associations.

As the state has legitimated these ethnic claims, a growing number of American scholars and a newly produced corps of professional "ethnics" have jumped on the ethnicity bandwagon and proclaimed a new American reality that is most often conveyed by the phrase the "new ethnicity." The primary assertion of this recent school of ethnic studies is that the heretofore presumed assimilated ethnic groups, such as the Italians, Irish, Slavs, Germans, Jews, and Catholics, have not, in fact, assimilated; that they retain many of the cultural attributes of their former origins. In the words of their leading guru, Michael Novak, they represent "unmeltable ethnics," groups that have maintained a high level of "cultural cohesion" despite the assimilation of individual members.[10]

An important aspect of this renewed emphasis on ethnicity is the degree to which several important scholars, disillusioned assimilationists for the most part, have provided a theoretical explanation (and justification) for its existence. One explanation is the naturalist brand of primordialism discussed in the previous chapter that simply asserts the unmeltability and affectivity of ethnic ties. A second, social explanation asserts that this new ethnic movement is to be expected because the nature of American society is changing from an industrial society to a "post-industrial" society in which class antagonisms have "lost efficacy" and, as a result, ethnic antagonisms become the basis for political interest-seeking behaviors.[11] The ascendancy of sociobiology has also provided theoretical justification for the movement, even though Pierre van den Berghe, who has staunchly maintained his universalist values despite his belief in the naturalness of ethnic ties, has seen through the ideology of the new ethnicity. In his words, "the white 'ethnic movement' is really not an ethnic movement at all. Ethnicity here is an alibi for race [antiblack sentiments] and class."[12]

In this chapter I want to demonstrate that the new ethnicity is, by and large, an expression of latent class sentiments that, in the absence of effective class organization in the contemporary United States, has taken on an ethnic form or appearance. Moreover, it really doesn't represent a movement at all in the sense of a mass-participation, grass-roots organization on the part of lower-class Italians, Irish, Catholics, or Poles. It is, for the most part, an ideological position that has been offered by upper- and upper-middle-class ethnic elites, most of whom have a stake in maintaining certain aspects of ethnic social organization—their economic and political influence over their claimed ethnic constituencies.[13]

Demystifying the new ethnicity involves two connected tasks. First, the basic assumptions underlying assimilationist theory need to be reexamined, since much of the recent scholarship on the new ethnicity seems to have been spurred by the inability of assimilationism to explain the lack of black Americans' assimilation. To a great extent, the new ethnicity has emerged as a theoretical alternative born out of the crisis of assimilationism itself. Second, the theoretical basis of the new ethnicity needs to be examined in order to show the inadequacy of the social theory on which it is based.

What Does Assimilation Mean?

The assimilationists have contributed most to social analysis by studying the assimilation process and outlining its complexity. Milton Gordon has been the most important assimilation theorist in this regard. Gordon defined assimilation as a process or series of stages through which people pass in the course of adapting to a new society. He defined the first stage as "cultural assimilation," more commonly referred to as acculturation. Acculturation—learning the language, values, and other modes of cultural discourse that predominate in the "host" society—is a necessary, but not sufficient condition for entering later phases of the assimilation process. In the United States what constitutes acculturation has always been clear: acculturation means, at a *minimum*, the adoption of the English language and some conformity to the dominant, European-originated values on which American social institutions are structured (the Constitution, the legal system, the economy, to name but a few). This means that acculturation is essentially a *one-way* process that requires non-English-speaking and/or non-European residents to change in the direction of the dominant culture, a process that most often results in the disappearance of the native language and culture of the acculturating person. Thus the history of acculturation in American society has always been, and continues to be, a process that Gordon termed "Anglo-conformity," in which immigrants were expected to shed their native traditions and adopt the cultural and linguistic patterns of the dominant Anglo-European tradition.

Despite the ideology of the "melting pot" that was prevalent during most of the twentieth century, American culture is not and has never been a blend of disparate and unique immigrant cultures, notwithstanding our appetites for Italian, Mexican, and Oriental cuisines. Moreover, the millions of non-English-speaking/non-Anglo-Saxon immigrants to the United States have both understood and accepted this reality out of practical necessity, if not always sympathy. There has never been a significant challenge against the dominance of the English language in the United States or to the Anglo-Saxon origins of our institutions. This is true even of the increasingly large Spanish-speaking population, whose calls for bilingual and multicultural education have been misrepresented as "anti-English, anti-American." Underpinning these programs is the genuine concern that cultural assimilation (learning English and Anglo-American values) almost always involves not only the acceptance of the dominant culture, but also the *rejection* of the assimilating person's native culture as inferior, backward, and unworthy. This rejection process often poses serious psychological problems for the assimilator, who comes to regard his or her *self* as inferior and unworthy, leading to, in serious cases, the marginal adaptation first identified by Park in which a person is psychologically trapped between the pushes and pulls of two contradictory cultures.[14] Bilingual and multicultural educational programs are designed to ease the acculturation process, remove the negative stereotypes impugned to the native culture, and lessen the likelihood of marginality. If they were anti-English, anti-American in intent, they would not be stressing bilingualism and multiculturalism, but rather unilingualism (Spanish) and the multicultural heritages of the Spanish-speaking New World.

It is certainly true that Afro-Americans and other minorities have challenged aspects of American culture, but this challenge has generally not been aimed at transforming it. Rather, it has been aimed at bringing the American reality into closer correspondence with American ideals. Thus, in terms of the acculturation process, almost all Americans, regardless of their origins and with the exception of only the most recent immigrants, have become competent in *and committed to* the language and culture of the dominant, European-based tradition. This is true even for many original Americans, Indians, who a century after conquest and a high degree of structural separation from mainstream institutions, are nevertheless highly acculturated. This is particularly true of anti-European Indian leaders, who, despite their rejection of the dominant culture and its brutal anti-Indian practices, can operate competently within it and in fact must do so to further the Indian cause.

What Gordon and the other assimilationists have recognized, however, is that acculturation to the dominant tradition, although a necessary first step to "total" assimilation, does not guarantee total assimilation. Gordon defined complete assimilation as the successful adoption of seven "stages" or variables that make up the assimilation process, of which acculturation represents only the first stage. After acculturation was what Gordon termed "structural assimilation." Individuals and groups became structurally assimilated to the degree that they entered the host society's institutions—its schools, factories, political organizations, and the like—and achieved "large-scale" entrance into the cliques and clubs of the dominant group. Once structural assimilation was well advanced, other types of assimilation, such as marital assimilation, "identificational" assimilation, civic assimilation, and others outlined by Gordon, would "naturally follow."[15]

Gordon's own analysis showed that all but the most recent immigrants to the United States had achieved the stage of cultural assimilation, and with the exception of "Negroes," other ethnic groups were at least partly or mostly assimilated on the other variables as well. Certain ethnic groups were more fully assimilated than others. Early immigrants of northern and western European origins had advanced further than later immigrants from southern Europe or those from non-European countries. And Afro-Americans, despite two or more centuries of residence in the United States and having fully acculturated, remained further behind all other groups with respect to structural assimilation. What Gordon found difficult to explain was that which needed most to be explained: if all racial and ethnic groups had successfully acculturated, what factors caused certain groups to achieve high levels of structural assimilation and other groups to lag behind?

Gordon understood the importance of this issue. He knew that the absence of structural assimilation meant the *presence* of ethnic and racial stratification—a class system that was heavily influenced by ethnic and particularly racial inequality. Although all ethnic and racial groups were characterized by internal class divisions, certain ethnic and racial groups were disproportionately "lower class." Irish and Italians, for example, had a larger percentage of working-class members compared with other whites than they had members in the upper and middle classes. And blacks, more so than any other group, were disproportionately present in the lower and under classes of American society.

The existence of ethnic and racial stratification, or, in assimilationist language, the absence of structural assimilation, constituted the anomaly that confronted assimilation theory. And it was the inability of assimilationism to explain this anomaly that ultimately posed what can be called a crisis in assimilationism. It was a crisis to the extent that the assimilation process was seen as an inevitable social process in modern society— inevitable because modern society was "modern" insofar as it did not use racial, ethnic, or other ascriptive bonds for the allocation of social roles. The institutions of modern society worked because they used achieved criteria such as education, experience, and other qualifications to fill the technical and other specialized positions characteristic of an industrial society.

The answers given by assimilationists to explain the persistence of ethnic and racial stratification took two major forms, neither of which involved a fundamental critique of the workings of modern society (i.e., advanced capitalist society) itself. One prevalent type of answer located the source or cause of continued racial and ethnic stratification in the psychological or personality characteristics of both whites and minorities, their needs or desires for prejudice and discrimination. This was the answer provided by Gordon himself:

If structural assimilation in substantial fashion has not taken place in America, we must ask why. The answer lies in the *attitudes* of both the majority and the minority groups and in the ways in which these attitudes have interacted. A folk saying of the current day is that "It takes two to tango." To utilize the analogy, there is no good reason to believe that white Protestant America ever extended a firm and cordial invitation to its minorities to dance. Furthermore, the attitudes of the minority group members themselves on the matter have been divided and ambiguous. (Emphasis added.)[16]

If Gordon asked the right question, he surely gave the wrong answer. To locate the cause of the problem in the prejudicial attitudes of both whites and blacks (and other minorities) placed him in the rather unenviable position of trying to explain just from where and how these prejudicial attitudes emerged. Perhaps anticipating the difficulty of such a task, he never attempted it. Writing about the situation of "Negroes" in the United States, Gordon eloquently described the symptoms of the race problem, but diagnosed the wrong disease:

With the racial minorities there was not even the pretense of an invitation [on the part of whites to participate in the host society]. . . . Consequently, with due allowance for internal class differences, [Negroes] have constructed their own network of organizations and institutions—their own "social world." . . . However, the ideological attachment of Negroes to their communal separation is, as we noted earlier, not conspicuous. Their sense of identification with ancestral African national cultures is virtually nonexistent, although Pan-Africanism engages the interest of some intellectuals and although "black nationalist" and "black racist" fringe groups have recently made an appearance at the other end of the communal spectrum.... Thus, there are here no "logical" ideological reasons for separate communality; *dual social structures are created solely by the dynamics of prejudice and discrimination rather than being reinforced by ideological commitments of the minority itself.* (Emphasis added.)[17]

Although Gordon did not elaborate on "the dynamics of prejudice and discrimination," such a diagnosis spurred a renewed interest in psychological theories of prejudice that had developed in the 1940s and 1950s. Two of these in particular received the most attention: Gordon Allport's *The Nature of Prejudice* (1958) and Theodore Adorno's *The Authoritarian Personality* (1950). The latter work especially, one of the most important studies in the history of American social science and a scathing critique of American society, was grossly misinterpreted—stood on its head, if you will—and used to argue that certain personalities (primarily those of the working class) were predisposed (genetically was the presumption) to exhibit "traits" for fascism, ethnocentrism, anti-Semitism, and racism. Thus racism and discrimination were ultimately caused by racist and discriminatory personality types who, for reasons largely unspecified, had infected the social structure with their own personal disease, resulting in a racist and discriminatory society.

Another attempt to answer the question "Why haven't some groups assimilated as fully as others?" produced what Micaela di Leonardo has called "ethnic family culture" studies. Historians, economists, and sociologists viewed the various rates of assimilation by different ethnic groups as a kind of "ethnic report card" in which those groups with the highest percentage of white-collar and professional employment received the highest ethnic grades. As di Leonardo suggests, these studies consistently "assumed that ethnic family structure is largely responsible for the relative white-collar outcome: differing 'cultures' determine the structures of ethnic families, and they in turn determine the economic status of the men associated with them."[18]

Such studies argued that Italians remained largely working class because of the continuing cultural influence of their peasant backgrounds; Slovaks were similarly lower class because the "Slovak community created social institutions emphasizing the value of order and maintaining the continuity of the ethnic group."[19] Jews, on the other hand, had succeeded in American society because of their willingness to adapt to new social and cultural conditions and their emphasis on certain values, particularly education, that would lead to assimilation.

Another variant of ethnic family culture studies was the now famous "culture of poverty" idea. The culture of poverty referred to a host of individual and family-centered characteristics such as "weak ego structures," fatalism, female-headed families, lack of deferred gratification patterns, and other improper attitudes that characterized the least assimilated groups—Puerto Ricans and blacks—and prevented them from achieving levels of success comparable to other groups.[20]

Regardless of whether the failure to assimilate was lodged in the personal need for prejudice and discrimination or the particular cultural values presumed to dominate within ethnic and racial families, assimilationists could explain the lack of assimilation only in terms of the personal or cultural inadequacies of the lower-ranking groups. Such "victim-blaming" explanations were the necessary outcome of the assimilationist model itself, a model that saw American social institutions as operating on "natural" or inevitable social processes that were taken for granted and not subject to critique.

By clinging to their assumptions about the nature of industrial society, the assimilationists were more or less forced to regard the absence of assimilation as the fault of the nonassimilated group and to reevaluate the power of society itself vis-à-vis individual genetic and psychological traits. It is this process that accounts for former assimilationists such as Glazer and Moynihan blaming blacks and Puerto Ricans for an unwillingness to assimilate,[21] and for others such as van den Berghe to reverse their social view of race and ethnicity for an individualist view. Even Gordon, in his most recent book, *Human Nature, Class, and Ethnicity*, now views the absence of assimilation as caused by the primordial strength of ethnic ties; ties that are rooted in the "biological organism of man."[22] Had they examined the social assumptions on which assimilationism was based, they might have moved in a quite different direction.

Assimilationism: Assumptions About the Nature of Society

What were these largely hidden assumptions about society that undergirded the assimilationist paradigm? In my view they were assumptions concerning three major aspects of the American social structure: assumptions pertaining to the nature of stratification, the nature of the economy or market, and the nature of the state. For all three aspects the assimilationists attributed a certain "behavior" or "kind of functioning" that was seen as natural or obvious. A brief examination of each and the assimilationists' view of them will help us to understand why assimilationism could produce its conservative offspring.

Stratification and Racial Stratification

If assimilationists saw racial and ethnic stratification as an anomaly, they saw stratification *itself* (that is, a class hierarchy characterized by unequal rewards) as both inevitable and beneficial to the proper functioning of a modern society. They followed the reasoning put forward by Kingsley Davis and Wilbert Moore in their classic article "Some Principles of Stratification." Davis and Moore argued that any society based on a complex division of labor would necessarily generate a significant degree of social inequality because the society must provide differential rewards in income, prestige, and other values in order to motivate or induce people to occupy "functionally important" roles necessary for society's survival. In their view, most functionally important roles were difficult to fill because they involve high levels of expensive training or such complex and far-reaching decisions that people would not seek such jobs unless they were accompanied by high levels of income and prestige. It is clear that Davis and Moore regarded social stratification to be a necessary, beneficial, and universal process: "Starting from the proposition that no society is 'classless,' or unstratified, an effort is made to explain, in functional terms, the *universal necessity* which calls forth stratification in any social system" (emphasis added).[23]

We now know that Davis and Moore's starting proposition was incorrect. Human societies were "classless" during the greater part of human history, and the origins of social stratification were not the natural outcome of increased functional complexity, but of war, conquest, and the institutionalization of surplus extraction.[24] Aside from this historical error, the Davis and Moore hypothesis has been thoroughly critiqued on other grounds as well: its failure to define "functional importance"; its ethnocentric view of "reward"; its inability to even suggest, let alone specify, how much inequality is necessary for the "proper functioning" of society; its failure to compare forms of stratification based on private versus public ownership (they regarded such differences as insignificant for stratification); and their complete disregard for the generational transmission of class position.[25]

Despite the theoretical deficiencies inherent in the "functional necessity of stratification" hypothesis, it is clear that assimilationists (again, excepting the early work of Park) regarded inequality itself as a natural feature of the American or any other complex social structure. As a result, the existence of inequality itself was a *nonissue* for assimilation theory, and the relation between racial inequality and inequality per se was not a prominent feature of their analysis. This is true even for Pierre van den Berghe, who, in his early work *Race and Racism*, explicitly treated racial stratification as a special case of stratification in general. But he did not critique the existence of stratification itself, presumably because he, too, regarded it as necessary (although deplorable). He was thus faced with the same dilemma as Gordon—given the existence of stratification, why does racial and ethnic stratification persist? His answer is not dissimilar from Gordon's:

Segregation and discrimination are the foremost mechanisms for the preservation of racial pluralism [racial separation] in the presence of cultural assimilation and other integrative pressures. Thus a competitive situation is one in which the ruling group deliberately maintains social pluralism [racial stratification] by force in order to protect its privileged position.[26]

Van den Berghe does not blame the racial minorities themselves for their lack of integration. In fact, he blames "the ruling group" for preventing structural assimilation as a way of maintaining its privilege. Unfortunately he does not tell us who this "ruling group" is (all whites?), what privileges they are trying to maintain, or the reasons underlying their "deliberate" (conspiratorial?) behavior. Because of this, their behavior strikes one as mysterious or irrational, and ultimately leads to an examination of racist personality types (or genes), which, as we now know, is precisely where van den Berghe was led.

The Market

Despite the necessity of stratification itself, why did assimilationism regard racial stratification as both an unnecessary and ultimately unimportant feature of modern industrial society? The answer is to be found in their implicit acceptance of a conservative neoclassical view concerning the nature of a capitalist economy. Simply stated, this view holds that racial and ethnic stratification will be eliminated because the "cost of discrimination"—that is, the cost to capitalists for taking into consideration "nonpecuniary" factors such as race, national origin, or other ascriptive criteria for hiring employees—will place employers at a competitive disadvantage vis-à-vis other employers who, following the strategy of profit maximization, hire a presumably productive labor force at the lowest possible labor cost. Thus, if we assume that both the black and white labor forces are comparable in terms of their predicted productivity, and if black labor is cheaper than white labor because of past discrimination and a resulting greater supply of black labor, then employers will favor black workers over white workers because a cheaper black labor force will increase the employer's profit.[27] This behavior will, over time, remove past inequities by placing blacks at a competitive advantage in the market in the short run, leading to, in the long run, the absence of racial stratification.

Thomas Sowell, one of the leading contemporary spokesmen for the conservative neoclassical view of race, puts it this way:

In general, job discrimination has a cost, not only to those discriminated against and to society, but also to the person who is discriminating. He must forgo hiring some employees he needs, or must interview more applicants in order to get the number of qualified workers required, or perhaps offer higher wages in order to attract a larger pool of applicants than necessary if hiring on merit alone. These costs do not necessarily eliminate discrimination, but discrimination—like everything else—tends to be more in demand at a low price than at a high price. The cost, of course, is of no concern to a businessman who is personally unconcerned about profit, but such businessmen are rare to begin with, and tend to get eliminated through competition, for their financial backers and creditors care about profitability even if they do not.[28]

Sowell admits that under special conditions, discrimination can be profitable. One condition is monopoly, where the holders of the monopoly can conspire to exclude members of a particular group from employment (as was the case with major league athletics not too many years ago). But even such conspiratorial actions are likely to be temporary because "as long as each individual is seeking to maximize his individual gains—not the collective gains of the group to which he belongs—each individual . . . has the incentives to violate the agreement."[29] This is precisely what happened in the case of professional athletics when, after Branch Rickey brought Jackie Robinson into major league baseball, the exclusionary racist practices of baseball "toppled like a house of cards."

I use this example offered by Sowell because he recognizes that blacks and other minorities were able to quickly expand into professional sports because they were "immediately prepared to enter [once] the exclusion" was broken, so prepared in fact that for other sports franchises to continue to discriminate against them placed them at a competitive disadvantage. The reasons for this are simple. Blacks had participated in baseball, basketball, and football for years in their own segregated neighborhoods and sports leagues. They had developed the skills necessary to compete at levels equal to whites despite the discrimination against them. Sowell uses this example as his basic market paradigm for arguing that blacks, *if they achieve skill levels comparable to whites in other areas of life*, would enter the labor force at all levels in numbers proportionate to their population. Sowell recognizes that blacks *do not* possess skill levels comparable to whites in areas in which high levels of education and training are necessary to even *enter* the market for "good" jobs. Moreover, he recognizes that the absence of black equality in these areas can be traced to past discrimination and segregation. But, he argues, just as black athletes learned their skills in inferior and segregated settings, so, too, can blacks learn marketable skills in segregated and inferior neighborhoods and schools (none of which he is in favor of, I need add). To do so, however, blacks will have to quit looking to the government to help them and reject the quick fixes implied by job quotas, charity, subsidies, and preferential treatment. Instead, they will have to rely on "those methods which have historically proved successful—self reliance, work skills, education, business experience."[30]

The problem of racial or ethnic inequality, then, does not lie in the operation of the economy, which, by its very nature, is nondiscriminatory. The problem ultimately lies with minorities themselves who do not possess the right attitudes toward education, business, community, and other areas that would be necessary for them to achieve equality with whites:

If the history of American ethnic groups shows anything, it is how large a role has been played by attitudes—and particularly attitudes of self-reliance. The success of the antebellum 'free persons of color' compared to the later black migrants to the North, the advancement of the Italian-Americans beyond the Irish-Americans who had many other advantages, the resilience of the Japanese-Americans despite numerous campaigns of persecution, all emphasize the importance of this factor, however mundane and unfashionable it may be.[31]

We are again transported back to "attitudes" as the basic cause of racial stratification (in this case the attitudes of the minorities) without any explanation as to *why* such attitudes are prevalent. Why don't blacks value self-reliance today as did, evidently, their antebellum forebears? Why can't blacks learn accounting, computer science and engineering, medicine and law, and business just as they have learned baseball, football, and basketball?[32] If the issue is, in some respects, a question of attitudes, then such theories must explain the *causes* of the attitudes themselves. In most of the assimilationist and "free market" literatures the implied causes of "bad attitudes" that prevent assimilation are located in either genes, personality types, or the cultural patterns of minorities. This is because the social structure itself—the stratification system, the economy—could not have been the cause because it operates on natural, impersonal, and universalist bases.

As I shall show in the final chapter, there is reason to locate the cause of certain attitudes (or lack of them) in the operation of the social structure itself. In particular, it is possible to show that the basic premise of the "nondiscriminatory market"—that there is a "cost" to capitalists for discriminating—is false; that instead capitalists can and do benefit from a racially stratified society, have an interest in maintaining it (or at least no compelling interest in dismantling it), and that the cost of it is born by both blacks and whites of the noncapitalist classes.

The State

A final assumption that helps us to understand the inability of assimilationism to explain continued racial stratification centers on the presumed roles or behavior of the state. A major aspect of assimilation theory was its recognition of the historical role played by government in *maintaining* and buttressing racial segregation and inequality, particularly in the South. Assimilationists were universally critical of laws and decisions at both the federal (*Plessy vs. Ferguson*) and state levels (Jim Crow laws, poll taxes, etc.) that directly or indirectly supported segregation and, to their minds, prevented racial integration. The state in fact was seen as the main culprit in the race problem insofar as its racist practices prevented the natural assimilating tendencies of the stratification system and the economy from taking hold. As a result, the state, by its legalization and legitimation of racial inequality, was the major barrier to the assimilation process.

For this reason assimilationists strongly supported the landmark Supreme Court decisions that struck down segregationist practices and generally affirmed the Civil and Voting Rights Acts, which gave Congress the power to enforce equal opportunity. Such enforcement powers were necessary in a society that was, owing to past discrimination, still heavily racially stratified, and thus subject to backsliding on racial matters. Following the same logic, many assimilationists also supported increased federal aid to educationally deprived school districts, increased maintenance programs for chronically poor households, and various job training programs designed to make blacks and other poor people more competitive in the market. Again, these compensatory programs were necessary to help blacks "catch up" to whites and attain those skills necessary to achieve parity. Thus assimilationists were, by and large, favorable to the liberal reforms of the late 1960s and beyond, and regarded the state as the proper institution to both mandate and enforce such reforms.

Why would assimilationists, whose theory was based on a conservative view of society insofar as it treated both stratification and the capitalist economy as "natural" systems, favor such an important and expansive role for government in solving the race problem? As I noted earlier, assimilationists generally blamed government for causing the race problem in the first place. It was easy to demonstrate that the state, at all levels, had passed and enforced laws that were clearly unconstitutional and that had the effect of discriminating against blacks in all areas of life, particularly employment, education, and housing. Historically, then, government had acted in ways that produced racial segregation and inequality, and it was the government's responsibility to repent for its *own* past sins by vigorously pursuing policies that would end discrimination. If government was the prime cause of the problem, it must be the solution to it as well.

The expanded role of government in racial matters produced a great deal of ambivalence among assimilationists, however, as the passages from Gordon and Glazer cited earlier make clear. The fear was that government would overstep its legitimate domain, be too exuberant in performing its penance, and try to *force* racial equalization through the institution of racial quotas, lowered standards for minorities, and other programs designed to produce equality of result instead of equality of opportunity. These practices were illegitimate not only because they, too, were unconstitutional ("reverse discrimination"), but also because they abandoned the universalist criteria that both the stratification system and the economy require for their proper functioning.

The "fear of government," then, was a fear that the state, in its zeal to redress past racial inequities, would require businesses (particularly those that rely on government contracts and over which the state could exercise some control) and its own agencies to give preferential treatment in hiring and promotion to minorities who, owing to past inequities or limitations of talent, might be *less* qualified for a particular job than a member of the dominant group. Such practices were to be condemned not only because they violated a person's "freedom," but also because they might, in the long term, spell economic and social disaster. Thus we can understand Gordon's antipathy to any governmental action "to create programs labeled and reserved for the benefit of any special racial group" and his insistence "that job hiring and promotion at all levels should be made on the basis of individual merit, not racial quotas, however 'benignly' the latter may be motivated."[33]

Despite the large role that many assimilationists advocated government play in the arena of civil rights, their view of the "proper role" of the state was essentially a conservative one. On the one hand, government should get out of the business of supporting segregation and discrimination, and enforce equal opportunity under the law. It was also proper for government to institute certain compensatory programs in the areas of education (some assimilationists supported busing to achieve better education for minorities, others opposed it) and job training that would help minorities historically discriminated against to better compete in a competitive society. On the other hand, government should restrain from any actions that meddled in the operation of social institutions, particularly the economy, since these institutions were already operating according to functionally necessary principles. The state's relatively large role in race relations, then, should be limited to righting the state's past wrongs and, in the area of compensatory programs, *temporary*.

From Out of the Ashes: A New Ethnicity or a New Ideology?

The failure of assimilationism to explain what it most needed and wanted to explain—the persistence of racial stratification—and its subsequent reduction to psychological and/or biological forms of reason produced a new version of reality that currently dominates American social science's view toward racial and ethnic relations. This new version of reality is generally called the "new ethnicity," a phenomenon that is "new" to the extent that ethnic movements have appeared with greater frequency and intensity in the past twenty years. Analytically, the new ethnicity can be subdivided into two interrelated positions: (1) the claim that ethnic and racial criteria have become major forms of *group*-based sociopolitical behavior because of the changing nature of industrial society; (2) the claim that ethnic and racial groups *ought* to maintain their separate boundaries and seek their separate interests provided such interests recognize and respect the multitude of other, different ethnic interests. The latter claim is usually referred to as the ethic of cultural pluralism—the belief that heterogeneous cultural traditions coexisting within the framework of a democratic state represent the "highest good" for a modern complex society.

Several important works have adequately critiqued the origins and ideology of the new ethnicity. Steinberg interprets it as a backlash by white working-class ethnics against the successes of the Civil Rights Movement. This backlash is rooted not merely in racial prejudice but "in the realities of a class society. . . . At bottom, the so-called ethnic backlash is a conflict between the racial have-nots and the ethnics who have a little and are afraid of losing even that."[34] Stein and Hill view the new ethnicity as "new" in the sense of a "revitalization movement," or a "crisis cult." For them, it is an inauthentic movement that "is both a symptomatic expression of a disintegrated life and an attempt to cope with this sense of personal disintegration through regression to an earlier stage in individual development. . . . The New Ethnic vogue is a 'false consciousness' in a deeply *Freudian* way."[35]

Orlando Patterson has unveiled the contradictory and reactionary implications of the "cultural pluralism creed" that is the ideological banner of the new ethnicity. The heart of his critique is that the pluralist creed, despite the good intentions of its liberal promulgators, consists of "intellectual malevolence." On the one hand, it is based on the logically inconsistent doctrine of relativism, which, in the context of an ethnically and racially stratified society, becomes an apologia for continued separation and inequality. Its liberal intentions have reactionary consequences. Additionally, the pluralist creed, despite its presumed consistency with individualism, both neglects individuality and places such an emphasis on *group* diversity that it in fact works against a respect for individuality.[36]

I want to demonstrate, in addition to these critiques, how the new ethnicity has emerged as a theoretical alternative to assimilationism, and one that has been embraced largely by former assimilationists. These scholars, owing to the failure of assimilationism to explain the persistence of race and ethnicity in American life, have been led to rethink their assumptions regarding American society. This rethinking has produced a new version of industrial society—one that Daniel Bell calls "post-industrial" society—in which the continued presence of racial and ethnic influences is to be both expected and celebrated. This supposed new social reality is misguided insofar as it is an incorrect description of advanced industrial society, and one that fails to grasp the nature of the racial and ethnic movements it seeks to explain.

The New Ethnicity and "Post-Industrial Society"

A central feature of the new ethnicity is the presumption that it is in fact "new" both in the United States and elsewhere. In the Introduction to their influential reader *Ethnicity: Theory and Experience*, Nathan Glazer and Daniel Moynihan argue that "there seem of late to be far more of such [ethnic] conflicts, and they are more intense."[37] They cite as examples the Anglophone/Francophone conflict in Canada, Catholic versus Protestant in northern Ireland, Walloon and Fleming in Belgium, Bengali and non-Bengali in Pakistan, Chinese and Malay in Malaysia, Jews and other ethnic minorities versus Great Russians in the Soviet Union, and more. Although Glazer and Moynihan make no effort to list either the frequency or the intensity of ethnic conflicts over various historical periods, they nevertheless state that "we think it can hardly be disputed that there has been a greater degree of ethnic conflict in the last ten or twenty years than most informed observers expected."[38] Although it may be true that "most informed observers expected" less ethnic antagonism than has occurred in recent times, that reflects more on the quality of observation than on either the frequency or intensity of ethnic conflicts.

As discussed in the previous chapter, the frequency and intensity of ethnic conflicts can be historically traced to the process of state formation (a process that began some 6,000 years ago) and its latter-day offspring, colonialism and imperialism, which together have incorporated literally hundreds and perhaps thousands of formerly autonomous, prestate societies under the authoritarian banners of new nations. To the extent that such processes have involved both brutally coercive and unequal postconsolidation social arrangements, these processes have spawned their own potential negation—what are often referred to as "ethnonationalist" movements all over the world designed to either reestablish a former autonomy or gain a more equitable position within their state framework. To suggest that such movements are contemporary inventions (even the examples cited by Glazer and Moynihan have roots several hundred years old) is to admit to a rather wide-ranging historical blind spot.

The operative word in the "new ethnicity" is surely not "new," nor is it primarily "ethnicity." Instead, the phrase "most informed observers expected" is more telling concerning the rise of the so-called new ethnicity. It is fair to suggest that the observers referred to are mostly American observers whose rediscovery of ethnicity is largely a response to the black protest movement of the 1960s, the state's subsequent definition and legitimation of that movement as an ethnic (but not primarily a class) movement, and the resulting increase in the United States of other ethnically defined movements by Hispanics, Asian-Americans, and "white ethnics," who, observing the "success" of black organization and the state's receptivity to it, have quite unmysteriously followed a similar tack. The new ethnic phenomenon is only a phenomenon to American scholars formerly wedded to assimilationism. It is *these* observers who expected less ethnic antagonisms, not only in the United States and other advanced industrial countries, but also in developing or "modernizing" countries in which it was believed that old ethnic and tribal loyalties would eventually lose their salience. Glazer and Moynihan, two of the most representative figures among these observers, state the case well:

Perhaps the best way of suggesting what is common is to refer to the *expectations* of most social scientists some time ago and even today as to the course of modern social development. In one of the chapters to follow, Milton Gordon refers to a "liberal expectancy"—the expectation that the kinds of features that divide one group from another would inevitably lose their weight and sharpness in modern and modernizing societies, that there would be increasing emphasis on achievement rather than ascription, that common systems of education and communication would level differences, that nationally uniform economic and political systems would have the same effect. Under these circumstances the "primordial" (or in any case antecedent) differences between groups would be expected to become of lesser significance.[39]

While assimilationists could argue that in developing countries these "leveling processes" were only incipient, and could thus account for the continued importance of primordial differences, they clearly could not do so for the United States (or Canada, for that matter). All of the processes that should level ethnic differences were well advanced, and thus the events of the "last ten or twenty years" *in the United States* is what shattered the "liberal expectancy" and called forth the new ethnicity.

If we grant the increased intensity and frequency of ethnic-based sociopolitical movements in the United States during the past twenty years, then we must also explain the *content* of such movements and the reasons for their emergence. With respect to the former requirement, trying to understand the basic content of ethnic movements, Glazer and Moynihan are basically correct when they suggest that:

one of the striking characteristics of the present situation is indeed the extent to which we find the ethnic group defined in terms of interest, as an interest group. Thus, whereas in the past a religious conflict, such as that which is tearing northern Ireland apart, was based on such issues as the free and public practice of a religion, today it is based on the issue of which group shall gain benefits or hold power of a wholly secular sort. Language conflicts—as in India—today have little to do with the right to the public use of language.... Today they have more to do with which language user shall have the best opportunity to get which job. ... It is clear the weight of these kinds of conflict has shifted: from an emphasis on culture, language, religion, *as such*, it shifts to an emphasis on the *interests* broadly defined of the members of the group.[40]

Although the examples cited above are taken from outside the United States, it is even more evident that the ethnic movements of blacks, Asian-Americans, Hispanics, and other minorities in America are *not* primarily focused on the recognition of their distinct ethnicity, whether it be race, language, culture, or national origins. These movements are rooted in inequality (that is, racial and ethnic stratification) as it has historically affected racial and ethnic groups. This inequality is manifest in almost all areas of American life, from housing conditions to educational opportunities, to market segregation and wage discrimination, to political participation and powerlessness.

Just as in the new states, in which primordial movements are attempts to attain some measure of autonomy and self-determination, in the highly developed states characterized by racial and ethnic stratification, ethnic movements are attempts to achieve greater equality. In the new states, in which state power is relatively weak and "still up for grabs" (usually because of the presence of large, still highly traditional primordial communities), ethnic movements tend to take the form of nationalist movements wherein the calls for autonomy and self-determination are often calls for separate statehood and independence. This is seldom the case in highly developed, powerful states, in which ethnic and racial groups have usually immigrated to an already developed state structure (or been forcibly abducted as in the case of Negro slaves), are numerically small compared with the dominant group, and are widely dispersed throughout the country. The exceptions to this are Canada, where Francophones are heavily concentrated in a single province, Quebec, and South Africa, where a numerically small, immigrant dominant group rules over a large native majority. In these cases ethnic movements have a national character, but given the power of these states and the reluctance of the world community to intervene and bring pressure on them, the outcomes of these movements are not likely to result in independence for the ethnic minorities. (In South Africa, for example, white rule is more likely to be overthrown and replaced with majority rule within the current boundaries of the state rather than a fragmentation of a single state into multiple ones.)

In the United States ethnic movements have not historically been national movements except in the case of American Indians, whose native claim to U.S. soil and preconquered status as independent, autonomous tribal communities have resulted in a complex and special relationship to the U.S. state that has been instituted through a policy of "dependent nations." In suggesting that ethnic movements in the United States have not been "nationalist," I do not mean to deny the existence or significance of the black nationalist movements led by Marcus Garvey or the importance of Communist party-led theorizing about the U.S. "black nation" during the 1920s and 1930s. The latter was particularly important to the extent that the theory was largely developed by influential American blacks such as Harry Haywood, who argued that the common oppression suffered by blacks under slavery and their geographical concentration in the southern Black Belt justified viewing American blacks as a "submerged nation."[41] Haywood himself realized, however, that the great majority of black Americans did not see themselves as constituting a nation, nor did he view the American state as sufficiently weak or receptive so as to be influenced by a black nationalist movement.[42] These important developments notwithstanding, black Americans have, by and large, viewed themselves as an oppressed race/class, sometimes emphasizing the racial aspects of their oppression and at other times emphasizing class oppression.[43] The practical thrust of this analysis has been geared to having the U.S. state recognize that blacks, because of their racial classification and racism, have been systematically relegated to inferior positions in the American social structure. Most black American movements (and certainly the most successful ones) have followed a two-pronged strategy designed to force the state to admit that blacks have been the victims of a special racial oppression and, having done so, force the state to grant greater access to the dominant institutional structure. In brief, most blacks have favored and pushed for an integrationist, not a separatist, policy designed to eliminate racial stratification.

In the United States, then, particularly in the past twenty years, ethnic sociopolitical movements have focused as much on *class* as on "ethnic" issues. To some extent, the new ethnicity recognizes this, although its proponents prefer the neutral and thoroughly uninformative term "interests" to what they regard as the "loaded" construct of "class interests." Having so recognized, they at least attempt to answer a crucially important question: Why have essentially class-based movements taken on an ethnic appearance or form in advanced industrial states such as the United States? Glazer and Moynihan suggest two reasons:

The first is the evolution of the welfare state in the more advanced economies of the world and the advent of the socialist state in the underdeveloped economies. In either circumstance, the *state* becomes a crucial and direct arbiter of economic well-being, as well as political status and whatever flows from that. In

such a situation it is not usually enough, or not enough for long enough, to
assert claims on behalf of large but loosely aggregated groups such as "workers,"
"peasants," "white collar employees." Claims of this order are too general to
elicit a very satisfactory response.....

[The second involves a modification of] the bald assertion that ethnicity becomes a *means* of advancing interests—which it does—by insisting that it is not
only a means of advancing interests. One reason ethnicity becomes an effective
means in the modern world of advancing interests is that it involves *more* than
interests. As Daniel Bell writes in his chapter, "Ethnicity has become more salient
[than class] because it can combine an interest with an affective tie." While, on
the other hand, in the case of class, "What had once been an *ideology* had now
become almost largely an *interest*."[44]

The first reason involves two related phenomena: first, the advanced
capitalist world and the evolving socialist world have seen a great expansion and increase in power of the state apparatus itself; second, these
powerful states do not respond to class challenges to their legitimacy
because such challenges are "too diffuse" to elicit a satisfactory response.
The first of these alleged phenomena is beyond dispute. The state has
greatly increased in power and scope in advanced capitalist societies such
that it now intervenes massively in affairs once considered beyond its
purview. It especially intervenes heavily in the economy by controlling
the money supply, arbitrating contracts, bailing out failing huge corporations, requiring affirmative action in hiring, and so on. In the United
States the expansion of the state since World War II has been such that
now nearly one in four jobs is provided by some form of state employment. But merely *recognizing* the expansion of the state only begs more
questions. Specifically, we must ask *why* the state in advanced capitalist
countries has become so large and interventionist? In other words, we
require a theory of state expansionism in the United States that suggests
the causes for the increasingly large role the state has assumed in everyday life.

An implication of the Glazer and Moynihan view of the state revolves
around the notion of "welfare state." By this they presumably mean the
direct role the state has assumed for maintaining an increasingly large
sector of the population that has found it impossible to meet basic needs
through normal economic channels. The aged, the poor, "dependent
families," and so on have literally become clients of the state and depend
on it for a meager livelihood. What the "welfare state" refers to, then,
is the increasingly large and direct *economic* role that the state has assumed
in the past thirty or so years. This recognition begs yet another question.
Why has the state had to assume so direct an economic role in the
maintenance of a rather large (about 15 percent) segment of the population? Glazer and Moynihan and others in the "new ethnicity" tradition

have no answer to this question, despite the fact that theories that explain precisely this question are readily available to them.

One example of such a theory is James O'Connor's *Fiscal Crisis of the State*. He argues that the state, in order to maintain its legitimacy, has had to play a large role in the economy (particularly with respect to maintenance of the poor) because the evolution of an advanced capitalist economy has created a large, poorly paid, and underemployed and unemployed labor force that it cannot incorporate. Thus the state has had to bail out the economy itself by introducing maintenance programs that both quell potential rebellion (and, in the case of black protest, actual rebellion) and keep the basic capitalist economy that ultimately supports the state intact.[45]

Theories of this sort have not been embraced by the new ethnicity's proponents because they violate a central assumption concerning what they see as the role of the state—that of a neutral referee that should meddle in neither economic nor social affairs, nor be biased in favor of any particular group or class. Yet the only theories that can explain both the expansion of the state and the particular economic role played by it adopt the view that the state is *not* neutral, that it has *particular* interests to serve, especially the viability of a private enterprise economy. Insofar as the new ethnicity recognizes the increased role of the state and its impact on race and ethnic relations, it is obligated to explain both the nature of and the reasons behind this increased role. This obligation requires a theory of the state and its relation to the larger society, a theory that the proponents of the new ethnicity do not provide.

The second aspect of Glazer and Moynihan's treatment of the state is the claim that the state is more responsive to ethnic movements than to class-based movements. This, too, is true but not for the reasons suggested by them. They argue that class movements "are too general to elicit a very satisfactory response," and that ethnic movements are sufficiently "small enough to make significant concessions possible." This is not historically the case. As a result of the severe labor strife that characterized the United States during the early part of this century, the government instituted a series of laws and agencies (such as the Taft-Hartley Act and the National Labor Relations Board) designed to regulate or institutionalize broad-based class conflicts and confine them to ever more restrictive contexts. Class conflict is not expressed in this country in either "general" or "diffuse" ways, but in quite specific and concrete situations in which unions (or the issue of unionization itself) press their demands on particular industries or specific companies within an industry. The advanced capitalist state has been successful in fragmenting and institutionalizing class conflict such that broadly based "workers'" movements (i.e., the "labor movement") are not currently effective. Ethnic movements, on the other hand, have in the past twenty or so years been much larger (and more diffuse) than workers' movements. This is particularly true of the black protest movement of the 1960s, which in both its organized and unorganized forms constituted a serious threat to the legitimacy of the state. The state had to respond to this movement because it revealed the central contradiction that has characterized the development of the U.S. social system—racial and ethnic stratification.

The existence of stratification or inequality *itself* has not posed a serious legitimation crisis for the state, particularly in the post–World War II period. There are three reasons for this. First, the state was, as mentioned earlier, successful in institutionalizing the serious class conflicts that erupted during the period between world wars I and II. The Franklin Roosevelt and Truman administrations, during which most of the current labor legislation was passed, successfully channeled these conflicts into the more benign (and ineffective) movements that characterize labor today. Second, the post–World War II economic boom generated unprecedented mobility and job opportunities, particularly for white men. In a world of expanding opportunity for the dominant group it becomes relatively easy for certain ideologies such as "the poor have only themselves to blame" or "you can become anything you want (even President) if you work hard enough" to take root. It is precisely the existence of such ideologies, especially what Tawney called "the religion of inequality," that constitutes the third reason for the absence of an effective movement against inequality itself in American life.[46] There is a widespread cultural belief in the United States (and in England and other Western nations as well) that a rather significant amount of inequality is inevitable and necessary in a complex, industrial society, and that the inequality observed is but a reflection of individual abilities, hard work (or lack of it), and "risk taking."

The existence of severe racial and ethnic stratification, however, has posed a legitimation crisis for the state. Insofar as class position was clearly linked to racial classification and black Americans had not shared in the economic prosperity of the post–World War II period; inasmuch as the very legal and moral basis of the United States proclaimed a nondiscriminatory and "all men are created equal" creed; and given the increased politicization of blacks and outright rebellion that brought into clear focus the contradiction between democratic ideals and economic reality, the state was literally forced to deal with the "ethnic claims" of black Americans. Moreover, despite the existence of pervasive racism—beliefs that blacks are inferior to whites—the state was hardly in a position, legally or morally, to adopt an official racist ideology to justify black inequality. On the contrary, it had to admit with consternation, as the Kerner Commission did admit, that the United States consisted of "two societies: one white, one black; separate and unequal."

In contrast to Glazer and Moynihan, my argument concerning the recent responsiveness of the state to "ethnic" rather than "class" claims has nothing to do with the allegation that the former are sufficiently "small," while the latter are too general and diffuse. Instead, it has everything to do with the *sociological fact* that class position has been historically linked to racial membership, and it is the existence of racial stratification, rather than stratification per se, that has produced the state's legitimation crisis and the subsequent attempts to manage this crisis.[47] This sociological fact explains why class issues have taken on an ethnic (or racial) appearance, and, as discussed earlier, why the state emphasizes the "racial" aspect of this relation rather than the "class" aspect. By defining the problem as a "race problem" rather than as a "class problem," the state is able to exploit the continued existence of racism without embracing it as ideology or policy and, at the same time, divert attention *away from* the fundamental problem that confronts many black Americans and other ethnic poor—their poverty.

This brings us to the final reason suggested by Glazer and Moynihan for the emergence of ethnic-based social movements in the United States during the past twenty years. The reason they approvingly offer is not their own, but one suggested by Daniel Bell, one of America's foremost sociologists. Bell suggests that ethnicity has become a new force in American life because ethnic movements "combine interest with an affective tie."[48] As Bell clearly admits, ethnicity has become effective in modern life because of its "primordial" character:

Ethnicity provides a tangible set of common identifications—in language, food, music, names—when other social roles become more abstract and impersonal. In the competition for the values of society to be realized politically, ethnicity can become a means of claiming place or advantage.

Ethnic groups—be they religious, linguistic, racial, or communal—are, it should be pointed out, *pre-industrial* units that with the rise of industry, became cross-cut by economic and class interests. In trying to account for the upsurge of ethnicity today, one can see this ethnicity as the emergent expression of primordial feelings, long suppressed but now reawakened, or as a "strategic site," chosen by disadvantaged persons as a new mode of seeking political redress in the society.[49]

Bell seeks to explain the new ethnicity in terms of what he regards as its double character: on the one hand, ethnicity is a means of "seeking political redress"; on the other hand, it is effective in doing so because of its "primordial" nature. Although this is an interesting juxtaposition, it is thoroughly unsatisfactory for several reasons. First, Bell does not tell us what interests ethnic groups are pursuing. He refers to them as "communal issues" without ever telling us what communal issues are or why they need redressing. Second, he uses a kind of social-psychoanalytic

reasoning by suggesting that ethnicity is a suppressed, primordial, preindustrial instinct that, in the modern world, is finally reawakening after
centuries of oppression by the superego—the industrial world and its
universalist values.

In order to understand Bell's ingenuous conception of the ethnic
factor in the contemporary world order, it is necessary to explore Bell's
theory of society. This is the theory of the post-industrial society outlined
by Bell in his book *The Coming of Post-industrial Society* (1973). As Bell
himself admits, this notion is more a description of advanced industrial
societies such as the United States and the Soviet Union than a theory
of their development or causation.[50] As such it is difficult to critique
because it paints a picture of the world that, lacking any explanation of
the world, one can choose to either like or dislike. Even as a picture it
is incomplete and misleading, since it cannot incorporate either the content or the objectives of recent racial and ethnic movements in the United
States.

Bell classifies the history of society into three basic categories: the
preindustrial world, the industrial world, and the postindustrial world.
He defines each category by means of what he calls "axial principles" in
"an effort to specify not causation [but] . . . centrality. [An axial principle]
seeks to specify . . . the *organizing* frame which the other institutions are
draped, or the *energizing* principle that is a primary logic for all the
others."[51] For the preindustrial world Bell identified "traditionalism and
land and resource limitation" as the axial principles; the industrial world
was characterized by economic growth with either the state or the private
sector in control of investment decisions; the postindustrial world has
the centrality and codification of theoretical knowledge as its axial principle.[52] Bell is primarily concerned with describing the differences between industrial society and postindustrial society and then "forecasting"
the impacts of such differences for the future of postindustrial society.
In a later article (1975) he attempts to use his model of postindustrial
society to explain the rise of the new ethnicity in the United States. The
following list is my summary of Bell's model in terms of its central
propositions: "Whereas industrial society was based on the coordination
of men and machines for the production of goods, post-industrial society
is organized around theoretical knowledge for the purpose of social
control and the directing of innovations and change."[53] From this basic
statement, Bell derives the following corollaries.

1. The economic order has been superseded by the political order in
postindustrial societies. The state rather than the economy becomes the
principle allocator of social values and positions.

2. The old class formations of the industrial order, principally the
capitalist class and the working class, have lost their significance and
been replaced by the new "knowledge class" of professional and technical

specialists. Thus class itself has "lost efficacy" as an organizing principle in postindustrial society. People no longer use economic interest as the primary interest pursued in the political arena. Additionally, there has been a general embourgeoisment of the working class such that most occupational roles require and are filled by technical and professional experts. The few capitalists and workers that remain are relatively unimportant in decision making or system functioning.

3. The new class formations of postindustrial society are not determined by one's relation to property, but by possession of "theoretical knowledge." Education is the primary vehicle to mobility, and the ownership and control of property has lost its importance ("the corporation may be a *private enterprise* institution, but it is not really a *private property* institution. [And] if ownership is largely a legal fiction, then one ought to adopt a more realistic attitude toward it"[54]).

4. In such a postindustrial world, interests other than class become ascendant, and such interests are sought in the political, not the economic, arena. Ethnicity thus becomes emergent in the post-industrial society because it has retained its affective basis (although it was temporarily suppressed during the industrial period) and is a particularly good political basis for organization, since the state is receptive to ethnic claims. In Bell's own words, "where class issues become attenuated, and communal issues come to the fore, understandably, the ethnic tie becomes more salient."[55]

Bell's entire notion of postindustrial society is a gross misrepresentation of the major trends that have occurred in the development of the United States during the twentieth century. If his model applies to any society (and I think it doesn't very well), it applies more to the Soviet Union, where the state is the dominant institution, where private property has lost efficacy, and where class position is a function of education provided one is faithful to the Communist party. Bell believes that his model applies to both the United States *and* the Soviet Union, and that the similarities between these two postindustrial giants far outweigh the differences.

I will argue later that in the United States the advanced *capitalist* economy remains the "organizing framework" within which to interpret recent developments, particularly developments in race relations. Here I need only suggest that Bell's notion of postindustrial society as applied to the United States simply cannot deal with the rise of ethnic movements, especially the most important of these—the Black Protest Movement. This is because Bell denies not only the existence of racial stratification, *but also the existence of stratification itself.* In his view all Americans have experienced "embourgeoisment," that is, a rise both socially and culturally into a middle class, and by implication, America has been successful in meeting the economic needs of its people. Holding such a view, Bell then sees the rise of ethnicity not as an economic matter, but as a matter of "status" in which groups attempt to enhance their individual status by pressing for the recognition of their group identification. As he puts it, *"what takes place, then, is the wedding of status issues to political demands through the ethnic groups"* (emphasis added).[56] Bell does recognize that in the contemporary world order there exists a proletariat, political oppression, chronic unemployment, and poverty—even misery, disease, exploitation, and starvation. But none of this exists in the United States (or at least not enough to be considered a social problem). These are characteristic of what Bell terms the "external proletariat" of the Third World, and not of the technologically advanced postindustrial world. Perhaps Professor Bell will forgive my impertinence and follow my suggestion that he leave his Harvard office and visit a Boston slum.

Whither Assimilationism?

Until recently assimilationism was the dominant paradigm for explaining racial and ethnic processes in the United States. Its dominance was based on its ability to define the nature of the assimilation process and show how numerous American ethnic and religious groups, particularly immigrants of European origins, gradually assimilated both culturally and structurally into American society. However, the inability of assimilationism to explain the continued presence of severe racism and racial stratification has led to its abandonment by many of its foremost proponents. The inability of assimilationism to account for the persistence of racial stratification lay in its assumptions concerning the workings of society's stratification system, the economy, and the state. Assimilationism's basic assumption concerning these institutions was that their inexorable, "natural" workings in a complex industrial society would inevitably lead to a diminution of racial and ethnic forms of social organization. The persistence of racial and ethnic organization in the United States produced a crisis in assimilation theory and has led many former assimilationists to argue that this persistence reflects either biological tendencies for the maintenance of ethnic and racial identities or sociopsychological theories that maintain that the failure of minorities, especially Afro-Americans, to assimilate is due to improper attitudes, lack of self-reliance, and other "victim-blaming" characteristics. Thus many of the "new" theories of ethnicity—sociobiology, primordialism, and the "new ethnicity"—are the offspring of assimilationism's crisis.

The failure of assimilationism and its illegitimate offspring to adequately account for the content and character of recent ethnic movements stems from a failure to critique the institutional structure of society and show its actual, as opposed to its assumed, workings. Moreover, the failure of assimilationism to analyze the historically specific role of Afro-

Americans in American society led to its viewing the "black problem" as similar to the problems faced by other American ethnic and racial groups. The remaining two chapters seek to do what assimilationism did not do—demonstrate the actual workings of dominant institutions both in the world and in the United States, and demonstrate how these institutions have both created and maintained racial and ethnic forms of social organization.

Notes

1. As James Geschwender tells us, this assumption was *not* embedded in Robert Park's work, but emerged later in the work of some of his students. Park himself analyzed race relations within the context of the expansion of capitalism worldwide and tended to view racial stratification as a form of exploitation that benefited capitalist interests (a view that was extended by a minority of his students). Even Park, however, thought that in the long run, racial organization would diminish in importance largely because of the efforts of minorities themselves to demand equal treatment. Cf. James Geschwender, *Racial Stratification in America*. Dubuque, Iowa: Wm. C Brown, 1978, pp. 19–26.

2. Milton Gordon, *Assimilation in American Life: The Role of Race, Religion, and National Origins*. New York: Oxford University Press, 1964, pp. 249–250.

3. Ibid., p. 251.

4. Racists would also argue that blacks cannot be expected to achieve parity with whites over time because of their alleged genetic inferiority to whites. Like the assimilationists, however, racists do not offer any critical examination of the social system in which racism exists.

5. Nathan Glazer, *Affirmative Discrimination: Ethnic Inequality and Public Policy*. Cambridge, Mass.: Harvard University Press, 1987 (1975), pp. 196–197.

6. I am not reducing the race problem to merely or only a class problem. Blacks, by virtue of their race, have been subject to special discrimination and ideologies that cannot be explained by a direct, monocausal "economism." I maintain in Chapter 6, however, that these special problems and their causes cannot be understood apart from their historical connection to the economic framework of American society.

7. Cf. William Julius Wilson, *The Declining Significance of Race*. 2d ed. Chicago: University of Chicago Press, 1978, esp. chs. 1 and 7.

8. Cf. Morton G. Wenger, "State Responses to Afro-American Rebellion: Internal Neo-colonialism and the Rise of a New Black Petite Bourgeoisie," *The Insurgent Sociologist*, 10(2), 1980, pp. 61–72.

9. The presumed cause-effect relation between governmental programs designed for blacks and white workers' economic deterioration has received impetus through the passage of a bill sponsored by Senator Jesse Helms that requires the U.S. Civil Rights Commission to investigate the effect of civil rights legislation on white ethnic males. But as I have suggested, those blacks who have benefited from governmental action are well-educated professionals who have not taken jobs that would have gone to non-college-educated white workers. Both black and white workers have suffered from shifts in the national economy

and the recent recessions, and black workers have suffered even more than their white counterparts.

10. Michael Novak, *The Rise of the Unmeltable Ethnics: Politics and Culture in the Seventies*. New York: Macmillan, 1971, pp. 270–271.

11. Daniel Bell, *The Coming of Post-Industrial Society*. New York: Basic Books, 1973, and "Ethnicity and Social Change," in Nathan Glazer and Daniel P. Moynihan, eds., *Ethnicity: Theory and Experience*. Cambridge, Mass.: Harvard University Press, 1975, pp. 141–174. Nathan Glazer and Daniel P. Moynihan, "Introduction," in Glazer and Moynihan, eds., *Ethnicity: Theory and Experience*, pp. 1–26.

12. Pierre L. van den Berghe, *The Ethnic Phenomenon*. New York: Elsevier, 1981, p. 228.

13. For an example see my article on ethnic politics in Toronto's Chinatown; Richard H. Thompson, "Ethnicity vs. Class: An Analysis of Conflict in a North American Chinese Community," *Ethnicity*, 6(Dec.), 1979, pp. 306–326.

14. Robert E. Park, "Personality and Cultural Conflict," *Publication of the American Sociological Society*, 25(2), 1931, pp. 95–110.

15. Gordon, *Assimilation in American Life*, p. 71.

16. Ibid., p. 111.

17. Ibid., pp. 113–114.

18. Micaela di Leonardo, *The Varieties of Ethnic Experience: Kinship, Class, and Gender Among California Italian-Americans*. Ithaca, N.Y.: Cornell University Press, 1984, p. 96.

19. Josef Barton, *Peasants and Strangers: Italians, Rumanians and Slovaks in an Industrial City, 1890–1950*. Cambridge, Mass.: Harvard University Press, 1975. Quoted in di Leonardo, *Varieties of Ethnic Experience*, p. 97.

20. Oscar Lewis' famous "culture of poverty" thesis is often cited as the seminal work concerning the existence of ethnic and racial family cultures that prevent assimilation and mobility on the part of minorities. Lewis' work ranks with Theodore Adorno's *Authoritarian Personality* as one of the most misinterpreted theories of recent times. Although Lewis did list a host of negative family and personality traits as characteristic of cultures of poverty, he was careful to "blame" the culture of poverty on American capitalism and not on poor people.

21. Nathan Glazer and Daniel P. Moynihan, *Beyond the Melting Pot: The Negroes, Puerto Ricans, Jews, Italians, and Irish of New York City*. 2d ed. Cambridge, Mass.: MIT Press, 1970.

22. Milton Gordon, *Human Nature, Class and Ethnicity*. New York: Oxford University Press, 1978, esp. pp. 67–89.

23. Kingsley Davis and W. E. Moore, "Some Principles of Stratification," *American Sociological Review*, 10(April), 1945, p. 242.

24. Cf. Robert Carneiro, "A Theory of the Origin of the State," *Science*, 69, 1970, pp. 733–738.

25. Cf. Leonard Broom and Robert G. Cushing, "A Modest Test of an Immodest Theory: The Functional Theory of Stratification," *American Sociological Reveiw*, 42, 1977, pp. 157–169; also, Dennis Wrong, "The Functional Theory of Stratification: Some Neglected Considerations," *American Sociological Review*, 24(6), 1959, pp. 772–782.

26. Pierre L. van den Berghe, *Race and Racism: A Comparative Perspective.* New York: John Wiley & Sons, 1967, p. 145.

27. Cf. Gary Becker, *The Economics of Discrimination.* 2d ed., Chicago: University of Chicago Press, 1971.

28. Thomas Sowell, *Race and Economics.* New York: David McKay Co., 1975, pp. 168–169.

29. Ibid., p. 169.

30. Ibid., p. 238.

31. Ibid.

32. An obvious answer to this question is that the means of production necessary to learn baseball, football, and basketball are cheaper and more readily available even to the poor than are those necessary for medicine, law, and the rest (a basketball + inner-city playground compared with a $50,000 or more education). They are also cheaper than golf and country clubs, the latter still a strong vestige of male and "white-only" practices, which probably accounts for the scarcity of black professional golfers.

33. Gordon, *Assimilation in American Life*, p. 251.

34. Stephen Steinberg, *The Ethnic Myth: Race, Ethnicity and Class in America.* New York: Beacon Press, 1981, p. 220.

35. Howard F. Stein and Robert F. Hill, *The Ethnic Imperative: Examining the New White Ethnic Movement.* University Park, Pa.: Pennsylvania State University Press, 1977, p. 9.

36. Orlando Patterson, *Ethnic Chauvinism: The Reactionary Impulse.* New York: Stein & Day, 1977.

37. Glazer and Moynihan, *Ethnicity: Theory and Experience*, p. 5.

38. Ibid., p. 6.

39. Ibid., pp. 6–7.

40. Ibid., pp. 7–8.

41. See Geschwender, *Racial Stratification*, pp. 70–80.

42. Even today various communist parties in the United States see the "Negro problem" as a national question instead of as a complex race/class question. Perhaps the clearest formulation of this point of view is Nelson Peery's *The Negro National Colonial Question.* Chicago: Workers' Press, 1975.

43. Cf. Oliver Cox, *Caste, Class and Race: A Study in Social Dynamics.* New York: Doubleday, 1948.

44. Glazer and Moynihan, *Ethnicity: Theory & Experience*, pp. 8–9, 19.

45. James O'Connor, *The Fiscal Crisis of the State.* New York: St. Martin's Press, 1973.

46. Richard Henry Tawney, *Equality.* 4th ed. rev., London: Allen & Unwin, 1952.

47. The relation between racial and ethnic membership and class status has long been noted by a minority of American scholars, who have used the concept of "internal colonialism" to describe this situation. Internal colonialism occurs when the stratification system of a multiethnic or multiracial society is based on what Michael Hechter has called a cultural division of labor, a situation in which a society "assigns individuals to specific roles in the social structure on the basis of objective cultural distinctions" (Michael Hechter, *Internal Colonialism: The Celtic Fringe in British National Development, 1536–1966.* Berkeley: University of Cali-

fornia Press, 1975, p. 39). Where internal colonialism prevails it has the effect of *maintaining the salience* of ethnic or racial distinctions that have served as the basis for stratification. For other analyses based on the internal colonialism model see Stokeley Carmichael and Charles V. Hamilton, *Black Power: The Politics of Liberation in America*. New York: Vintage Press, 1967; Robert Allen, *Black Awakening in Capitalist America: An Analytic History*. Garden City, NY: Doubleday, Anchor Books, 1970; Robert Blauner, *Racial Oppression in America*. New York: Harper & Row, 1972.

48. Bell, "Ethnicity and Social Change," p. 169.
49. Ibid.
50. Bell, *Coming of Post-industrial Society*, p. 10.
51. Ibid.
52. Ibid., p. 117.
53. Bell, "Ethnicity and Social Change," p. 20.
54. Bell, *Coming of Post-Industrial Society*, pp. 294–295.
55. Bell, "Ethnicity and Social Change," p. 168.
56. Ibid., pp. 170–171.

5

Ethnicity and the Capitalist World-System

One of the major difficulties that has prevented social theorists from understanding and explaining so pervasive and complex a phenomenon as interethnic relations has been the absence of a theoretical framework that is sufficiently general to embrace the totality of ethnic expression worldwide and, at the same time, account for the diverse forms that ethnic expression takes at different times and in different places.

Sociobiology, for example, asserts a universal genetic tendency for ethnically based forms of social organization, but is incapable of explaining either the absence of ethnic organization or its different forms except by reference to social and cultural processes. Assimilationism, on the other hand, has identified such processes as acculturation and structural assimilation that describe the gradual disappearance of ethnic organization, but has difficulty accounting for both the maintenance and the creation of racial or ethnic organization in advanced industrial societies. Also, within the assimilationist worldview, ethnicity is regarded as a traditional, premodern social form that continues to exist in the premodern, lesser developed world. In so-called Third World countries such as those in Africa, Latin America, and Asia tribal and other primordial communities still predominate, and the ethnic processes associated with them are simply regarded as historical holdovers from a traditional, preindustrial past. The problem with this view is that it fails to recognize that ethnic processes in the underdeveloped world have been relatively *recent* historical creations of colonialism and imperialism and the subsequent post-colonial period in which primordial communities have become integrated into new and often unstable state structures. Thus there is little that is "traditional" or premodern about ethnic processes in Africa,

Asia, or Latin America. They are part and parcel of a contemporary world and perform critical functions for the continued evolution of that world.

In 1974 a theory appeared that satisfies many of the problems mentioned above. The theory was developed by sociologist Immanuel Wallerstein, who called it the "modern world-system" and which today is generally referred to as "world-system theory." In his original work Wallerstein concentrated on the origins of this world-system, and in subsequent writings has applied his basic conception to the contemporary world and, on occasion, to ethnic and racial organization.[1] World-system theory is one of a class of theories that are often called "dependency theories" because they interpret the underdevelopment of the Third World as the result of the penetration of and exploitation by the advanced capitalist countries. Underdeveloped countries have thus become dependent on the developed countries whose economic interests are seen as inimical to development in the Third World. There are important differences among the varieties of dependency theory that have been examined and critiqued in detail elsewhere.[2] I have selected Wallerstein's theory because he has applied it specifically to various ethnic and racial situations, and because of its considerable influence on American social science in particular.

As regards race and ethnicity, world-system theory has the following characteristics that distinguish it from those theories discussed in the previous chapters. First, it is a general *social* theory that interprets ethnic processes within the framework of more general, nonethnic developments. Second, it interprets ethnic social organization as a particular form or kind of social stratification; that is, the analysis of inequality is basic to understanding contemporary ethnic processes. Third, it is a holistic theory that specifies a single, unitary framework for understanding ethnicity and at the same time seeks to account for its different and complex manifestations in different parts of the world. Finally, it claims to be a historical, and hence dynamic, theory that enables us to understand certain past events and, on this basis, makes certain predictions concerning future developments in ethnic social organization.

In this chapter I present an outline of world-system theory calling particular attention to its application to race and ethnicity. In so doing I seek to demonstrate the value of viewing ethnic processes within a world-system framework and yet highlight what I consider to be its major deficiencies. The basis of the next chapter, "Race and Ethnicity: Neo-Marxian Explanations and a Reformulation," will follow from the critique of world-system theory presented here.

What Is the Modern World-System?

The modern world-system refers to the *capitalist world-economy* that originated in northwestern Europe during the sixteenth century and has

since expanded to encompass the entire world and its inhabitants. As
Wallerstein describes it:

We live in a capitalist world-economy, one that took definitive shape as a European world-economy in the sixteenth century . . . and came to include the whole
world geographically in the nineteenth century. Capitalism as a system for production for sale in a market for profit and appropriation of this profit on the
basis of individual or collective ownership has only existed in, and can be said
to require, a world-system in which the political units are not coextensive with
the boundaries of the market economy.[3]

There are three major aspects of the world-system contained in this
description. The first aspect concerns the question "When is capitalism?"
At what point does capitalism emerge as a mode of production, and
when can we establish its dominance as the only mode of production?
The answer to this question hinges on a definition of capitalism, and
Wallerstein's definition has been subject to much criticism. I shall return
to this issue later, when I compare Wallerstein and his critics with respect
to their conceptions of capitalism.

A second feature of the world-system notion is that the contemporary
world consists of a single mode of production, capitalism, in which production for profit in a world (as opposed to a national or regional) market
is the defining characteristic. Again, this raises the definition issue, but
equally important is whether the contemporary world *is* a capitalist world
or whether it is *dominated* by a capitalist world. The thrust of Wallerstein's
position is clearly the former, a position he upholds through a definition
of capitalism that can have many forms of production for profit, including forms such as slavery and coerced labor arrangements such as
the Spanish *encomienda* system. For Wallerstein neither private property
nor "free" wage labor is essential to capitalism as a mode of production.
He thus downplays the significance of the differences between capitalist
countries based on private property and so-called socialist countries in
which property is owned collectively or by the state. For Wallerstein
there is little difference between production for profit by individuals (or
corporations) or production for profit by states—both forms of production are capitalist to the extent that they produce commodities for a
world market and seek either their individual or collective advantages
in that world market. Socialist economies such as the Soviet Union,
China, and Cuba are thus referred to as "state capitalist" economies,
which, despite their differing property relations, are nevertheless forced
to compete in the capitalist world-economy with countries based on private ownership.

A third aspect of Wallerstein's conception of the capitalist world-
economy is the recognition that it transcends and is not "coextensive"
with the political boundaries of the world's states. Wallerstein emphasizes

the relationship between the world-economy and the hundreds of states located within it to argue that the world-economy thrives on the absence of a single world government, which, if it existed, might have the power to regulate and even transform the world-economy. The development, spread, and dynamics of the current world-system results from struggles between and among states, or actors within states, for dominance in the world-economy. Thus capitalism is not truly a "free enterprise" economy, since, as Wallerstein states, "within a world-economy, the state structures function as ways for particular groups to affect and distort the functioning of the market."[4] In Wallerstein's view the state is an instrument of capitalist interests insofar as states are compelled to act in ways that further their standing in the world-economy. Thus competition for market advantage and profit becomes translated into a political struggle among competing states, with war, colonialism, and imperialism among this competition's more frequent outcomes. This "instrumentalist" view of the state is another aspect of the world system that is subject to critique.

Core, Semiperiphery, and Periphery

Basic to Wallerstein's conception of the capitalist world-economy is its outline or shape. What does the world-economy look like? How is such a world-economy constituted, and how do the parts that make up the whole interrelate with one another? Wallerstein has identified three structural *relations* that together constitute the capitalist world-economy. I say "relations" rather than "points" or "positions" to emphasize the dynamism and change that, Wallerstein stresses, are basic to the world-system. These relations are the core, the semiperiphery, and the periphery. Historically, there existed what Wallerstein termed "external areas," areas of the world that were not integrated into the world-economy. During the formation of the capitalist world-economy in the sixteenth century, for example, the world-economy centered on Europe and encompassed mainly Europe and Spanish America. Asia, which was connected to Europe largely through the trade of luxury items, was not yet part of the world-economy, and was thus an "external area." The development of capitalism from the sixteenth century to the present has now literally reached world proportions such that there no longer exist external areas. All regions, in Wallerstein's view, are now enmeshed within a single world-economy and occupy one of the three structural relations mentioned above. It must be noted, however, that individual regions and states can and have changed their position within the world-economy. The United States, for example, was a semiperipheral state in the nineteenth century and has only become a core state during the twentieth. The capitalist world-economy is a dynamic world-system in which the capitalist or other ruling classes are constantly competing, often through their state structures, to attain and maintain core status.

What, then, are the criteria that define a region's or state's position as either core, semiperipheral, or peripheral? To answer this I must emphasize two critically important features of the world-economy. First, the very existence of a *world*-economy implies, for Wallerstein, the existence of a single international division of labor. Second, this division of labor is characterized by relations of *inequality* in which the surplus generated by that labor is expropriated by a relatively small class of capitalists or, in the case of socialist countries, by the state. A particular state's or region's standing in the world-system, then, might be defined in terms of the degree to which they are, in terms of the world market, surplus-extracting states or regions (the core) or surplus-producing states or regions (the periphery). Core states are those whose economic power is such that they control a large share of the world market, usually by virtue of having indigenous capitalist enterprises that are technologically sophisticated and worldwide in scope (e.g., multinational corporations). Peripheral regions and countries, on the other hand, are generally at the financial (and military) mercy of core states, lack both an industrial base and a large indigenous capitalist class, and tend to produce labor-intensive agricultural and industrial products for export in firms in which the producers of these products do not own the means of production. Wallerstein describes the core-periphery distinction in the following way: The core-periphery distinction "differentiates those zones in which are concentrated high-profit, high-technology, high-wage diversified production (the core countries) from those in which are concentrated low-profit, low technology, low-wage, less diversified production (the peripheral countries)."[5] Standing intermediate between the core and the periphery are semiperipheral zones, whose "productive activities ... are more evenly divided." That is, in terms of the internal division of labor, the nature of production in the semiperiphery (be it industrial or agricultural), and the power of the state apparatus itself, exhibits some of the features of core zones and some of the features of the periphery. Wallerstein says this is because "in part they act as a peripheral zone for core countries and in part they act as a core country for some peripheral areas."[6]

As Wallerstein himself recognizes, the core-semiperiphery-periphery structure superficially resembles the conceptualization of First World (advanced industrial countries)–Second World (socialist bloc countries)–Third World (preindustrial, premodern countries) advocated by modernization theorists. But there are fundamental differences between the two conceptualizations. One of the most important differences is Wallerstein's insistence that there are not three worlds with their own distinctive characteristics, but a *single* world in which the characteristics observed at the core are connected to and perhaps causative of characteristics observed at the periphery. Because the capitalist world-economy is a system of *unequal* production and exchange, surplus extraction by the core necessarily produces impoverishment and dependency at the periphery. The very functioning of the world-economy is based on wealth at one pole and poverty at the other, or to use Wallerstein's own words, "the key factor to note is that within a capitalist world-economy, all states cannot 'develop' simultaneously *by definition*, since the system functions by virtue of having unequal core and peripheral regions."[7]

The following table shows the current makeup of the capitalist world-economy according to the core-semiperiphery-periphery model. Although the table does not include all the world's zones or regions, it lists those that Wallerstein himself has identified at various places in his writings according to three major variables that will be important to the analysis of race and ethnic relations. The zones (and the states centered on these zones) are designated as core, semiperipheral, or peripheral, according to their *current* location in the world-system, a location that may change for several of them in the not-so-distant future, depending on their ability to adjust to the fits and starts of the capitalist economy. The world-economy itself is a dynamic totality that experiences alternating cycles of expansion and consolidation, upturns and downturns, and so on. The capitalist world-economy is a structure of crisis with each crisis and its resolution producing new alignments of states and regions within states, new contradictions to be managed, and, perhaps ultimately, the transformation of the world-economy itself.

The dynamism inherent in capitalism is based on what Wallerstein terms "its three central antinomies" or contradictions, which are continually being managed in an attempt to serve the basic goal of capitalism—accumulation. These antinomies are:

1. *The contradiction between the economy and the polity (or the state).* "Economy is primarily a 'world' structure but political activity takes place primarily within and through state structures whose boundaries are narrower than those of the economy."[8]

2. *The antinomy of supply and demand.* "World supply is primarily a function of market-oriented 'individual' production decisions. World demand is primarily a function of 'socially' determined allocations of income."[9]

3. *The antinomy between capital and labor.* "Capital is accumulated by appropriating surplus produced by labor, but the more capital is accumulated, the less the role of labor in production."[10]

It is not possible to predict in a precise way how these antinomies will manifest themselves in the future, since each historical crisis produces

The Current Makeup of the Capitalist World System

Nature of the State Apparatus	Nature of the Class Structure	Relation Between Class and Ethnicity	Country (examples)
Core Zones			
Very strong, stable states	Relatively large indigenous bourgeoisie or state-owned enterprises	Bourgeoisie and professionals mostly from the dominant group	U.S.
High degree of bureaucratization			U.S.S.R.
Large, sophisticated militaries and/or alliances	Large professional class; large proletariat	Proletariat mixed between dominant and minority groups	Western Europe Japan
	Very small semiproletariat or subproletariat	Subproletariat, mainly ethnic or racial minorities	
Semiperipherial Zones			
Relatively strong state structures and increasing bureaucratization	Relatively small indigenous bourgeoisie	Bourgeoisie and professionals mostly from the dominant group	Canada
			China
Often large but technologically less sophisticated militaries	About evenly mixed between a fully proletarianized labor force and a semiproletarian labor force	Proletariat mainly from the dominant group	Australia
			Mexico
			Venezuela
Often dependent on core states for economic and military aid		Semiproletariat former "tribal" or other ethnic groups distinct from dominant group	Egypt
			Saudi Arabia
Peripheral Zones			
Relatively weak, unstable state structures	Very small indigenous bourgeoisies and professionals mostly tied to international bourgeoisie	Bourgeoisie mainly from "Europeanized" dominant group	Bolivia
			Zaire
Inefficient, corrupt bureaucracy		Proletariat mostly from rural-to-urban migrants	Ethiopia
			Afghanistan
	Small proletariat		Kampuchea
Unsophisticated but often repressive military and paramilitary forces	Large semiproletariat	Semiproletariat still rural and ethnically distinct from the majority	

a somewhat new reality that produces new problems and prospects. Wallerstein suggests that it is possible, however, to identify basic trends in the movement of the world-economy as a whole that are mandated by the operation of these central tensions. First, the supply/demand antinomy requires the continual *expansion* of the world-economy—"the pushing of outer boundaries of the world-economy to the limits of the earth."[11] The limits of such expansion are being approached today. Second, the joint workings of the supply/demand and capital/labor antinomies feed *proletarianization*, the process by which subsistence producers such as peasants and "tribesmen" are stripped of their means of production and transformed into wage or other types of laborers and market-consumers. Third, there is the *politicization* that accompanies proletarianization and that takes the multiple forms of political parties, workers' movements, national (and "ethnic") liberation movements, and so on.[12] It is this third tendency, the relation between proletarianization of the world's subsistence producers—*particularly as this occurs along racial and ethnic lines*—and their resulting politicization that is the cornerstone for analyzing racial and ethnic relations within a world-system framework. A brief discussion of the foregoing table will illustrate Wallerstein's basic position regarding the relation between the world-economy and racial and ethnic forms of social organization.

The table defines the core-semiperiphery-periphery distinction in terms of three major variables: the nature of the state, the nature of the class structure, and the relation between class structures and ethnic (or racial) groups. Wallerstein asserts that there is a close correspondence between a country's standing in the world-system and the strength of its state apparatus. Core countries tend to develop states that are stable over time; are highly bureaucratized with a large and professional corps of civil servants or cadres; have large professional militaries increasingly based on nuclear technology; and generally possess a high degree of legitimacy among their constituents. In his original work (1974) Wallerstein discusses how the emergence of strong states in the sixteenth and seventeenth centuries was a crucial development for extending capitalism's boundaries worldwide, and how this expansion in turn reinforced the development of a strong state system. Conversely, states that consist mainly of peripheral zones, many of which have only emerged as "independent" states in the past century (a process that has been accelerated by the very development of the world-economy), tend to be unstable; have a small and, compared with the core states, an unprofessional and inefficient bureaucracy; have relatively small armies that function mainly to keep internal order rather than international defense; and often lack legitimacy among their constituents.

The existence of such "weak" states reflects their dependency on core states, a dependency that is both economic and political. Moreover, the core states have an interest in maintaining this dependency, since it underscores the unequal exchange relations that underlie the core-periphery distinction. This is true both for core capitalist states such as the United States and for core socialist states such as the Soviet Union. For example, from a world-system perspective, the U.S. state has an interest in supporting repressive and unpopular regimes in Central America inasmuch as social revolutions there might lead to an alteration of current economic and political alignments that favor certain American companies such as United Fruit that are clearly based on "unequal exchange."[13]

The response of the Reagan administration to the Nicaraguan revolution illustrates how core states seek to maintain their influence over peripheral regions within their sphere. Nicaragua experienced a highly popular revolution that forcibly ousted a repressive regime with close ties to U.S. business interests. The widespread support for the revolution permitted Nicaragua to develop a state apparatus of considerable strength and legitimacy, one committed to reducing the extreme gaps in wealth between the masses of poverty-stricken peasants and the small, indigenous bourgeoisie. During the Carter administration the Nicaraguan revolution was seen as a positive development because it was clear that the new government would end the human rights abuses of the Somosa regime. Also, Nicaragua quickly announced its policy of nonalignment, asserting that it sought to be independent of both U.S. and Soviet alliances. It has only been due to the Reagan administration's quite overt attempts to destabilize and overthrow the Nicaraguan government that the Sandanista regime has become more repressive internally and moved closer to Cuban and Soviet alliances.

I cite the current crises in Central America for two reasons. First, it illustrates the degree to which peripheral countries that seek independence in a dependent world risk the wrath of core countries. A similar case can be made for Soviet domination of Hungary, Czechoslovakia, Poland, and Cuba. Second, it illustrates the degree to which competition among the core states is quite directly centered on peripheral zones, a situation that would be difficult to explain in the absence of a world-system framework. Third, while much of the world's conflict is *understandable* within a world-system framework, it is not necessarily *predictable*. Had the Carter administration been reelected, for example, the current situation in Central America might be very different (and, of course, it might be much the same).

The second major variable that defines the core-semiperiphery-periphery relation is the nature of the class structures that predominate in states, according to their standing in the world-economy. These class structures define how a region's population is distributed in the international division of labor. Wallerstein identifies four major classes that together make up the international division of labor: the *bourgeoisie*, the owners and high-level managers of capitalist enterprises or, in the case of state-owned enterprises, state executives and factory managers, who are almost always high-ranking members of the ruling Communist party; the *professional class* of highly educated and trained workers such as engineers, accountants, professors, middle-level managers, and professional civil servants; the *proletariat or working class*, including both skilled and unskilled wage laborers who occupy lower-level positions in enterprises, such as clerks, factory workers, and laborers; the *semiproletariat* and the *subproletariat*, two quite distinct classes, the former concentrated in peripheral countries and the latter, in core countries. The semiproletariat refers to people who are only partially integrated into the world labor market as wage laborers and who still retain some of their own means of subsistence. Examples are highland peasants in South America, who still till their own small farms but are increasingly pressed to seek part-time wage work in lowland cities, and African tribesmen, who still engage in traditional forms of production such as cattle raising but are increasingly forced to enter a cash economy and produce for a national market. The subproletariat, on the other hand, refers to people in core countries who are permanently unemployed or underemployed and have no means of subsistence other than that generated by occasional wage labor or by direct government assistance.

The relative proportion of a country's population in the international class structure can be used as a primary indicator of that country's position in the world-economy. Core countries have a large bourgeoisie relative to semiperipheral and peripheral countries (although the bourgeoisie is only a very small percentage of the population even in core countries), a large professional-managerial class, a large proletariat, a small but significant subproletariat, and practically no semiproletariat.[14] In the United States, for example, the bourgeoisie is perhaps 2 to 3 percent of the labor force, the professional-managerial class approximates 25 to 35 percent, the proletariat constitutes anywhere from 40 to 50 percent, while the subproletariat hovers between 8 and 12 percent. The absence of a semiproletariat in core areas is indicative of the degree to which proletarianization is practically complete. Few people in core countries directly produce their own means of subsistence and remain isolated from the market economy.

In peripheral regions and countries the class structures take a much different shape. The bourgeoisie is very small and often has links through multinational corporations to the bourgeoisies of core states. The professional and technical classes are similarly small, as is the proletariat compared with core countries, but the latter is rapidly increasing as proletarianization advances. Conversely, there is a large but decreasing semiproletariat and an expanding subproletariat of marginally employed workers drawn mostly from the ranks of the former semiproletariat.

This description of the class structures in core and peripheral zones should be interpreted as general trends in the international division of labor stemming from the antinomies mentioned earlier. Because they are general, however, they cannot be facilely applied to any one country. Class structures are rather more complex than this fivefold division implies, but as a general description of the international division of labor of the world-economy as a whole, this class model is quite accurate.

Race and Ethnicity in the World-Economy

The international class structure is crucial to understanding Wallerstein's basic position concerning race and ethnic relations in the capitalist world-system. In several articles collected in a volume of essays titled *The Capitalist World-Economy* (1979) Wallerstein applies his conception of the world-system to the analysis of racial and ethnic processes.[15] Based on these essays I have summarized his position concerning race and ethnicity in the following propositions:

1. Just as the development of the capitalist world-economy has benefited from the presence of multiple political structures (states), it has also benefited from the presence of multiple *cultural* units (ethnic and racial groups). The historical evolution of the world-economy has been a process whereby dominant core zones (mainly European) have expanded to incorporate small, weak, and culturally and racially distinct peoples into the international division of labor. The existence of multicultural units with different values, languages, and forms of production has facilitated the expansion and consolidation of the world-economy primarily because of the ease with which their labor could be controlled. Such "coerced labor" forms as slavery and the "second serfdom" of Eastern Europe were crucial to capitalism's early accumulation and expansion, as were later forms of coerced labor under colonialism. As the incorporation of culturally distinct peoples into the world-economy advanced, racism developed as a pseudoscientific ideology that both rationalized and justified European domination of nonwhite, non-Western peoples.

2. The central (though perhaps not only) variable to grasp for understanding ethnic processes is the correspondence between racial and ethnic groups and their standing or position in the international division of labor. That is, one should examine the degree to which racial and ethnic groups are confined to or overrepresented in particular classes or occupations within classes in the international division of labor. For Wallerstein racial and ethnic stratification throughout the international

division of labor is the prime cause of racial and ethnic classifications, sentiments, and forms of organization. He thus regards racial, ethnic, and other "status" groups as "blurred collective representation(s) of classes."[16]

3. Racial and ethnic divisions of labor benefit (or are "functional" for) the capitalist world-economy for several reasons. First, the confinement of racial and ethnic groups to particular occupations or forms of production tends to reinforce racial and ethnic boundaries, maintains the salience of racial and ethnic differences, and heightens ethnic consciousness. This in turn tends to inhibit the development of class consciousness inasmuch as *the essentially class concerns of racial and ethnic minorities are often defined in racial or ethnic terms* both by themselves and by the dominant group. Second, racial and ethnic divisions of labor are the breeding grounds for ideologies that assert that certain forms of labor are best suited for certain racial or ethnic groups (blacks are best suited for slavery because they lack ambition, are intellectually and morally inferior, and so on; Chinese are suited to restaurant and laundry work, and so on). Such ideologies reinforce ethnic stereotypes, inhibit the development of class consciousness, and, to the extent that they continue to be effective, tend to keep labor costs down and ensure the continued recruitment of racially and ethnically distinct workers. Over time, however, racial and ethnic divisions of labor tend to be unstable because their integration into the world-economy may lead to cultural assimilation, a process that tends to break down ethnic differences (though not always racial differences) and leads to increased class consciousness. The overall relation between race and ethnicity and class is, historically, one of "dialectical tension," with certain forces (the ethnic division of labor itself) pushing toward greater racial and ethnic solidarity and other forces (proletarianization and integration into the world-economy) pushing toward greater class solidarity. This "tension" can be observed in almost all racial and ethnic movements throughout the world, which are usually complex blends of racial and ethnic sentiments overlayed by calls for greater equality and autonomy.

4. The differences observed in ethnic movements worldwide can be explained by the core-periphery distinction. Core zones tend to have different forms of ethnic organization and "modes of ethnic consciousness" than peripheral zones.[17] Although in both core and peripheral regions ethnic movements stress cultural renaissance and greater political and economic equality, the particular forms that these movements take are different. In core countries racial and ethnic minorities are usually a small percentage of the population, and tend to live in urban areas, where they fill subproletarian roles in a highly industrialized economy. Cultural assimilation may be well advanced, but structural assimilation is lagging. Moreover, despite their concentration in urban ghettos

or other population pockets, ethnic minorities in core countries are usually dispersed throughout the country, and thus lack territorial cohesiveness and territorial claims. Under these circumstances the movements of low-status ethnic groups such as blacks in the United States tend to be urban-based movements with strong subproletarian elements. The movements themselves may range politically from radical revolutionary stances to more "legitimate," center-left concerns for greater economic and political equality within the current framework of the state. Seldom, however, are such movements truly nationalist calls for a separate state with internationally recognized borders and rights to self-determination and national sovereignty. Exceptions are those few cases (such as Quebec and American Indians) in which a minority does have territorial cohesiveness and separatist claims can be advanced. But given the strength of core states and many semiperipheral ones such as Canada, the success of separatist movements is practically nil.

The situation in peripheral countries is quite the opposite. Ethnically and racially distinct populations are still largely rural, and have the status of semiproletarians who are being transformed into proletarianized workers, mainly in agricultural industries (coffee, rubber, and other cash crops) or rural, primary extraction industries such as mining. Thus proletarianization is often confined to a local area in which the racial or ethnic minority is a majority of the population and in which its own language and customs still predominate. Integration into the national culture is not well advanced primarily because universal education in peripheral countries is rudimentary. Ethnic movements in peripheral zones thus have the advantages of territorial and cultural cohesiveness, and their primary mode of ethnic consciousness is nationalism. As Wallerstein states, "nationalism has as its major slogan 'self-determination,' and to have self-determination one must logically have a determinate unit . . . nationalism tends to be attached to territorial units, either already in existence or that can be seen as potential."[18]

These four propositions fairly represent Wallerstein's theory of racial and ethnic relations and their connection to the modern world-system. In its general outline it is a powerful theory because it can account for the historical development of racial and ethnic movements (as these are tied to the overall development of the world-economy), the different forms they take, and how, over time, they may lose their force or become transformed into national or class movements. The reader should also note the extent to which Wallerstein's theory can incorporate Geertz's notion of primordial sentiments as the dialectic between ethnicity and the state in the new (or peripheral) states. Similarly, one can appreciate the ability of the world-system perspective to explain racism and racial stratification in the United States as a functional benefit for capitalism, rather than as an anomaly or "quirk" in the social structure, which is how assimilationism tends to view it. I shall say more about the functions of racism and racial stratification in the United States in the next chapter.

Weaknesses in the World-System Approach

Despite the explanatory power of the world-system perspective and my own view that it is a necessary framework within which to understand race and ethnic relations, it contains several theoretical weaknesses that prevent me from embracing it as a sufficient theory. To illustrate these weaknesses and to set the stage for introducing correctives, I have "reduced" the world-system perspective to the following three axioms:

1. The dominance of the capitalist world-economy forces *all* states, regardless of their particular economic and political organizations, to act in ways that further, or are perceived to further, their position along the core-semiperiphery-periphery continuum.

2. "Socialist" states, therefore, act in ways that reflect their standing in the world-system more so than in ways dictated by the socialist organization of polity and economy. The same also applies to capitalist countries.

3. Thus core states, both capitalist and socialist, have the tendency to pursue the same policies or practices with regard to their ethnic minorities, which will differ from the policies pursued by peripheral or semiperipheral states, notwithstanding the political economies of the latter.

Wallerstein has provided us with an application of these axioms in a paper comparing ethnic relations in the United States and the Soviet Union.[19] In this article he predicts that ethnic relations in the Soviet Union will soon approximate those in the United States because the U.S.S.R. will soon face the requirement of filling subproletarian statuses with ethnically distinct workers from Soviet Central Asia. This is because the Soviet Union, an industrial core country, must continue to industrialize and urbanize in order to maintain or enhance its standing in the world-economy. Increased industrialization and urbanization will necessitate the widespread importation of laborers from Soviet Central Asia and other agricultural areas into Russia's cities, where they will perform the subproletarian roles formerly filled by European Russians. What will occur, in other words, is urban-based ethnic stratification of the sort found in the United States, which in turn may lead to the development of urban ethnic consciousness along lines similar to those found in core capitalist countries.

Wallerstein does not cite any evidence that the Soviet Union is, in fact, moving toward ethnic stratification of this sort. Instead, he seems to base his prediction on the general theoretical assertion that the Soviet Union is compelled by its place in the capitalist world-economy to develop forms of social organization similar to those in other core countries—even other *capitalist* core countries. The problem with this assertion is that the Soviet Union is *not* a capitalist country, and in fact might best be defined as an *anti*capitalist country. One of the weaknesses in Wallerstein's theory, then, is his claim that the differences between capitalist and socialist countries are not very meaningful or, at least, secondary and derivative, when compared with their standings in the world-system as either core, semiperipheral, or peripheral. To state it another way, Wallerstein would argue that the United States and the Soviet Union will pursue policies more similar to one another than to those of either Canada or China, both of which he classifies as semiperipheral countries. With the significant exception of the nuclear arms race and other defense policies, I can scarcely think of convergences in U.S. and Soviet policy, whereas convergences between the United States and Canada come readily to mind (particularly in the area of ethnic relations). To be more specific, *the world-system perspective grossly underspecifies the differences between and among states with different modes of production and different social formations* with the resulting effect that such differences are seen as unimportant or not even as true differences.[20] Wallerstein admits as much when he categorizes socialist countries as "state capitalist," implying that the differences between countries based on private enterprise and state enterprise are, in all important respects, the same.

This example shows several deficiencies of the world-system perspective that critics have identified and that I mentioned at the outset in the description of the world-economy. These criticisms have come in the main from scholars using a Marxian perspective who, in recognizing Wallerstein's debts to Marx and his contributions to a Marx-inspired theory of development, nevertheless think Wallerstein has miscast Marx's basic insights concerning the nature of capitalism, and that this has led him to a theory that is fundamentally flawed. Wallerstein has been influenced by Marx's theory of capitalism (as indicated by his embrace of certain key constructs such as the labor theory of value and the falling rate of profit among others), but he regards the world-system perspective to be an *alternative* to Marxian theories of development rather than an extension of Marxism per se. At issue is whether Wallerstein's alternative is a better account of world-system processes than those more closely tied to Marxian theory.

Wallerstein's critics have focused on three interrelated aspects of the world-system paradigm: (1) the definition of capitalism; (2) the existence of a single or "unitary" capitalist world-economy versus a world-economy dominated by capitalism but consisting of other, noncapitalist modes of production; and (3) what has been termed Wallerstein's "passive" view of the periphery. I will briefly discuss each of these criticisms and then provide an example contrasting two distinct types of ethnic relations that lends credence to them.

What and When Is Capitalism?

The definitional issue is by no means trivial, since one's view of the very nature of capitalism, especially its dynamics and historical expansion, rests on one's conception of its "essence" as a mode of production. For Wallerstein

the essential feature of a capitalist world-economy ... is production for sale in a market in which the object is to realize the maximum profit. In such a system production is constantly expanded as long as further production is profitable, and men constantly innovate new ways of producing things that will expand the profit margin.... Calculations of maximum profitability are made and which therefore determine over some long run the amount of productive activity, the degree of specialization, the modes of payment for labor, goods, and services, and the utility of technological invention.[21]

On this view Wallerstein defines capitalism *as* the existence of a world market, and considers the expansion of that market and/or producers within it to be the simple motivation for profit (greed?) combined with "calculations of maximum profitability" within that market. The particular forms and social relations of production that obtain within the world market are unimportant so long as they permit the surplus extractors (be they capitalists, land barons, the state, or whatever) to expropriate the surplus product of the direct producers (be they industrial workers, slaves, or serfs). Given the definition of capitalism as coterminous with the world market, Wallerstein thus maintains that capitalism originated in the sixteenth century, has expanded to cover the entire globe in the twentieth, is carried forth by the never-ending greed for profit, and is compatible with any system of production that realizes profit.

Wallerstein's view is considered by most scholars to be so broad as to obscure the underlying dynamics of the world-system, particularly because of his focus on relations of exchange rather than on relations of production. As Eric Wolf puts it in his recent book *Europe and the People Without History*:

[Wallerstein's model] collapse(s) the concept of the capitalist mode of production into the concept of the capitalist world market. Furthermore, in defining capitalism as production for a market in order to earn profits, this approach identifies the expansion of Europe since the fifteenth century with the rise of capitalism in its entirety....

What we must be clear about, however, is the analytical distinction between the employment of wealth in the pursuit of further wealth, and capitalism as a qualitatively different mode of committing social labor to the transformation of nature. . . .

Only when the stock of wealth can be related to human energy by purchasing living energy as "labor power," offered by sale for people who have no other means of using their labor to ensure their livelihood; and only when it can relate that labor power to purchased machines—embodiments of past transformations of nature by human energy expended in the past—only then does "wealth" become "capital."

In contrast to . . . Wallerstein, therefore, I argue that the capitalist mode of production did not come into being until the latter part of the eighteenth century. Before that time, European expansion produced a vast network of mercantile relations anchored in noncapitalist modes of production. The worldwide movement of commodities generated prices and money-begetting money, without as yet subsuming both means of production and labor power under capital. The capitalist mode produced, at one and the same time, a new form of deploying social labor and a change from a mercantile to a capitalist market. *The rise of capitalist relations of exchange is thus predicated upon the development of the capitalist mode of production, not the reverse. The enormous escalation of these relations to the level of a worldwide capitalist market was fueled by the dynamism of that newborn mode.* (Emphasis added.)[22]

Wolf's view is consistent with other critics of Wallerstein, particularly Robert Brenner, who see the dynamism and expansion of the current world-system as the result of the contradiction between specifically capitalist relations of production (i.e., between capitalists per se and "free" wage laborers) and the technical forces of production, primarily sophisticated technology designed to increase the amount of *relative* rather than simple surplus value. This contradiction (which produces the tendency for the rate of profit to fall) has historically compelled capitalists to expand their system globally and, in the process, subdue, transform, or abolish the noncapitalist and precapitalist modes that it has confronted worldwide. Thus capitalism is not only inconsistent with forms of production based on slavery, serfdom, or other "nonfree" relations, but also antithetical to them to the point where, if the capitalist mode is to succeed, they must be eliminated.[23]

Georg Lukacs, one of the most important interpreters of Marx, also stresses the specificity and relative recentness of the capitalist mode. For Lukacs the essence of capitalism is the dominance of the "commodity-structure," whose "basis is that a relation between people takes on the character of a thing and thus acquires a 'phantom objectivity,' an autonomy that seems so strictly rational and all-embracing as to conceal every trace of its fundamental nature: the relation between people."[24] The commodity-structure makes episodic appearances throughout history, but only through capitalist relations of production (i.e., those based specifically on the capital/wage-labor relation) is the commodity-structure "able to influence the *total* outer and inner life of society"[25] such that it becomes the "universal structuring principle" of that society.[26]

Lukacs insists on this "narrow" definition of capitalism not only because it is consistent with Marx's own view, but also because it is only when capitalism is understood through the commodity-structure that one can observe the particular forms of subjective consciousness (i.e., the reification inherent in commodity fetishism) it produces and that differentiates it from other profit-taking and market-based forms of production (such as slavery or serfdom):

The commodity can only be understood in its undistorted essence when it becomes the universal category of society as a whole. Only in this context does the reification produced by commodity relations assume decisive importance both for the objective evolution of society and for the stance adopted by men towards it. Only then does the commodity become crucial for the subjugation of men's consciousness to the forms in which this reification finds expression and for their attempts to comprehend the process or to rebel against its disastrous effects and liberate themselves from servitude to the "second nature" so created.

And *this* development of the commodity to the point where it becomes the dominant form in society did not take place until the advent of modern capitalism. Hence it is not to be wondered at that the personal nature of economic relations was still understood on occasion at the start of capitalist development, but that as the process advanced and forms became more complex and less direct, it became increasingly difficult and rare to find anyone penetrating the veil of reification. Marx sees the matter in this way: "In preceding forms of society this economic mystification arose principally with respect to money and interest-bearing capital. In the nature of things it is excluded, in the first place, where production for the use-value, for immediate personal requirements, predominates; and secondly, where slavery or serfdom form the broad foundation of social production, as in antiquity and during the Middle Ages. Here, the domination of the producers by the conditions of production is concealed by the relations of dominion and servitude which appear and are evident as the direct motive power of the process of production."[27]

These criticisms lead to a view of the capitalist world-system quite distinct from Wallerstein's and consistent with Ernest Mandel's characterization of the world-system as "an articulated system of capitalist, semi-capitalist, and pre-capitalist relations of production, linked to each other by capitalist relations of exchange and dominated by the capitalist world market."[28] As Wolf suggests, Mandel's definition accomplishes three things:

First, it draws a distinction between the capitalist mode of production and the "capitalist world market." The capitalist mode of production may be dominant within the system of capitalist market relations, but it does not transform all the peoples of the world into producers of industrial surplus value. Second, it opens up the question of how the capitalist mode relates to other modes of production. Third, it allows us to take note of the heterogeneity of the different societies and subsocieties making up the system rather than obliterating that heterogeneity in dichotomies such as "core-periphery" or "metropolis-satellite."[29]

These criticisms call into question Wallerstein's insistence that the proper unit of analysis is a single, unitary capitalist world-economy,[30] and argue instead that the capitalist mode of production *and its articulation with semicapitalist, anticapitalist, and precapitalist modes is the primary focus of analysis.* Critics agree that capitalism is the *dominant* mode of production in the world-economy, and that it exerts enormous pressures on all countries and regions regardless of their particular mode of production. But capitalism is not the *only* mode of production and is in fact in real and potentially fatal competition with anticapitalist modes of production (usually called "socialism" or "market socialism") that are seeking to defeat and transform it. As I will demonstrate shortly through a comparison of ethnic policies in Canada and China, Wallerstein's failure to consider the quite fundamental differences between capitalist and noncapitalist modes of production can lead to incorrect analyses of ethnic relations.

A third weakness in Wallerstein's approach is his implicit treatment of the periphery as a "passive victim" that inevitably responds to the dictates of the core.[31] Basic to Wallerstein's position is the claim that development of the core countries produces *underdevelopment* in the periphery such that capitalist development in the periphery, however dependent such development on the capitalist world-system might be, is precluded. This position implies that peripheral regions merely react to the dictates of the core zones and that the internal institutions, modes of production, indigenous cultures, and class structures of the peripheral countries play little role in the historical development of the world-system or even within their own national system. Such a passive view causes Wallerstein to dismiss the analysis of *concrete situations of dependency as they exist in specific peripheral regions* and to minimize the dialectical interplay of "external" (i.e., world-system) and "internal" factors. This critique has been elaborated mainly by Latin American scholars, particularly Fernando Cardoso and Gabriel Palma.[32] They agree with Wallerstein that the central dynamics that affect development in peripheral regions are the "general determinants" of the capitalist world-system such that *"the analysis therefore requires an understanding of the contemporary characteristics of the world capitalist system."*[33] But Palma adds:

The system of "external domination" reappears as an "internal" phenomenon through the social practices of local groups and classes, who share its interests and values. Other internal groups and forces oppose this domination, and in the concrete development of these contradictions the specific dynamic of the society is generated. It is not a case of seeing one part of the world capitalist system as "developing" and another as "underdeveloping," or of seeing imperialism and dependency as two sides of the same coin, with the underdeveloped or dependent world reduced to a passive role determined by the other....

There are of course elements within the capitalist system which affect all the Latin American economies, but it is precisely the *diversity within this unity* which characterises historical processes. *Thus the effort of analysis should be oriented towards the elaboration of concepts capable of explaining how the general trends in capitalist expansion are transformed into specific relationships between men, classes and states, how these specific relations in turn react upon the general trends of the capitalist system, how internal and external processes of political domination reflect one another, both in their compatibilities and their contradictions, how the economies and politics of Latin America are articulated with those of the centre, and how their specific dynamics are thus generated.*[34]

The major weakness in the world-system perspective thus stems, ironically, from its strength—that it is a holistic, global perspective that seeks to interpret world events by means of a single, unifying framework. The tripartite division of the world's states into core, semiperiphery, and periphery is a useful way of categorizing hundreds of different polities to illustrate the structural links among them. But this division is useful only for the most general comparative purposes, such as describing the United States or Japan's shares of the world market or the nature of Brazil's dependency on foreign capital and cheaply produced export commodities. For more specific and more important analytical purposes, the core-semiperiphery-periphery distinction is not only of limited use, but also obscures crucially important differences among states who occupy the same standing in the world-economy. More relevant to my purpose, these limitations bear directly on the analysis of race and ethnic relations in the world-system. To demonstrate this, I compare below two countries, Canada and China, both of which are classified as semiperipheral countries by Wallerstein.[35] The purpose of this comparison is to demonstrate the inadequacy of the core-semiperiphery-periphery distinction to distinguish important differences between countries that, despite their same standing in the world-economy, greatly affect the policies pertaining to ethnic groups and the resulting forms of ethnic organization. The most important differences that the world-system ignores or obscures are the different tendencies or "rationales" that guide capitalist and, what I prefer to call, market socialist (as opposed to Wallerstein's characterization of them as "state capitalist") countries, and how these different rationales impose different restrictions on states organized by them. I want to illustrate these differences by considering the ethnic policies of China and Canada to show how they reflect the different modes of production in which they are set. To do so I will first discuss the relation between the state and the economy in capitalist and market socialist countries, since it is this relation, more than any other, that defines the different rationales underpinning the two modes of production. I will then briefly discuss the ethnic policies of China and Canada to show how these different modes lead to quite different forms of ethnic organization.

This comparison constitutes a limited test of the world-system perspective by arguing that two semiperipheral countries do not, as world-system theory suggests they should, necessarily produce the same forms of ethnic social organization. This is particularly the case when the two countries in question are based on fundamentally different modes of production. I have chosen China and Canada for comparison because of my own knowledge of and experience with the ethnic policies of these countries. Other comparisons between two or more countries with the same standing in the world-system and with different economic and political organizations would, I suspect, serve equally well.

The Nature of the State in Capitalist and Socialist Societies

Wallerstein's view of the relation between the state and the economy in capitalist societies seems quite consistent with neo-Marxian writings concerning this relation. The general question of the nature of the state in capitalist economies has been framed by three, more specific questions: Whom does the state represent? What are the constraints or limits to state action imposed by a capitalist economy? How powerful or powerless are these constraints to affect state actions; that is, how much autonomy does the state have to act in ways contrary to the basic laws of capitalism?

Marxian-oriented social scientists (this would include Wallerstein) agree that in capitalist countries, the state is a "class state" that generally, though not in every instance, represents the basic interest—profit accumulation—of the capitalist class. This is hardly a simple relation, for the state must also maintain its legitimacy among most sectors of the population, most of whom are neither capitalist nor beneficiaries of a capitalist economy.[36] Black Americans, for example, have been historically confined to the least favorable sections of the labor market and have, with increased political power and sophistication, been able to press the state for certain guarantees concerning minority-owned businesses, university enrollments, and the like, which serve to distort the normal functioning of the capitalist economy. The increased role that the state has come to play in the management of the economy has led some theorists to argue that the state in core capitalist countries is very "interventionist" and is no longer constrained by the "laws" of value, anarchy, and falling rate of profit, which Marx identified as the basic tendencies that guide the development of capitalist economies.[37] In this view the state has become dominant over, or at least separated from, the economy such that it exercises a high degree of autonomy. To some it appears that the capitalist economy has become politicized to the extent that it is now as much directed by the state as vice versa.

A second view, most clearly articulated by Milton Fisk,[38] maintains that the state, although it does play a larger role in advanced capitalist economies than during the earlier periods of capitalist development, is still constrained by the basic laws of the economy outlined by Marx. In this view the state is more "reactive" to the demands of capitalism than interventionist. Ralph Miliband, a leading authority on the relation between the state and capitalist economies, provides a succinct summary of the reactive state: "The state does of course 'intervene' massively in the life of advanced capitalism, and sustains it in a multitude of ways which cannot all by any means be labelled 'economic.' It *mainly* does so in accordance with the 'rationality' of the capitalist mode of production, and within the constraints imposed upon it by that mode of production."[39]

It is this second view—that the capitalist economy is still highly determinative of the state's actions—that is most consistent with Wallerstein's world-system perspective. The world-economy is still dominant over the political structures that attempt to manage it. The state is still subservient to the basic demands that the capitalist economy foists on it to the point that any state administration that seeks to ignore or contradict these demands would be short-lived indeed. In my view Wallerstein and others are correct in asserting that in capitalist countries, it is the economy that wags the state, not vice versa.

Less attention has been given to the role of the state in socialist countries, although a few writers, especially Miliband, have suggested useful lines of inquiry. There is widespread agreement, however, that in socialist countries the state clearly directs the economy and does so in accordance with political "laws" rather than economic ones. Compared with capitalist states, socialist states are decidedly directive and have much greater autonomy and "freedom." This is because the socialist state does not represent any single class or group, although, as Miliband suggests, this does not imply that it represents "the whole people" either.[40] Rather, the state is the executive arm of the Communist party and whomever controls the party controls the state. Although Communist parties are "mass" parties, they are nevertheless rigidly hierarchical and subject to domination by a relative few. The power wielded by party elites in socialist countries is much greater (with respect to their management of the economy) than that of their counterparts in bourgeois parties in advanced capitalist countries, a power that makes them more susceptible to antidemocratic and totalitarian tendencies.

Despite the much greater autonomy of socialist states, they, too, are subject to structural constraints that give them a particularly socialist character. These constraints are *internal* to market socialism as a mode of production and define, within broad limits, the kinds of policies pursued by socialist states. Miliband suggests that "collectivism" and "anti-capitalism," though less limiting than capitalist "laws," are nonetheless formidable constraints that impose "an altogether different 'rationality' upon those who control collectivist societies, and who are in this sense controlled by the collectivism over which they preside."[41] Socialist regimes must respond to the real and significant constraints imposed by exogenous factors such as events in the capitalist world-system in ways that do not contradict the rationality of the socialist mode of production—a rationality that is fundamentally different from, in fact opposed to, the rationality of capitalism. Certain policy options are not available to socialist regimes, in particular, options that would permit the expropriation and accumulation of profit through capitalist enterprises and the subsequent emergence of *widespread* private property-based social class relations.[42]

A necessary addition to the world-system perspective, then, is the recognition that states based on different modes of production will respond to events according to the basic tendencies of that mode of production. This recognition does not diminish the importance or necessity of understanding world-system factors, but places them within a more concrete framework. The central question is the extent to which the capitalist world-economy exerts a determining force on state actions greater than the internal forces stemming from a particular mode of production as it is defined and organized in a particular, historically specific country. In short, are we able to understand and explain the domestic and foreign behaviors of the United States and the Soviet Union by simply noting, as the world-system perspective notes, that both countries are core, industrial states in the world-economy? Or do we explain their behaviors better through a framework that, in addition to taking account of their dominant core status, also recognizes that one is capitalist and the other is state-planned, market socialist? By comparing ethnic policy in two semiperipheral states, one of which is capitalist (Canada) and the other socialist (China), I can demonstrate how countries with different modes of production produce quite different forms of ethnic social organization in spite of their similar standing in the world-economy.

Ethnic Policy in Canada and the People's Republic of China

Canada and China are both semiperipheral countries in Wallerstein's categorization, yet it is difficult to imagine two other countries whose origins, history, culture, and current social organization are more dissimilar. Canada is a state of recent origin that, from its beginnings as a colonial battleground of the French and English, was quickly incorporated into the world-economy and has, despite its "dependency" on European and American corporations and personnel, developed into a thoroughly modern society with a class structure similar to its core-status southern neighbor. Canada is not only a capitalist country, but an *advanced* capitalist country with a very high standard of living, a nonexistent semiproletariat, and an increasing subproletariat whose ranks are being swelled by immigrants from Africa, Asia, and other peripheral zones. The capitalist economy is so dominant that it has practically no competition from precapitalist forms of production, while the "threat" it does face (one that, for the time being, has diminished greatly) is from an equally modern, linguistically distinct, yet fully Europeanized province that advocates, officially at least, independence and a protosocialist economy.

China, on the other hand, is neither advanced nor capitalist, despite its overwhelming desire to become the former without capitulating to the latter. China is one of the world's first states, firmly consolidated by the time of Christ, and exhibiting an unparalleled continuity of culture and administration. Perhaps as late as 1800 China was not only the world's most populous country, but arguably its most powerful as well, having developed a sophisticated civilization out of the collective toil of its millions of agriculturally sophisticated peasants. During the course of its history China faced numerous, sometimes successful threats from "barbarian" invaders such as the Mongols and Manchus, but the ability of the Chinese to Sinicize even these conquering foreigners and integrate them into the traditional Chinese state enabled China to maintain an autonomy and independence that can only be described as remarkable.

The course of Chinese history was irrevocably changed, however, when, in the mid-nineteenth century, newly industrial England attempted to forcibly integrate China into its colonial empire through the Opium Wars. China was virtually helpless against the onslaught of Western war technology, in some part owing to its own inclination to ignore it. But neither England nor later imperialist ventures by France, Germany, and even the United States were able to colonize China outright. Only the Japanese war machine during the 1930s and 1940s truly occupied China, and even this invasion was restricted to the northeastern part of the country. Nevertheless, the development of the world-capitalist system changed China immeasurably, producing a century of internal turmoil and anarchy that ultimately resulted in the great peasant-socialist revolution of 1949.

Today China, though a stable and increasingly powerful state, is still an overwhelmingly agricultural country in which socialism, the dominant mode of production, is still in competition with its very recent precursor—subsistence agriculture based on private property and the Confucian values that supported it. The dominance of the Communist Party of China (CPC) makes this "competition" appear rather one-sided, although the recent displacement of the commune system with the household responsibility system is some indication that the party will take whatever steps it thinks necessary to modernize, including the "capitalist road." In this drive to industrialize, the CPC nevertheless directs the economy in ways that would not be possible in any capitalist country. There is, then, a profoundly different relation between the state and the economy in socialist countries than that which obtains in capitalist countries. Moreover, the CPC has to manage many non-Chinese ethnic groups that inhabit the crucial northwestern and southwestern border areas of China and that, in addition to being hostile to ethnic or "Han" Chinese, were historically engaged in forms of production such as slash-and-burn agriculture and pastoral nomadism, which the CPC, in its pseudo-Marxian classification of history, regards as "backward" and "feudal." A basic mission of Chinese policy has been to "transform" these traditional economies according to socialist principles of production, a mission that has led to a particular ethnic policy and forms of ethnic organization. China is a country, then, in which socialism (which in CPC terms is "socialism with Chinese characteristics"), not capitalism, is the dominant mode of production; but one that is still being imposed on the remnants of nonsocialist, precapitalist forms.[43]

Superficially, at least, Canada's ethnic policy of "bilingualism within a multicultural framework" and China's ethnic policy of "regional autonomy" appear remarkably similar. Both policies permit the expression of ethnic differences (or pluralism) within multinational states. The "ethnic question" is also an important issue in both countries, although for different reasons. The current Canadian federation in which Anglo-Europeans have historically played the dominant role has been seriously threatened by the Francophone minority in Quebec and the increasing politicization of hundreds of thousands of recent immigrants from underdeveloped countries. China, on the other hand, although not seriously threatened by its numerous ethnic groups, has nearly 60 percent of its territory inhabited mainly by its 6 percent non-Chinese minority nationalities. These minorities, culturally distinct from the Chinese and engaged in traditional forms of production such as pastoral nomadism, occupy lands rich in natural resources and strategically situated along China's northwestern and southwestern borders.

The importance of state-ethnic group relations has led both Canada and China to develop a complex ethnic management formula that Cynthia Enloe calls "vanguard assimilation cum pluralism."[44] As Enloe defines it, "as the awkward phrase suggests, this formula is full of ambivalences. It is intended to achieve ends for the state roughly akin to those of the simpler vanguard assimilationist strategy [i.e., under-

mining ethnic communal differences while maintaining the leading position of the dominant ethnic group], but to do so without openly
admitting it."[45] All policies promulgated by states toward their constit-
uent ethnic groups have a distinctly ideological component. That is, states
attempt to define just what ethnicity *is* and what aspects of ethnic expression are legitimate and nonlegitimate. In the "vanguard assimilation cum
pluralism" formula the ideological component of the policy is as important as the specific provisions of the policy per se, since the primary
purpose of the formula is to create the illusion of multi-ethnic harmony
and equality without seriously undermining the dominant ethnic group's
hold on state power. Thus various specific provisions of the policy such
as the recognition of ethnic languages, immigrant services, and so forth
are motivated mainly to the extent that they further the pluralist ideology. For example, the expressed intent of Canada's policy of bilingualism within a multicultural framework is to establish "an equal
partnership of the two founding races" (French and English) and to take
"into account the contribution made by other ethnic groups to the cultural enrichment of Canada and the measures that should be taken to
safeguard that contribution."[46] Chinese writings on regional autonomy
have a similar ring. They portray the People's Republic as a "unitary,
multinational state" in which all the nationalities have contributed to
Chinese civilization and culture and live "united and equal," in a "big
fraternal co-operative family."[47] Note the emphasis of both policies on
"equality," "unity," and respect for ethnic differences, a sure sign that
inequality, conflict, and assimilationist pressures lie at the heart of interethnic relations in both countries. Both Canada and the People's Republic of China have invested enormous time and expense managing
and propagating ethnic policies whose contents and goals are similar—
convince the ethnic minorities that their cultures will be retained on the
one hand, while on the other inculcating and institutionalizing the dominant values that underpin the state. At the level of policy, then, China
and Canada are pursuing essentially the same goals. *But the effects of these
similar policies have been very different because each policy is set in different
modes of production that impose their different rationales on the implementation
of the policies.*
    Canada pursues its ethnic policy as a way of managing contradictory
tendencies in the capitalist economy. Canada has historically used ethnically distinct immigrant populations to supply manpower for the competitive sectors of the economy, mainly service and construction
industries and textile manufacturing. In these sectors either technology
has not sufficiently increased productivity so as to maintain an acceptable
rate of profit, or multinationals with Third World bases, particularly in
garments, have required domestic firms to hire immigrant labor to stay
competitive. Moreover, there has historically been a severe overrepre-

sentation of Americans and British (be they immigrants or Canadian residents) in the managerial and professional occupations, a fact that, in addition to the dominance of Anglophone institutions, has led the French-speakers in Quebec to see themselves as a national minority. Canada has a deeply entrenched system of ethnic stratification, and one that has intensified in the twenty years since the passage of new immigration regulations during which nearly four million new immigrants, mostly from peripheral countries, came to Canada.[48] This new immigration, coupled with a general slump in the Canadian economy during the 1970s and 1980s, has caused the "ethnic problem" to progress from acute to chronic, and reflects the failure of the state to perform what O'Connor described as the delicate balancing act required by all capitalist states: further capital accumulation and at the same time enhance the state's legitimacy.[49]

Canada faces the same "Catch–22" as that encountered by other capitalist states such as the United States, which have historically relied on ethnic divisions of labor to fuel the economy in times of expansion and to bear the brunt of underemployment and unemployment in times of recession—how to further the growth of capitalism and the commitment to stratification that that necessarily entails and, at the same time, remove ethnic stratification. Realistically, the Canadian state does not have the autonomy or power to legislate the removal of ethnic stratification. As a result it has developed the ingenious and complex policy of "bilingualism within a multicultural framework," which is first and foremost an effort by the state to show its respect for ethnic differences, and thus enhance legitimacy, without seriously altering the ethnic stratification that produced the "legitimation crisis."

The Chinese People's Republic (CPR) has its ethnic difficulties, too, but they stem from different contradictions. China is trying to solve a much different problem than Canada is trying to solve: how to integrate non-Chinese ethnic groups into the socialist economy and polity *without resorting to ethnic stratification* and, at the same time, maintain certain ethnic differences such as native languages and some customs. It may be argued that China has no commitment to maintaining ethnic distinctions, that it is pursuing a strictly assimilationist policy designed to remove all traces of non-Chinese culture. But there is sufficient evidence that the CPR has instituted many programs designed to maintain certain aspects of the minorities' cultures so long as they are not seen as a hindrance to socialist reconstruction or as a threat to state security. China, like Canada, has only a quasi-commitment to ethnicity, and one that is designed primarily to achieve legitimacy in the eyes of the minority nationalities. But the history of Chinese-minority relations and the requirements of a socialist mode of production have led to a commitment quite different from Canada's.

When the CPR extended firm political control over the now designated fifty-five minority nationalities in 1949–1951, it found native societies that not only had an intense dislike for the Han Chinese, but also whose economies and social relations the state regarded as backward and feudal. In order to counter the distrust and dislike the CPR immediately proclaimed its respect for ethnic differences and countermanded the blatantly assimilationist programs of Chiang Kai-shek's Kuomintang.[50] Soon, however, the Chinese made it clear that the socialist reconstruction policies that would be implemented among the mass of Chinese peasants would be applied to the minority nationalities as well, though perhaps more slowly and with suitable sensitivity to ethnic languages and customs. The state thus set about to transform the backward economies of the Kazakh, the Uzbek, the Mongols, the Miao, the Yi, and other nationalities, a process that the Chinese defined as eliminating the feudal class relations on which these economies were based. This involved the importation of thousands of Han Chinese, mostly members of the army, who introduced "scientific" methods of agriculture and animal husbandry, important medical and sanitation advances, and, of course, the thought of Marxism-Leninism-Maoism communicated mostly in Chinese. Vigorous campaigns were launched criticizing certain customs (such as homage to certain deities and "chiefs"), and traditional leaders hostile to the aims of the party were either isolated or co-opted.

It is difficult to determine just how far the transformation of native economies and social systems has gone, since all information is transmitted through the Chinese press. Certainly the Chinese have proferred assimilationist policies, insofar as the state language is Chinese and traditional practices considered a hindrance to socialist reconstruction have been criticized or eliminated. But the CPR has instituted other policies to counter these assimilationist ones. They have vigorously pursued the restoration of minority histories and languages. They seem to have been more successful in multicultural education than Canada has been. But the specific policies emanating from China's program of regional autonomy (despite the lack of true autonomy) differ in one fundamental respect from Canada's policy of bilingualism and multiculturalism. Whereas Canada has consistently developed ethnic divisions of labor, China has sought to develop its ethnic minorities along socialist lines and *prevent* the emergence of ethnic stratification by integrating the minorities into the educational, occupational, and political structures. If Chinese data are reliable, the state has expended in minority areas two and one-half times the revenue that it has extracted. Second, representation in the People's Congresses in the autonomous regions is heavily non-Han, though in no case are they the majority. Third, minority cadres and party members now approximate the percentage of the minority populations, and millions of minorities are in primary and middle schools and universities. Lastly, the life expectancies, populations, and general standards of living of most of the minorities have increased greatly since 1949, which indicates that the Chinese have not resorted to genocide to "solve" the ethnic problem.[51]

In the final analysis, however, the CPR is not likely to succeed in maintaining ethnic differences while removing the structural basis of "backward" modes of production. Its own theorizing on the ethnic question suffers from a flaw as fatal as liberal theorizing in capitalist states—the belief that economic transformation need not lead to cultural transformation. This is an issue that the current so-called Marxist-Leninist states have not adequately solved, nor will it be solved in such hierarchical, antidemocratic, and bureaucratic states as China. Thus the Chinese state stands accused of a form of ethnocide, if not genocide, not because it so intended, but because it has so far treated ethnicity as an obstacle to its national development.

Several factors in the world-system have no doubt played important roles in the development and execution of ethnic policies in Canada and China. Canada's relatively advanced standing in the world-economy has permitted it to attract millions of immigrants from the underdeveloped world. The serious external pressures faced by China, particularly from the Soviet Union, account for many of the policy shifts and timing of ethnic policy there. But at no time has either state implemented policies that contradict the logic of their respective modes of production.

Conclusion

In this chapter I have sought to demonstrate the necessity of analyzing race and ethnic relations from a world-system perspective. This perspective treats race and ethnic relations as particular forms of social organization connected to the international division of labor. This means that racial and ethnic relations are kinds of production relations that have been produced by the expansion of the capitalist economy worldwide. The particular structure of these relations varies from country to country, depending on their standing in the world-economy, the makeup of their internal class structures, their racial and ethnic composition, and the particular historical role they have played in the evolution of the world-economy. The world-system perspective also argues that racial and ethnic divisions of labor have benefited the capitalist world-economy not only because racially and ethnically distinct peoples from underdeveloped countries were more easily coerced into the international division of labor, but also because ethnic divisions of labor inhibit the development of international and national class consciousness and lead to conflicts that are essentially caused by inequality, but are defined on racial and ethnic, rather than class, grounds.

I have also tried to show, however, that there are certain important weaknesses in the world-system perspective, the most important of which is the inability of the world-system approach to distinguish different forms of race and ethnic relations existing in societies with drastically different histories and based on different modes of production. What a sufficient theory of race and ethnicity requires, then, is a more general theory of modes of production as they exist within and are influenced by the dominant capitalist mode of production. If the issue itself appears rather straightforward, the solution of it is not. Social science has failed in what I consider its basic task—the development of theories of modes of production and the principles that govern them. Part of this failure stems from the lack of an adequate method by which to analyze societies and by the very complexity of concrete societies themselves in which one dominant mode of production is often interconnected with very different modes of production.

Fortunately the dominant mode of production in the world today, capitalism, has been eviscerated theoretically, most especially by Marx, by means of a method, dialectical materialism, which enables us to examine its inner workings. The dominant capitalist country, the United States, has also been studied by numerous Marx-inspired scholars, many of whom have applied his method to the analysis of race and ethnic relations. In the next chapter I hope to provide a general outline of a more adequate theory of race and ethnicity based on a neo-Marxian perspective and several important studies of race and ethnic relations in the United States.

Notes

1. Immanuel Wallerstein, *The Modern World-System: Capitalist Agriculture and the Origins of the European World-Economy in the Sixteenth Century.* New York: Academic Press, 1974; *The Capitalist World-Economy.* Cambridge: Cambridge University Press, 1979. The following articles in *The Capitalist World-Economy* deal with aspects of race and ethnicity: "Social Conflict in Post-Independence Black Africa: The Concepts of Race and Status Group Reconsidered," pp. 165–183; "The Two Modes of Ethnic Consciousness: Soviet Central Asia in Transition," pp. 184–192; "Class and Class Conflict in Contemporary Africa," pp. 193–201; "American Slavery and the Capitalist World-Economy," pp. 202–221.

2. Consult Gabriel Palma, "Dependency and Development: A Critical Overview," in D. Seers, ed., *Dependency Theory: A Critical Overview.* London: Francis Pitner, 1981, pp. 20-78, for the relationship between Wallerstein and other "schools" of dependency theory.

3. Wallerstein, *Capitalist World-Economy*, p. 66.

4. Ibid., p. 61.

5. Ibid., p. 97.

6. Ibid.

7. Ibid., p. 61.

8. Ibid., p. 273.

9. Ibid.

10. Ibid.

11. Ibid., p. 278.

12. Ibid., p. 279.

13. Walter Lefeber presents an excellent analysis of U.S. policy with respect to Central America in *Inevitable Revolutions*. New York: W. W. Norton, 1984.

14. There is a "sixth" class of independent owners and producers, the petty bourgeoisie, which includes artists, independent craftsmen, and others who own their means of production and individually produce their commodities. In the contemporary world this is a very small class, and one that is located outside the capitalist mode of production (though still very much affected by it).

15. These are the articles listed in note 1 above.

16. Wallerstein, *Capitalist World-Economy*, p. 181.

17. I. Wallerstein, "The Two Modes of Ethnic Consciousness: Soviet Central Asia in Transition," in Wallerstein, *Capitalist World-Economy*, pp. 184–192.

18. Ibid., p. 186.

19. Ibid., pp. 184–192.

20. This is the basis of an excellent critique of the world-system perspective by Dupuy and Fitzgerald, who argue that Wallerstein's lack of the concepts of "mode of production" and "social formation" prevent him from correctly analyzing social (including ethnic) relations even in capitalist countries. Alex Dupuy and Paul V. Fitzgerald, "Contribution to the Critique of the World-System Perspective," *The Insurgent Sociologist*, 7(2), 1977, pp. 113–124.

21. Wallerstein, *Capitalist World-Economy*, pp. 15, 222.

22. Eric Wolf, *Europe and the People Without History*. Berkeley: University of California Press, 1984, pp. 297–298.

23. For an early, yet excellent and comprehensive critique of this and other aspects of Wallerstein's model consult Robert Brenner, "The Origins of Capitalist Development: A Critique of Neo-Smithian Marxism," *New Left Review*, 104, 1977, pp. 25–93.

24. Georg Lukacs, *History and Class Consciousness*. Cambridge, Mass.: MIT Press, 1967, p. 83.

25. Ibid., p. 84.

26. Ibid., p. 85.

27. Ibid., p. 86. By "modern capitalism" Lukacs is clearly referring to capitalism at its most advanced stages in Europe and America in the nineteenth and early twentieth centuries. He would thus take issue with Wallerstein's contention that capitalism arose in the sixteenth century, although he might agree that its incipient forms (mercantilism and the period of "primitive accumulation" especially) developed during this time. During this incipient phase we can identify instances of reification, but not until capitalism is firmly entrenched as a mature mode of production is reification a dominant aspect of consciousness.

28. Ernest Mandel, *Late Capitalism*. London: Verso, 1978, pp. 48–49 (first published in German in 1972).

29. Wolf, *Europe and People Without History*, p. 297.

30. Wallerstein has attempted to answer his critics, particularly Ernesto La-

clau, in an article titled "The Rise and Future Demise of the Capitalist World-System: Concepts for Comparative Analysis," in *Capitalist World-Economy*, pp. 1–36.

31. See K. E. Trimberger, "World Systems Analysis: The Problem of Unequal Development," *Theory of Society*, 8, 1979, pp. 101–106; and June Nash, "Ethnographic Aspects of the World Capitalist System," *Annual Review of Anthropology*, 10, 1981, pp. 393–423, for a more extended discussion of this.

32. F. H. Cardoso, "Dependency and Development in Latin America," *New Left Review*, 74, 1972, pp. 83–95; F. H. Cardoso and E. Faletto, *Dependency and Development in Latin America*. Trans. by M. M. Urquidi. Berkeley: University of California Press, 1979; Palma, "Dependency and Development," pp. 20-78.

33. Palma, "Dependency and Development," p. 60.

34. Ibid., pp. 61–62.

35. I. Wallerstein, "Semiperiphal Countries and the Contemporary World Crisis," in Wallerstein, *Capitalist World-Economy*, pp. 95–118 (especially p. 100).

36. An excellent analysis of the role of the state in advanced capitalism is James O'Connor's *Fiscal Crisis of the State*. New York: St. Martin's Press, 1973.

37. "Interventionist" views of the state have been given by Michael Harrington, *The Twilight of Capitalism*. New York: Simon & Schuster, 1976; Nicos Poulantzas, *Classes in Contemporary Capitalism*. Trans. by David Fernbach. London: Verso, 1974; Erik Olin Wright, *Class, Crisis and the State*. London: New Left Books, 1978.

38. Milton Fisk, "The State and the Economy," *Midwest Studies in Philosophy*, 7(February), 1982, pp. 42–65.

39. Ralph Miliband, *Marxism and Politics*. Oxford: Oxford University Press, 1977.

40. Ibid., p. 114.

41. Ibid., p. 111.

42. Market socialist countries such as China, Yugoslavia, and the Soviet Union do permit a degree of independent, "petty bourgeois" enterprises, but their production systems as a whole are scarcely affected by such private property-based relations, nor do they resemble truly capitalist production relations.

43. In a recent book Michel Chossudovsky argues that the dominance of the capitalist world-economy may be pushing China toward a capitalist restoration. This restoration may be observed, he suggests, by the post-Mao reforms instituted by the Deng Xiao-ping–led Chinese Community party. Although these reforms clearly reflect an attempt by China to integrate its economy more closely with the capitalist West and Japan, and attests to the dominance of the capitalist world market, China has not yet restored private property as the basis of its production systems in either industry or agriculture. See Michel Chossudovsky, *Towards Capitalist Restoration? Chinese Socialism After Mao*. New York: St. Martin's Press, 1986.

44. Cynthia Enloe, "Internal Colonialism, Federalism, and Alternative State Development Strategies," *Publius*, 7(4), 1977, pp. 145–160. Enloe regards the ethnic policy of China as an example of "vanguard assimilationism" *without* the "cultural pluralism" aspect attached (p. 153). Chinese policy as it was implemented during the ill-fated Great Leap Forward (1958–1959) and the Cultural Revolution (1966-1975) was assimilationist, for it clearly emphasized the mod-

ernization of the national minorities with little regard for native customs and languages. With the exception of these atypical periods, however, Chinese policy has generally been "pluralist" inasmuch as it has recognized and, to a great extent, legitimated ethnic characteristics. Current Chinese theorizing on this issue stresses the necessity of accepting nationalities' (ethnic) differences under socialism so long as they do not underpin class differences. Policies during the Great Leap and the Cultural Revolution have been criticized as "left-wing mistakes" for confusing the "national question" with the "class question." Thus the Chinese are, in my opinion, promulgating a cultural pluralist strategy, although the Han Chinese are certainly the "vanguard" ethnic group. For an insightful discussion of recent Chinese analyses on this issue, see "Is the National Question Essentially a Class Question?" *Renmin Ribao* (People's Daily), July 15, 1980.

45. Ibid., p. 154.

46. Royal Commission on Bilingualism and Biculturalism. *Book IV. The Contributions of the Other Ethnic Groups.* Ottawa: Queen's Printer, 1970, p. 11.

47. Yin Ming, *United and Equal: Progress Among China's Minority Nationalities.* Peking: Foreign Language Press, 1977.

48. The classic work on ethnic stratification in Canada is John Porter, *The Vertical Mosaic.* Toronto: University of Toronto Press, 1965. New immigration regulations (1962, 1967, and 1977) have led to increased immigration from Asian, African, and other peripheral regions.

49. O'Connor, *Fiscal Crisis of the State.*

50. See June Dreyer, *China's Forty Millions.* Cambridge, Mass.: Harvard University Press, 1976.

51. Data taken from *Beijing Review*, March 10, 1980.

6

Race and Ethnicity

NEO-MARXIAN EXPLANATIONS
AND A REFORMULATION

In the previous chapter I argued that the central difficulty confronting Wallerstein's world-system approach is his definition of capitalism *as* the capitalist world market and his locating the dynamics of the world-system in the ensuing competition among countries that strive to enhance their standings within the world market. This definition leads Wallerstein to treat as similar what are essentially different forms of race and ethnic relations, such as those between the United States and the Soviet Union, and Canada and China. This error stems from Wallerstein's failure to situate both the forms and the dynamics of race and ethnic relations within the modes of production that structure or organize these and other relations in particular countries or "social formations."

What distinguishes neo-Marxian approaches to the study of race and ethnic relations from non-Marxian or even Marx-inspired approaches (such as Wallerstein's) is the centrality of *mode of production analysis* for understanding both the forms and the dynamics of race and ethnicity in the modern world. Such an analysis must consider the effect of world market forces, but interprets the impact of these forces as they work on and through modes of production rather than their being determining in themselves.

I refer to these theories as "neo-Marxian" rather than as "Marxian" for two reasons. Marx himself wrote little about the dynamics of race and ethnicity in the context of either capitalism or the world as a whole. His greatest achievement was laying bare the structures of capitalism as a mode of production with primary reference to England and Western Europe, and he did not explicitly incorporate the racial, ethnic, or gender hierarchies present there into his analysis. Second, Marx also did not develop a model centering on the expansion of capitalism worldwide and the impact of that expansion on the backward nations of the world. As Gabriel Palma suggests, Marx clearly foresaw the need for worldwide capitalist expansion primarily to counter the tendency for the rate of profit to fall, but he did not develop a "world-system" theory (or even the theory of imperialism, which Lenin did develop).[1] Thus there is no "Marxian" theory of race and ethnicity if we take that to mean one that Marx himself elaborated.

Marxism, understood as the totality of Marx's writings and the relatively coherent body of thought that this represents, has stimulated thousands of more particular analyses such that there are now numerous varieties of Marxism, many of which seem to bear little relation to either one another or to the theory and method of Marx himself. These varieties are a complex web of sometimes cross-cutting, sometimes mutually incompatible approaches that go by various labels. There are empiricist, historicist, functionalist, structuralist, and poststructuralist approaches; positivist, postpositivist, dialectical, critical, and hermeneutical approaches; "democratic" versus "authoritarian" approaches; so-called orthodox versus nonorthodox and "Western" versus "Eastern" varieties, to name only the most prominent. All of these are in some sense neo-Marxian to the extent that they trace their intellectual heritage to Marxism, but have sought to amend, apply, or otherwise extend Marx's analyses to practically every domain of social life in both capitalist and noncapitalist modes of production. Marxism and neo-Marxism thus represent one of the most enduring, complex, and diverse theoretical worldviews in Western social science.

Neo-Marxian theories of race and ethnicity are similarly numerous, and reflect the bewildering variety of approaches alluded to above. I shall make no attempt to survey or critique all of these, but will instead focus on those theories that have been developed to explain ethnic and, especially, racial inequality in the advanced capitalist countries. There are several reasons for this focus. First, Marx himself concentrated his analysis on capitalism in the West such that we are able to connect and compare neo-Marxian approaches situated in the capitalist countries directly with Marx's analysis in *Capital*, clearly the centerpiece work for later analyses of race and ethnicity. Second, theories of race and ethnicity pertaining to noncapitalist or anticapitalist modes of production are both few and incomplete, owing to what I regard as undeveloped theories of noncapitalist modes of production in general. Although there are numerous discussions and analyses of race and ethnic relations in socialist states and the newer states of Africa and Asia, these are seldom carried out within a Marxian framework based on mode of production analysis, inasmuch as the development of such an analysis is only in the beginning stages. We are only now addressing the structural bases of precapitalist and noncapitalist modes of production and how these impact on racial and ethnic groups, and it is by no means apparent that the Marxian framework developed for the capitalist mode of production is directly transferable to other modes.[2] Finally, important critiques of neo-Marxian approaches have been raised almost exclusively against those theories that have been developed to explain racial and ethnic inequality in the advanced capitalist countries. Thus current debates and controversies are centered on the questions of race and ethnicity as these manifest themselves within the capitalist mode of production.

In this chapter I discuss three interrelated issues central to a neo-Marxian understanding of race and ethnicity. First, I outline the major criticisms that have been leveled against neo-Marxian approaches in order to situate the locus of debate. Second, I discuss three neo-Marxian formulations of race and ethnicity that are widely cited as typical of such an approach, and show the degree to which the aforementioned criticisms apply. I then suggest a framework for what I consider to be a more genuine approach to race and ethnicity, that is, one consistent with the method and analysis of Marx himself in *Capital*, and certain other writers who have commented on and extended Marx's views. I do not develop a full-blown theory of race and ethnicity based on this framework such that I add a new (or another) neo-Marxian variety to the already lengthy list (this would require a volume or volumes in itself). Rather, I attempt to shift future analyses to a more open-ended view of Marxism as this might apply to race and ethnicity by answering the criticisms against such an approach, and addressing weaknesses in previous neo-Marxian formulations.

Critiques of Marxist Approaches to Race and Ethnicity

There are two major categories of criticism applied to Marxian analysis in general and to more specific applications of Marx's thought. In one category are those critiques that simply dismiss any kind of Marxian approach, usually on the grounds that insofar as Marx's "prediction" of socialist revolution in capitalist countries has not occurred, Marx's general theory is invalidated. Such criticisms are grossly "theory-centric" because they are offered by social scientists who impose a positivist reading on Marx's writings. They reduce his analysis to a set of predictive or law-like statements concerning some future state of affairs, the non-occurrence of which requires abandonment (or at least substantial revision) of these statements. These criticisms can be dismissed on the following grounds: Marx's theory is clearly nonpositivistic, and is in fact opposed to positivist approaches that argue for the possibility of a value-free, predictive theory modeled on the natural or physical sciences. Marx's theory is an example of a very different kind of social science, what Brian Fay calls "critical social science"—theories that "explain a social order in such a way that it becomes itself the catalyst which leads to the transformation of this social order."[3] If this is granted, positivist critiques of Marxism violate a central principle of theoretical criticism by using a particular theoretical worldview (positivism) as a metatheory for judging the adequacy of another worldview. This is inappropriate, given positivism's failure to achieve metatheoretical status.

Another category of criticisms, however, needs to be considered. These are critiques that, like Marxism, treat racism, ethnism, and sexism as forms of social inequality and oppression, and recognize the importance of capitalist relations of production for understanding these forms. They nevertheless regard a Marxist approach as *fundamentally* deficient because of its insistence on the centrality or primacy of mode of production analysis. A recent book by Brittan and Maynard titled *Sexism, Racism and Oppression* (1984) illustrates well the substance of these critiques:

Primary oppression refers to those direct consequences of the unequal possession of . . . economic, cultural, and social resources. . . . In the case of social and economic oppression, the main argument is usually based on the assumption that the "mode of production" and "class" are the ultimate determinants of all other kinds of oppression. Hence, racism and sexism are not explained in their own terms, but are seen as being dependent upon the class antagonisms of this or that society. . . .

So [we] will not be concerned with the search for a general theory of oppression incorporating "race," gender, and class. We do not subscribe to the view that such a theory exists, or even is desireable. Accordingly, we find it difficult to reduce racism and sexism to class. [Original emphasis.][4]

Later, Brittan and Maynard extend this critique specifically to Marxist approaches:

Marxism has played a major role in elucidating the class position of out-groups and in explaining how this position arose and is maintained. However, difficulties arise with both the orthodox and neo-Marxist arguments due to their implicit insistence that the terms of the debate can only be couched from *within* the context of capitalism and its class system. Such an approach immediately opens up the danger of reductionism and indeed some writers have almost mechanistically explained racism (and sexism, too), in both its institutionalized and personalized forms, in terms of the needs and interests of capital. The demands of the "system" are regarded as paramount and almost anything can be reduced to, and thus explained by, the "system's" requirements.[5]

There are several specific criticisms contained in this argument: (a) that racism, ethnism, and sexism are viewed as "secondary," derived phenomena that are subordinate to, a reflection of, and perhaps even caused by capitalist relations of production; (b) that racial and sexual oppression are required by the "needs" of the capitalist system; that is, racism and sexism are "functional necessities" of capitalism such that they would have to be invented if they did not already exist; (c) that "Marxism" improperly reduces racial and sexual forms of oppression to class or "economic" oppression, thereby denying both the social and phenomenal significance of these types of oppression and their "autonomy" from class relations. This is objectionable not only theoretically, but also because "Marxists" have argued that racial and sexual minorities should subordinate their interests in (and their movements for) racial and sexual equality to the workers' struggle to eliminate capitalist relations of production. These criticisms lead Brittan and Maynard to suggest that the Marxist "insistence that the terms of the debate can only be couched from *within* the context of capitalism" is fundamentally wrong.

A brief response here to these criticisms will serve to establish the nature of my more detailed arguments that follow. A Marxist account of race and ethnicity does insist on interpreting these forms of oppression from within the context of the mode of production in which they are present. If that mode of production is capitalism, then capitalism is the proper *context* for analysis. This means that what I will call the "economic framework," understood as the dialectical relationship between the forces of production and the relations of production, is the primary or central aspect within which the other aspects that make up the totality of any capitalist social formation must be interpreted. Contrary to Brittan and Maynard's assertions, however, an insistence on the primacy of the economic framework *does not*, if properly applied, lead to an account of race and ethnicity that is reductionist, nor to one that views racial and ethnic formations as secondary or epiphenomenal to class formations, nor denies either the autonomy or significance of their everyday oppression or their struggles for equality. Stated positively, I shall argue for a non-reductionist, but nevertheless Marxian approach to race and ethnicity that is capable of meeting the objections usually raised against it.

It remains the case, however, that the criticisms raised against neo-Marxian approaches are, with respect to *certain* of these approaches, valid. Some theories have mechanically and reductionistically applied basic tenets of Marx's analysis to racial and ethnic relations. In the following sections I summarize several important varieties of neo-Marxian analyses that illustrate the main criticisms above, but that also, on a careful reading, can lead us to a nonreductionist account of race and ethnicity.

Oliver C. Cox and the Origins and Functions of Racism

Oliver Cox's classic work on *Caste, Class and Race* published in 1948 is still often cited as the "orthodox Marxist" treatment of race relations and its relation to the capitalist mode of production. This is somewhat unfortunate, inasmuch as the book itself deals with much more than race relations within capitalism, and also because Cox does not explicitly link his analysis to Marx's writings. Nevertheless, his central arguments concerning racial antagonism are clearly rooted in a Marx-inspired analysis, and Cox can rightfully be regarded as an early, and still important, contributor to a neo-Marxian theory of race.

Cox developed his theory around three central concerns: (1) differentiating what he called "race prejudice" or racism from other forms of social intolerance, (2) investigating the historical origins of racial antagonism, and (3) analyzing the situation of Negroes in the United States as an aspect of "political-class relations." For all three concerns the nature of capitalism as a mode of production is the critical variable that must be considered.

Cox goes to great lengths to distinguish racial prejudice from other historically important forms of intergroup and interethnic hostility. In particular he distinguishes among ethnocentrism, social intolerance, and racism. Ethnocentrism—the "we" feeling of any community as over against "others"—is, he argues, a sentiment common to all groups that functions to maintain group solidarity, but seldom does ethnocentrism correspond to feelings of racial antipathy toward others.[6] What Cox calls "intolerance," on the other hand, is often mistaken for racial prejudice, particularly when this intolerance is directed against a group that is racially distinct (or thought to be so). Specifically, he argues that anti-Semitism is an instance of social intolerance applied to a distinguishable group that is often mistaken for racial prejudice, but that is categorically different:

Anti-Semitism, to begin with, is clearly a form of social intolerance, which attitude may be defined as an unwillingness on the part of a dominant group to tolerate the beliefs or practices of a subordinate group because it considers these beliefs and practices to be either inimical to group solidarity or a threat to the continuity of the status quo. Race prejudice, on the other hand, is a social attitude propagated among the public by an exploiting class for the purpose of stigmatizing some group as inferior so that the exploitation of either the group itself or its resources or both may be justified. Persecution and exploitation are the behavior aspects of intolerance and race prejudice respectively. In other words, race prejudice is the socio-attitudinal facilitation of a particular type of labor exploitation, while social intolerance is a reactionary attitude supporting the action of a society in purging itself of contrary cultural groups.[7]

Cox thus distinguishes between social intolerance and racial prejudice on three dimensions. First, racial prejudice is applied to groups that are *physically distinguishable* from the dominant group, rather than culturally distinguishable. Whatever cultural differences may exist between a racial group and the dominant group are secondary to their classification on the basis of physically identifiable traits. This makes it possible to stigmatize racial groups solely on the basis of color even in the absence of cultural differences. Social intolerance, however, is primarily cultural intolerance, with presumed racial differences occupying a secondary place. Second, racial prejudice, as defined above, is restricted to those situations in which the racial minority is exploited by the dominant group for its labor or resources, or both. Social intolerance need not involve such exploitative relations, inasmuch as the cultural differences on which it is based may be sufficient, given its cultural "distance" from the dominant culture, to be abhorred by the dominant group. Third, racial prejudice is necessarily an ideology of inferiority stemming from presumed biological (racial) differences. Such an ideology is necessary to justify the exploitation of the racial minority by the dominant group. Social intolerance, on the other hand, not being rooted in such exploitation, need not imply cultural inferiority of the stigmatized group. In fact the dominant group may fear the cultural distinctiveness of the minority as a potential competitor or threat to its own cultural dominance.

These differences are not merely "definitional" for Cox, but imply very different forms of social relations and, as such, spawn different reactions by the dominant group toward the respective cultural or racial minority groups. Continuing the analogy between Jews and Negroes, Cox writes:

The dominant group is intolerant of those whom it can define as anti-social, while it holds race prejudice against those whom it can define as subsocial. . . . Thus we are ordinarily intolerant of Jews but prejudiced against Negroes. In other words, the dominant group or ruling class does not like the Jew at all, but likes the Negro in his place. To put it still another way, the condition of its liking the Jew is that he cease being a Jew and voluntarily become like the generality of society, while the condition of liking the Negro is that he cease trying to become like the generality of society and remain contentedly a Negro. . . .

We want to assimilate the Jews, but they, on the whole, refuse with probable justification to be assimilated; the Negroes want to be assimilated, but we refuse to let them assimilate.[8]

Given his definition of racial prejudice as an ideology of inferiority rooted in physical differences and necessitated by the exploitation of a racially distinguishable group by another, Cox argues that the beginnings or origins of racial prejudice and racial antagonism arose only in recent times. Specifically, he argues "that racial exploitation and race prejudice developed among Europeans with the rise of capitalism and nationalism, and that because of the world-wide ramifications of capitalism, all racial antagonisms can be traced to the policies and attitudes of the leading capitalist people, the white people of Europe and North America."[9]

Cox surveys the history of intergroup conquest and conflict beginning with the Greeks and discussing in turn the Romans, "Asiatics," "Mohammedans," the Moors, and the Portuguese, detailing the forms of interethnic relations they characteristically produced. Cox maintains that in all these situations of interethnic conflict, however brutal, what was at issue was "cultural conversion" by slaves, "barbarians," or other conquered peoples to the religion and/or culture of the conquering group. Even the Portuguese incursions into Africa and the beginning of the slave trade produced no clear sense of racial antagonism, both because such a view was undermined by the Catholic emphasis on converting "heathens" and also because the economic and rationalistic basis of racism had not yet developed among them: "The Church received its share of African servants; as yet, however, it had no idea of the economic uses of segregation and 'cultural parallelism'—of the techniques for perpetuating the servile status of the black workers. It had developed no rationalizations of inborn human inferiority in support of a basic need for labor exploitation."[10]

It is the European conquest of the New World, and its subsequent exploitation of Indians and, later, African slaves, that marks the beginnings of racial antagonism as Cox conceptualized it. As he correctly argues, the idea of racial inferiority did not precede the use of Indians and Africans as servile laborers in the mines or on the plantations of European conquerers. In fact, he argues, had white laborers been available in sufficient numbers they might have been substituted. It was the "historical availability" of Africans especially (such "availability" having resulted from superior European military power, expansionism, and the ensuing slave trade) that led to the widespread use of nonwhites. Only *subsequent* to the use of "colored" labor and *the continuing need to maintain that labor in a servile status in order to assure profits* did ideologies of racial inferiority develop. Cox points to the Spanish theologian Gaines de Sepulveda's argument concerning the "barbarous" nature of Indians as among the earliest racist treatises, but goes on to add that "it remained for later thinkers, mainly from northern European countries, to produce evidence that 'native peoples' have an inferior, animal-like capacity for culture."[11]

The development of doctrines of racial inferiority was an ongoing process that reached its zenith in the latter part of the nineteenth century when, Cox argues, "the sun no longer set on British soil and the great nationalistic powers of Europe began to justify their economic designs upon weaker European peoples with subtle theories of racial superiority and masterhood."[12]

Implicit in Cox's argument concerning the codevelopment of early capitalist expansion and racial antagonism was the "need" of a new economic order, one rooted in profit under conditions of preindustrial, labor-intensive technology, to *prevent* the cultural assimilation of the servile group. Cox's analysis, though not explicitly linked to Marx's writings, is nevertheless consistent with Marx's own views concerning forms of labor control in the colonies. Servile labor was indispensable to what Marx called "primitive accumulation, . . . the historical process of divorcing the producer from the means of production."[13] It is "primitive" because it forms the prehistory of capitalist development and is the starting point of later, mature capitalism based on wage labor. This "starting point," Marx maintained, began in the sixteenth century and was based on the "enslavement of the worker."[14] In Europe this "enslavement" was the expropriation of the land from the peasant, while in the colonies it took the form of enslavement per se, owing to a labor market that was, with respect to free people, always understocked.[15] Thus the economic need for a docile, unfree labor force that would not be permitted to assimilate to the dominant country was the underlying material basis of racial antagonism.

What Cox does not explain is *why* ideologies of racial inferiority should accompany this need to maintain a servile labor force. Certainly the Europeans possessed power sufficient to enforce their rule such that ideological hegemony was hardly necessary. Moreover, as Cox himself argues, the Hellenistic and Roman regimes—themselves based on slavery—had not resorted to racist ideologies, despite their need for servile labor. The answer to this lies as much in the cultural basis of European society in the seventeenth and eighteenth centuries as in the economic. The origins of capitalist development and expansion were justified in the "natural rights" philosophy of the Enlightenment, a philosophy that was rooted in the idiom that all men are created equal and therefore have rights to just entitlements (particularly property). Maintaining such a philosophy was important to undermining feudal privileges based on heredity. Connected to this general philosophy was the logically necessary view that human differences as expressed in lifestyle, manners, customs, and other habits—particularly those of the commoner and merchant classes—resulted from environmental and historical conditions, not immutable biological characteristics.

This "environmentalist" view of man ultimately came into contradiction with forms of labor control in the colonies, particularly slavery in America, as European "masters" were increasingly called on to justify bondage by antislavery advocates. As George Fredrickson argues, this contradiction took more than two centuries to develop such that only in the nineteenth century, when attacks on the morality of forced labor systems reached their zenith, was the environmentalist philosophy of the Enlightenment replaced with a racist defense by southern slaveholders and sympathizers:

Although gradual emancipation had been instituted in the North, slavery in the South had survived the Revolutionary era and the rise of the natural-rights philosophy without an elaborate racial defense—without, indeed, much of an intellectual defense of any kind; for the institution had never actually been seriously threatened. Antislavery forces had been so weak and hesitant in the post-Revolutionary South that emancipation proposals had not even come up for full public consideration, even though there was little difficulty at the time in gaining theoretical assent from many slaveholders to the abstract proposition that slavery was an undesireable institution which posed a threat to republican government, national unity, and economic progress.[16]

It is only when slavery and other forms of coerced labor came under direct attack from a maturing capitalist order based on an ideology of free labor that racist arguments rooted in biological inferiority were zealously created and vigorously defended. Cox's general argument that racial prejudice originated with the rise of European capitalism has, by and large, been supported by subsequent historical analyses. But this was neither an "automatic" nor "necessary" outcome of capitalism as a mode of production in either its nascent, "primitive" forms or its developed form under the factory system. To thus suggest, as both critics and admirers of Marxism often have, that capitalism *caused* racism, or "needed" racism is a mistaken reduction of complex economic, social, and cultural forces as they combined historically. It would be equally mistaken, however, to claim that the rise of racial ideologies in the West had little or nothing to do with capitalism, particularly what would become the emerging conflict between an agrarian-based, labor-intensive economic formation rooted in coerced labor and a developing manufacturing system based on "free" labor. It is only within this economic context that the development of racism and racial antagonisms is understandable at all. Racism was not, then, some necessary outcome of an abstract "capitalism" or a historical accident. It was an ideological creation of individuals committed to an increasingly arcane and stagnant economic and cultural formation that was in a revolutionary struggle with an expanding and aggressive new order.

The old order based on slavery was defeated, but its creation of racism was to find new vigor in the maturing capitalism that replaced it. The bulk of Cox's analysis of race relations in the United States concerns the functions of racism in the post–Civil War South, with relatively little attention devoted to race relations in the more industrialized North (an entirely appropriate emphasis in the late 1940s). His discussion is wide-ranging and provocative, with brilliant treatments on the psychology of dehumanization as it affects Negroes' abilities to press for equal treatment, and the fundamental role of lynching in the maintenance of Southern segregation. He also critiques at length the two major figures in the sociology of race relations, Robert Park and Gunnar Myrdal, for retreating to "mysticism" in their explanations of the race problem when confronted by (to Cox's view) the superior, but "tabooed" analysis of Karl Marx.[17]

Cox's own treatment of Marx is not particularly systematic, however, and, to the extent that Cox's view is still considered the "orthodox" extension of Marx's theory applied to race relations, has contributed to the aforementioned criticisms of Marxian approaches. Cox's statement of the relation between capitalism and race relations can be summarized by the following principles.[18]

1. Industrial capitalism must, in order to exist, proletarianize the masses of workers; that is, it must "commodotize" their capacity to work. To "commodotize" is to conceptualize, consciously or unconsciously, as inanimate or subhuman, these human vehicles of labor power and to behave toward them according to the laws of the market, that is, according to the fundamental rules of capitalist society. Human labor power must be viewed as an impersonal, purchaseable, abstract quantity, a commodity in the cost of production rather than a great mass of human beings.

2. Given the existence of labor power as a cost of production to be bought and sold like any other commodity, a cheap labor supply is an immediate and practical end for the maximization of profits.

3. It is in the immediate pecuniary interests of capitalists to develop ideologies that facilitate proletarianization. Capitalists thus strive to show by any irrational or logical means available that the working class of their own race or whole peoples of other races, whose labor they are bent on exploiting, are something apart: (a) not human at all, (b) only part human, (c) inferior humans, and so on.

4. In the United States ideologies of racial inferiority have become especially efficacious, owing to the racial division of the working class into white and black. Racism, particularly in the South, has had three main consequences: (1) maintaining the entire Negro race as an easily exploitable labor force; (2) hindering, through segregation or other means, any "sympathetic contact" between the white and black masses; and (3) retarding the development of proletarian organizations, particularly strong unions, by dividing black and white laborers.

In light of these principles Cox's neo-Marxian theory of race relations can be summarized as follows: (a) Blacks are exploited *primarily* by their class position as proletarians. They are exploited racially as well, subject as they are to racist ideologies of inferiority. Negroes thus face "double exploitation" or "superexploitation" compared with white workers. This is what Cox meant when he insisted on the necessity of viewing American race relations as a form of "political-class" domination and not, as Park and Myrdal had argued, as a problem of values, attitudes, or assimilation. (b) Racism and the racial division of labor benefit the capitalist class and, by extension, harm the entire proletariat, white and black, by dividing white workers and black workers such that their common interests as workers are obscured by racist ideologies. These ideologies are effective to the extent that capitalists threaten white labor with cheaper black labor, a common practice in the late nineteenth and early twentieth centuries designed to prevent unionization, break strikes, and otherwise undermine the security of white workers.

Cox was perhaps the first scholar to clearly understand the functions of racism as part of a divide-and-rule strategy used by employers to discipline labor:

Today it is of vital consequence that black labor and white labor in the South be kept glaring at each other, for if they were permitted to come together in force and to identify their interests as workers, the difficulty of exploiting them would be increased beyond calculation. Indeed, the persistence of the whole system of worker exploitation in the United States depends pivotally upon the maintenance of an active race hatred between white and black workers in the South.[19]

By treating the "Negro problem" as essentially one of class position complicated by racism, Cox's prognosis for the future of race relations in the United States was guardedly optimistic. He noted that blacks suffered less racial prejudice in the Northern states because capitalism was further advanced there than in the South. This had led to greater power of the Northern proletariat as the developed factory system produced greater worker solidarity and class consciousness. As the white proletariat achieved power in the North, so also, Cox argued, had the condition of Negroes advanced. Conversely, in the South the status of the white proletariat was weak, owing in part to the even weaker condition of the black proletariat.

Given this analysis, Cox believed that blacks must unite with white workers and build strong labor alliances. Both blacks and whites must see the problem as one of "political-class struggle" against the bourgeoisie. Black workers must be willing to unite behind "white democratic forces" in order to advance their particular struggle rather than go it alone, a strategy that Cox believed would only intensify the degree of racial hatred. Cox thus believed that the race problem was a peculiar manifestation of the American social formation, particularly the regional discrepancy between North and South, whose solution was nevertheless tied to ending the general exploitation of the working class under capitalism. He stated this position clearly at the end of his book: "The problem of racial exploitation, then, will most probably be settled as part of the world proletarian struggle for democracy; every advance of the masses will be an actual or potential advance for the colored people."[20]

The aid of forty years' hindsight makes it easier to locate Cox's theoretical shortcomings. He clearly underestimated the ability of Negroes to mobilize under their own leadership and take the lead in dismantling the system of racial segregation in the South. He also overestimated the progress of blacks in the North as well as the willingness and consciousness of the white proletariat to take up the black cause. These "mistakes" are attributable in part to Cox's reduction of the race problem to the class problem and his view that the position of black workers in America was, *structurally*, the same as that of white workers, though worse in degree. Both were proletarians whose convergent interests would become apparent through interracial coalitions. Despite these problems, Cox's analysis established a neo-Marxian framework for studying race relations within the context of capitalism as a mode of production, and outlined the major issues that would come to be debated by future scholars. Two of these issues—the structural position of blacks in the American economy and the question of who benefits from racism—have been at the center of subsequent analyses.

Michael Reich and the Class Conflict Theory of Racial Inequality

Michael Reich may be considered the modern-day heir to Cox's initial formulation of the relation between capitalism and race relations, although his analysis is much more sophisticated and empirically grounded. Whereas Cox simply asserted that racism hurts both white and black workers and benefits capitalists, Reich saw this as a hypothesis that required demonstration, and sought to do so in his book *Racial Inequality* (1981). Reich, an economist, set about to compare, by means of econometric analyses, the relative adequacy of neoclassical approaches to the issue of persistent racial inequality with that of a Marxian approach rooted in a class conflict model.

As I noted in Chapter 4, one of the failings of the assimilationist model was its implicit acceptance of a conservative analysis of the capitalist economy. This view holds that the operation of the competitive market will gradually eliminate racial economic differentials once legal barriers to market entry and to institutions such as schools (which impact on market qualifications) are removed. This model, most closely associated with Milton Friedman and Thomas Sowell, argues that competition among employers for labor will eliminate wage differentials between whites and blacks by driving out of business those employers who refuse to hire cheaper, but equally productive blacks.

This analysis has been called into question not only by radical scholars, but also by liberal neoclassical economists who agree with Reich that despite some gains by blacks resulting from the desegregation of the

South, racial inequality in the marketplace has persisted with little change since World War II:

First, it is true that blacks have made significant gains in recent decades. These changes are most evident in the areas of civil and political rights, in the depiction of blacks in the mass media, and, to a lesser extent, in black representation in elected offices. It is also true that a notable change has taken place in the black class structure. For example, the proportion of blacks employed in professional and managerial occupations rose from 4 percent in 1949 to 12 percent in 1969, while the proportion working in agriculture fell from about 10 percent in 1949 to about 2 percent in 1969.

Nonetheless, economic inequality for most blacks has persisted virtually unchanged in this period. Using black/white earnings ratios as a measure of racial inequality, I find that the last major era of relative gains for blacks in private industry occurred during the 1930s and 1940s, the decades of the formation and growth of the industrial union movement and World War II. *Since 1949 the economic position of blacks relative to whites has not changed markedly in industry and in the major metropolitan areas.* (Emphasis added.)[21]

The conservative response to the problem of continuing inequality argues that blacks continue to suffer in the marketplace because past discrimination has not enabled them to achieve skills and qualifications ("human capital") on a par with whites. But the human capital thesis has never accounted for more than half of the wage gap between whites and blacks, nor sought to account for observed racial differences in human capital.[22] These problems with the conservative analysis led several liberal neoclassicists to entertain the hypothesis that blacks might still experience discrimination in the marketplace even in the absence of legal barriers to employment.

Reich goes into considerable detail describing the models developed within a neoclassic framework to explain continuing racial inequality. He considers those put forward by Becker (1971), Anne Kreuger (1963), Lester Thurow (1969), Barbara Bergmann (1971), Finis Welch (1967), and Kenneth Arrow (1972).[23] Although these models stress different "causes" for the persistence of racial differentials (from employers who have a "taste" for discrimination, to monopolistic cartels, to black crowding into low-wage occupations, to shop floor friction between white and black workers), they agree that racial inequality persists because it economically benefits white workers or all whites collectively (employers and workers) to the detriment of blacks. Reich tested these models by means of a complicated cross-sectional analysis based on nationwide SMSA (Standard Metropolitan Statistical Area) samples from the 1960 and 1970 censuses. These results indicated that most black *and* white workers lose income from racism while rich whites benefit, a finding opposite to that predicted by liberal neoclassic approaches.[24]

Reich then examines the assumptions of neoclassical theories in order to explain why they cannot account for the finding that racism harms black and white workers. He identifies four failings in the neoclassical model that, taken together, lead to an incorrect view of the workings of a modern capitalist economy. The first weakness, what Reich calls the "logical incompleteness of the paradigm," is a "technical criticism," but the remaining three criticisms are important as both critiques of neo-classicism and as indicators of an alternative theory. Reich summarizes criticisms 2 through 4:

(2) The neoclassical approach lacks a theory of the distribution of factor endowments. It therefore incorrectly specifies the institutional class relations that distinguish capitalist economies from other market economies. (3) The neoclassical approach incorrectly construes labor to be a commodity, failing to see that workers sell only their capacity to work, that is, their labor power to capitalists. It therefore obscures the character of the labor process in capitalist production ....(4) The neoclassical approach neglects collective action by workers and capitalists. Its incorrect individualistic assumptions about human behavior obscure the bases of widespread collective behavior not only in regard to the determinants of government action, but also in regard to economic activity inside and outside the workplace.[25]

Reich proposes a more "realistic model" of a modern capitalist economy rooted in Marx's conception of the antagonism between the capitalist and working classes. This view assumes that capitalists and workers have different interests, owing to struggle over the surplus product (profit), a struggle that is played out repeatedly within capitalist firms. In Reich's words:

This alternative approach takes the analyses of class conflict and of markets as the starting points of its understanding of political and economic processes. It views the determination of income distribution as resulting both from market processes and processes of power and conflict between workers and capitalists. The workplace is now understood as contested terrain, where capitalists organize work and workers with the objective of extracting the most work for the least pay, while workers resist these efforts, both individually and collectively. Profitability therefore depends on limiting worker collective action. The organization of jobs, including bureaucratic structures that exploit the existence of racial and other divisions among workers, becomes a key variable....

The class conflict theory indicates the outlines of a formal analysis that suggests why racial inequality is reproduced over time in a capitalist economy.... It offers an explanation of why the market by itself does not eliminate racial inequality and suggests, in contrast to neoclassical theories, that most white workers do not benefit from racial inequality while capitalists do.... The evidence presented here contradicts the neoclassical theories and supports the class conflict analysis.[26]

The evidence Reich presents indicates that racism undermines both black and white workers in two ways. First, racial antagonisms inhibit union bargaining strength and militancy. In short, racism divides white workers from black workers and serves to obscure their common interests. Second, racial antagonisms result in a reduced effective supply of public services, such as public schooling and welfare, that are available to low- and middle-income whites.[27] These problems combine to lower the ability of poor blacks and whites to organize "poor people's coalitions" that would press for societywide reforms pertaining to full employment, more effective social services, and more adequate housing and transfer payments.

In Reich's view the historical legacy of racism in the United States has resulted in a social formation that, compared with other capitalist countries, lacks a significant socialist movement, has a weak labor movement, and is characterized by a state that has little commitment to either social welfare or full employment. He argues that the relatively low level of working-class economic and political power and the continuing degree of racial inequality are not just parallel developments, but are inextricably linked.[28] In no sense does Reich claim that capitalism caused racism. He does show how racism can be functional for the capitalist class, how racial antagonisms can be maintained and reinforced in a modern market economy in which profitability remains the prime motive for production. He can thus explain the operation of racism within the context of an advanced capitalist system. But Reich's contribution goes beyond this, for he also demonstrates how racial antagonisms have played a major role in the very shaping of that system. It is racism that has, in Reich's view, been a primary cause in shaping the *particularity* of American capitalism.[29] Racism and continuing racial stratification in the United States is not a secondary or derived need of some abstract capitalist system. Racism is, in fact, a primary—indeed indispensable—aspect of the American social formation, inasmuch as the United States is not merely a capitalist state, but a *racist* capitalist state. Understanding race relations in the United States, especially within a Marxian framework, requires an understanding of the degree to which race has and continues to be a basic aspect of the social structure, one that tends to persist because it remains functional for capitalist relations of production. The power of Reich's neo-Marxian analysis lies in its ability to account for continued (and even worsening) racial antagonisms in a way that does not reduce race to some "secondary oppression," nor dismisses it, as most non-Marxian models do, as an anomalous characteristic of the system.

Reich's analysis shares some similarities with that of Cox. Both see the race problem as inextricably tied to the class system, and the continuing concentration of blacks at the lower levels of that system. They also stress the functional aspects of racism, that is, the degree to which racial antagonisms benefit the capitalist class by maintaining divisions within the working class. For example, the statement below by Reich is similar to those given by Cox with regard to the effects of racism on unionism, but the optimism expressed by Cox for improved race relations in the postwar period has given way to a soberer appraisal warranted by Reich's examination of the empirical evidence since 1945:

Racism has weakened the labor movement and hurt most white workers in the postwar period. Unionism remains weakest in the South because of the strength of racism in the region. The resultant low wages in the South have hurt white and black Southern workers directly. Northern workers have also suffered as a result. Wage gains by Northern workers have increased regional wage differentials, impelling many Northern employers to relocate their plants in the South.[30]

Nevertheless, both Reich and Cox believe that the development of strong interracial alliances, particularly in labor, are necessary to ameliorate the effects of centuries-long racism. This does not mean that blacks must subordinate their interests in overcoming racism to movements stressing worker solidarity or socialism, with race taking a back seat to other interests. It means that race must be understood as a *primary* issue that affects workers' movements both actually and in potential. As Reich argues, "the presence or absence of antiracism as a popular theme will be crucial not only for immediate economic interests of blacks and whites, and not just for the realization of reformist programs, but also for the entire social and cultural character of coming decades."[31]

Reich's theory of racial antagonisms demonstrates how it is possible to locate important causes of a noneconomic sort (and to thus be neither economistic nor reductionistic) without abandoning the economic relations of production as the basic framework within which these other causes operate. Moreover, it is both possible and, if required by the evidence, necessary to consider how such noneconomic causes might alter, in some fundamental way, the economic relations of production. That is, causes of a noneconomic nature may be sufficient, given their impact on the economic framework, to revolutionize or otherwise transform the economic basis of society.

Sidney Wilhelm's "Anti-Marxist" Marxism

People familiar with the work of Sidney Wilhelm will no doubt be surprised (including perhaps Wilhelm himself) by my inclusion of his writings as representative of a neo-Marxian approach to black/white relations in the United States. This is because his two major treatises, *Who Needs the Negro?* and *Black in a White America*, are in part devastating critiques of what Wilhelm calls "Marxian views of racism."[32] But Wilhelm's critique and his subsequent provocative analysis of black/white relations are very much consistent with the kind of neo-Marxian analysis I have been arguing for, and provide evidence for the necessity of what I have been calling "mode of production analysis."

While recognizing that there are numerous varieties of Marxist approaches to racism, Wilhelm nevertheless regards most Marxian approaches as fundamentally flawed, owing to their reliance on what Wilhelm calls the "Marxist fallacy of materialism":

If materialism, the mode of processing products through tools of production, creates the networks of social relations of production and race relations, Marxists leave much to be explained not only about the conduct of their working class but about their notion of race and racism. If the fundamental strife in capitalist America is the class struggle, then how is it possible for the working class to succumb to a nonmaterialistic quality about capitalism, namely, racism? How can the nonmaterial force of race "derail" workers from their common interests? . . . Many Marxists acknowledge that, historically, time and time again, racism diverts workers from the class struggle by creating divisions within the working class itself. But if racism is so powerful as to undermine a proletarian assault against capitalists by sapping the vigor of a workers' unity against a common class enemy, it must be a factor transcending the economic interests of the entire working class.[33]

This passage is one of many by Wilhelm in which he excoriates so-called Marxists for their inability to come to terms with racism except as a functional need for capitalism or as an ideology that prevents workers from understanding their "objective" class interests. It is also indicative of Wilhelm's consistent misunderstandings concerning "materialism" as it is used by Marxists. Racism may be considered a noneconomic phenomenon, but it is not a "nonmaterial" phenomenon as Wilhelm states. It is in fact a very "material" phenomenon (as ideas and practices of a noneconomic sort *can* be) that has both economic and noneconomic consequences. Despite this and other misunderstandings, however, Wilhelm does point to weaknesses in Marxian formulations that need to be revised to accord with late-twentieth-century realities if neo-Marxian views of race relations are to be compelling to whites and blacks alike. Whereas Wilhelm sees these weaknesses as casting doubt on the validity of any Marxian approach, I shall argue that they can be accommodated by a Marxian framework and that his own reformulation of the problem *requires* such a framework. The major criticisms offered by Wilhelm against Marxian approaches are as follows:

1. *Marxian analyses cannot treat racism as a cause in its own right independent of class issues.* This leads certain Marxists to unwittingly embrace the very racism they claim to eschew:

As is the case for so many theories and theorists, it is all too commonplace for Marxists eventually to slip into racism. By rejecting the reality of racism as an experience in its own right, which only Black people endure because they are Black—not because they are of the working class and are superexploited due to the economics of capitalism—and imposing upon Blacks themselves the "need" for remaining true only to a working-class interest, Marxists are transformed into the very racists they fail to perceive within the dynamics of capitalism."[34]

This is the familiar claim of reductionism or "economism" that, in my discussions of both Cox and Reich, I have argued against. Racism has and does operate as a "cause in its own right," but understanding the *effects* of such a cause requires situating racism within the relations of production, an argument that Wilhelm himself makes with considerable force:

We must come to comprehend how White America's racism accommodates to shifting economic processes throughout the nation's history. This task will require the realization that racism exists in its own right, an autonomous determining force that is not a class phenomenon but which has the capacity of "shaping and directing behavior, not merely reflecting it." Racism cut across class lines—it prevails within White America in spite of class differentiations—but *how* racism is used reflects class divisions among Whites. That is, racism exists regardless of class distinctions yet it will be implemented in ways that reflect class interests. Whites upholding property interests rely upon racism to preserve their economic needs depending upon the historical moment; their tactics shift over historical periods in terms of the economics of agriculture, industrial, and now, postindustrial production. White workers likewise alter their racial tactics in keeping with their economic circumstances which reflect the conditions of laboring under capitalism. (Original emphasis.)[35]

Wilhelm, in castigating Marxism, makes the very Marxian statement that racism, even when viewed "autonomously" (though I am not sure what is meant by that), can only be understood as it operates through the forces and relations of production. Racism is *different* insofar as it occurs in different economic contexts (agricultural, industrial, or postindustrial) and has different effects as these contexts vary. Far from invalidating a Marxian framework, Wilhelm himself demonstrates the utility of such a framework when he says, "There is a need for a perspective which blends racism as a variable within the economic relationships of production."[36]

Wilhelm is correct on another important matter, however. Racism does transcend class differences to the extent that all blacks, regardless of class, are subject to the stigma of racial inferiority. For Wilhelm this is significant insofar as calls for blacks to subordinate their "race" interests to a generalized "worker's interest" on the grounds that socialism will automatically eliminate racism deny the relative autonomy of racial an-

tagonisms from the economic arena and lead many Marxists to thus fall
into the racist trap of "color-blind" policies.

Racism within the Marxian analysis becomes just as apparent when Marxists
propose overturning capitalist America as *the* only alternative for overturning
racism. Since racism is supposedly a "prop for capitalism," the destruction of
capitalism will immediately eliminate any economic necessity for the continuation
of racism. Marxists call for the replacement of capitalism with socialism, a form
of economics supposedly free from any dependence upon racism for production.
. . . Marxists have no need to perceive a Black perspective or to consider what
kind of socialism will be suitable for Black interests. There is no Black interest
in capitalism and hence there is no Black interest when formulating the composition of a socialist society. [Marxists] are not compelled to come forth with a
socialist vision which is compatible to Blacks and not just to a proletariat.[37]

Again, Wilhelm is arguing for the primacy of race as it has existed
and continues to exist in the American social formation, and insists,
properly so, that Marxists should neither relegate racism to the background of some generalized class interest, nor advocate a socialism in
which the particular interests of blacks *as* blacks are denied. Any call for
socialism in America must place the race issue at the center of discussion,
if only to prevent the emergence of a socialism that pays no heed to the
special characteristics and circumstances of blacks and that, in the absence of such attention, might reproduce a new racism even in a radically
different mode of production. Wilhelm does not deny, however, that
blacks have an "interest" in socialism, but only that too many Marxists
fail to analyze the centrality of the race issue when speaking of socialism.
But what are the particular or special circumstances that affect blacks
that differentiate them from the white proletariat, and require that a
"black face" be put on a socialist program? This question is answered in
Wilhelm's second criticism of Marxian analyses of race.

2. *Marxist approaches focus on the problem of black labor and its relation to
white labor. The black "experience" is thus equivalent to the black proletariat, a
view that not only underestimates the impact of racism on all blacks regardless
of class, but also leads to a misinterpretation of the structural position of blacks
in late-twentieth-century capitalism.* This criticism is more important than
economism or reductionism, for it calls into question the typical Marxian
emphasis on black labor and leads to an analysis of racism substantially
different from those by Cox, Reich, and other neo-Marxian writers.
Wilhelm argues that by treating racism as essentially a problem of black
labor, even labor that is marginal and "superexploited," Marxists fail to
comprehend the most significant problem facing blacks today: their *permanently unemployed status*:

Whenever Marxists seek to confirm their notions about the role of black labor,
they invariably rely only upon data which is compatible to their notions of labor

exploitation. They often turn to tables of distribution of occupations that deal with *employment* characteristics to demonstrate the labor value themes of exploitation to sustain the contention of a working-class Black people being relegated to the "lowest paying, dirtiest and most dangerous jobs." This procedure dismisses unemployment as a category. Marxists...do not give any particular significance to the extraordinary high rates [of unemployment] (relative to Whites) besetting Blacks since the 1950s.... Yet, the *fundamental* economic quality that sets Blacks apart from White workers is not the peripheral status of Blacks ...as it is the Black worker's acute vulnerability to be among the *permanently unemployed*, while White laborers struggle to survive labor exploitation and layoffs due to *temporary* joblessness. That is, Blacks in America are becoming increasingly *inconsequential* to capital's *entire labor market* as their *labor* becomes more irrelevant for production; Blacks are being *disengaged from the workforce* and are *not* being reallocated to the Marxist's reserve army. (Original emphasis.)[38]

Wilhelm is making the forceful argument that to view blacks as especially oppressed members of the proletariat is to completely miss their primary structural position in the economy as *redundant and useless*; they are increasingly not "labor" at all. This structural position has been progressively developing since the end of World War II as the United States has moved from an industrial economy to an increasingly "postindustrial" economy based on automation and computerization: "The advent of automation exposes the possibility of a strictly technological system displacing the social organization of industrial production. This latest tooling system means the displacement of both nature and people. It is explicitly designed to disengage humans from the act of production."[39] This "disengagement process" that makes human labor of any kind increasingly unnecessary has had an especially devastating effect on blacks:

With the means of production remaining in the hands of private ownership, the computer revolution makes it necessary to usher in not only new forms of social organization for production and political relations, but also an entirely new disposition toward labor itself, namely that workers are unnecessary people. In the postindustrial era people become superfluous for the accumulation of wealth by the owner of production. And it is at this moment, unlike any other moment in the history of Black/White relations, that the fate of Blacks in America takes a dramatic turn. Automation, the continued growth in the concentration of wealth within the multinational corporations vigorously enhanced through government policies to assure high rates of profit...and the massive abandonment of the city by business (at just the moment when Blacks have increased their percentage as urban dwellers) all combine with racism to make Blacks disposable commodities and hence, expendable as people....

Blacks become victims of neglect as they become useless to an emerging economy of automation. They are moving out of their historical state of oppression into one of uselessness. Increasingly, they are not so much economically exploited as irrelevant.... Blacks are not needed; they are not so much oppressed as unwanted; not so much unwanted as unnecessary; not so much abused as ignored.[40]

Wilhelm's argument, hyperbole notwithstanding, must be taken seriously as evidence to support it increasingly mounts. Even using government data—data that notoriously underestimate the levels of employment and unemployment—the increasing marginality of blacks relative to whites is apparent. The Census Bureau's reports of poverty status in the United States, perhaps the best indicator of economic uselessness, show how grim the situation has become. As of 1983 there were 35,266,000 poor people in the United States, that is, people living in households in which the income was below $10,178. This figure represented an increase of more than six million persons since 1979, and more than 12 million since 1973. The poverty rate among all Americans had increased during this same time from 11.1 to 15.2 percent of the population. Among Afro-Americans there were 9,885,000 poor, 35.7 percent of the black population in 1983, an increase of 2.5 million persons over 1973. The poverty rate among blacks, which has always been more than triple the rate for whites, increased nearly 20 percent during this period. Since 1966, the first year statistics were compiled by race, the poverty rate for blacks has remained fairly stable, fluctuating from a low of 30.3 percent in 1974, down more than 10 percent since 1966, and back to more than 35 percent for 1983.[41]

These figures demonstrate that the removal of legal barriers to discrimination, the passage of civil rights laws, the provision of equal opportunity, and even the dimunition of white racism have not altered the economic circumstances of more than one-third of the black population. As Wilhelm suggests, there exists today a relatively permanent and increasing mass of underemployed and unemployed blacks *whose connection to the labor market is weak or nonexistent, regardless of whether the economy as a whole is recessionary or expanding.*

The historical context of black/white relations enables us to understand why blacks, much more so than whites, have become increasingly irrelevant to late capitalist production in America. Their positions as slaves in a system in which alleged racial inferiority was taken for granted was a legacy they carried with them well after the dismantling of the plantation system. As Afro-Americans moved from agricultural labor into the competitive industrial labor market they found themselves at a disadvantage compared with white workers. Not only were they late arrivals on the industrial scene, and thus relegated to the least desirable jobs within an increasingly complex division of labor, but the firmly established racist attitudes of American society made them convenient scapegoats both for employers who sought to undermine organized labor and for white workers who believed that discriminating against black labor would advance their own positions in the economy. Later the extremely heavy concentration of blacks who moved to large urban areas seeking industrial employment coincided with a decentralization of corporate industrial locations and a shift away from heavy industry toward high-paying professional and technical occupations, on the one hand, and relatively low-paying, irregular service occupations, on the other. This shift has had a particularly adverse impact on blacks, a near majority of whom are concentrated in overcrowded, substandard urban ghettos where the bulk of employment "opportunities"—such as they are—are low-paying, stultifying, and undesirable. As Fusfeld and Bates explain, "a condition of permanent depression prevails in urban poverty areas. In the ghettoes, unemployment remains high, even when the rest of the economy is prosperous, and at levels that would signal a serious depression if they were present in the economy as a whole."[42]

Wilhelm understands the history recounted above; a history that again underscores the primacy of racism in accounting for the particular oppression suffered by blacks. But he also understands that this particular oppression stems from a *general* tendency in the capitalist mode of production—a continuous revolutionizing of the forces of production (i.e., automation and computerization) that ultimately serves to transform the existing relations of production (an increasingly redundant and unnecessary laboring population). He credits Marx with the following insight:

Modern industry never looks upon or treats the existing form of a production process as final. The technical basis of that industry is therefore revolutionary, while all earlier modes of production were essentially conservative.... We have seen how this absolute contradiction between the technical necessities of Modern Industry, and the social character inherent in its capitalistic form, dispels all fixity and security in the situation of the laborer; how it constantly threatens, by taking away the instruments of labor, to snatch from his hands his means of subsistence and ... to make him superfluous.[43]

Marx observed that a central structural tendency in capitalism was the systematic production of what he called "a relative surplus population or industrial reserve army," a redundant working population that, on the one hand, can be employed in times of capitalistic expansion and, on the other hand, be discarded during periods of stagnation and decline. Marx tied the production of this surplus population to the "general law of capitalist accumulation" and the historical motion or path that this law characteristically followed. He argued that as the accumulation of capital progresses in any one industry, there occurs a *qualitative* change in its composition such that the ratio of what he termed "constant capital" (machinery, physical plant, and other fixed capital components) to "variable capital" (the mass of labor power employed) increases. This changing composition of capital occurs because increasing technological inputs (assembly lines and computers, for example) greatly increase labor productivity (which generates greater amounts of relative surplus value) and permit maximum production *by an ever diminishing labor force.* Thus there is the tendency in the development of any one area of industry for capital to need fewer and fewer workers to meet its valorization requirements. It is this process, as it has historically unfolded, that continually "sets workers free." As the accumulation process develops, and along with the increasing productivity of labor, the increases in the total social capital make it possible for industry to expand into new areas of production that require new masses of workers. The surplus population that has been "set free" by the changing composition of capital in one area provides the mass of workers needed for accumulation in new areas of production.

What Marx demonstrated was not an abstract "law" of capital accumulation, but a historical process for which he found empirical support in the still infant capitalist economy of England. He was able to show how the actual development of capitalism, through the basic accumulation process, created and re-created a surplus working population that was always greater in size than capital's ability to employ it: "But in fact it is capitalist accumulation itself that constantly produces, and produces indeed in direct relation with its own energy and extent, *a relatively redundant working population, i.e., a population which is superfluous* to capital's average requirements for its own valorization, and is therefore a surplus population" (emphasis added).[44]

This process, as it has occurred in the United States, has most seriously affected Afro-Americans. Those industries in which blacks achieved their greatest participation in the labor force—large-scale manufacturing in war-related industries, steel and automobile manufacturing—have required fewer and fewer workers, both because of increased labor productivity resulting from automation and because of a decline in the profit rates of these industries. (To take one example, the U.S. automobile industry in the 1980s, a period of record production and high profits, employs 250,000 *fewer* workers than it did during the recessionary years of the 1970s.) At the same time capital has expanded into new areas of production that are either located away from heavy concentrations of the black population, or has invested in new financial and technical enterprises that most blacks are less able to compete for. It is this motion of capital in the United States (and overseas), alongside the revolutionary changes in the forces of production, that has led to the disengaging of an ever-increasing mass of the black population, particularly in the urban ghettoes.

Wilhelm is aware of Marxian arguments that link the progressive impoverishment of blacks to the progressive development of a surplus population or industrial reserve army. But as indicated in note 38 above, Wilhelm rejects this explanation: "Blacks are being *disengaged from the workforce* and are *not* being reallocated to the Marxist's reserve army." Wilhelm is arguing against liberal and Marxian arguments that have portrayed the black lower class as an *underclass* of semiemployed or underemployed subproletarians. He wants to emphasize their *declassed* position and draw attention to their increasing marginality and irrelevance to the labor market.

I have no quarrel with this emphasis, but with Wilhelm's attempt to dissociate his position from the reserve army thesis. As Wilhelm probably knows, Marx stated that "the relative surplus population exists in all kinds of forms. Every worker belongs to it during the time when he is only partially or wholly unemployed."[45] Depending on the worker's relative disengagement from the economy, he might fall into what Marx termed the "floating, latent, or stagnant" levels of the reserve army, levels that varied by the degree to which workers were regularly or irregularly employed. But Marx also noted as part of the surplus population that "lowest sediment [which] . . . dwells in the sphere of pauperism."[46] Here dwell those completely disengaged from the labor force—*those able to work but unable to find work* (Wilhelm's "permanently unemployed"); those unable to work owing to injury or age; women, orphans, and pauper children—in short, those discarded by the production system who are dependent on the state for subsistence or welfare. As Marx indicated, the development of pauperism (or what today we would call chronic poverty stemming from unemployment or other causes) is as much a condition of capitalist development as is the production of a more active reserve army: "Its [pauperism's] production *is included in that of the relative surplus population, its necessity is implied by their necessity*; along with the surplus population, pauperism forms a condition of capitalist production, and of the capitalist development of wealth. It forms part of the *faux frais* [incidental expenses] of capitalist production: but capital usually knows how to transfer these from its own shoulders to those of the working class and the petty bourgeoisie." (Emphasis added.)[47]

As Marx observed the progressive development of a redundant working population, he also foresaw the effects of this population on the employed laboring class. He noted that

the industrial reserve army, during periods of stagnation and average prosperity, weighs down the active army of workers; during the periods of over-production and feverish activity, it puts a curb on their pretensions. The relative surplus population is therefore the background against which the law of the demand and supply of labour does its work. It confines the field of action of this law to the limits absolutely convenient to capital's drive to exploit and dominate the workers.[48]

This connection between what we can call, using Wilhelm's terms, the engaged and disengaged workers establishes the basis for the general condition of the working class as a whole: "Taking them as a whole, the general movements of wages are exclusively regulated by the expansion and contraction of the industrial reserve army...by the varying proportions in which the working class is divided into an active army and a reserve army."[49] Given this connection, Marx argued that working-class organizations must embrace both employed and *unemployed* workers. American labor has almost never made the unemployed a target either of organization or political policy and has in fact generally fallen into the trap of capital's own despotism by attempting to protect its employed from encroachments by the reserve army. This has enabled racism to be an effective divide-and-rule strategy and helps to explain why many blacks are hostile to whites in general rather than to capitalists in particular.

What I have argued with respect to Wilhelm's analysis is that his understanding of the structural position of blacks in the United States is rooted in a mode of production analysis in which the contradiction between the changing forces of capitalist production and concomitant changes in the relations of production provide the backdrop or framework within which to situate the current condition of Afro-Americans. Put less abstractly, the position of blacks in the United States has resulted from two factors: a set of *structural conditions*—the progressive production of a redundant surplus population rooted in the capital accumulation process—and a set of *historical* causes—the particular history of racism as it has affected both blacks and whites. Both of these factors are necessary in the sense that they have interacted with each other at all levels of the society, the political and cultural as well as the economic, and the operation of one factor cannot be understood independent of the other. These factors do operate at different levels, however. The very notion of "structural condition" or structural cause implies relative fundamentality, an aspect endemic to a particular social structure, in this case capitalism, even at an abstract, nonhistorical level. Marx's general "law" of capital accumulation, of which the progressive development of a surplus population is a corollary, is a structural condition in this sense. Such structural forces are not causes in the sense of direct human agency, but in the sense that they set limits to and exert pressures on the kinds of direct, historical causes (those stemming from human agency) that are likely to both originate and take hold in the structure. But structural conditions have no meaning independent of the historical causes, "the shaping and creative force" of racism, for example, which over time can alter the very workings of—even to the point of ultimately transforming—the structure. For this, after all, is how one mode of production comes to be superseded by another. We can, then, accord factors such as racism with a primacy that is not incompatible with insisting on the mode of production as the underlying structural framework within which such causes operate. Wilhelm is wrong when he suggests that a Marxian analysis must view America's pattern of race relations as "a direct and inevitable consequence of a structural need, namely, the economic imperative for capitalists to enhance profits by the superexploitation of a Black people."[50] Structural forces do not *act* in either a direct or inevitable way in the sense that they predetermine historical outcomes and the human behaviors that produce such outcomes. Wilhelm's own thesis that blacks increasingly lack any economic usefulness for capitalist America and are, therefore, becoming irrelevant is clearly compatible with Marx's ideas of structural conditions and, I have argued, must be interpreted within such a structural framework.

By unnecessarily rejecting a Marxian framework, and consequently rejecting any interest by blacks in socialism, Wilhelm's profound, sobering, and otherwise brilliant analysis promotes a nihilistic vision concerning the fate of blacks in America:

Unlike the past, there is no economic imperative necessitating economic exploitation of Black people.... The emergence of automation permits the exclusion of Blacks from the labor force—hence the sustainment of permanent unemployment which, relative to White rates of unemployment, is at an unprecedented level—and may come to tolerate the introduction of "conditional genocide" rather than the toleration of a people "regardless of color." For the first time in the history of White America, Black labor is neither wanted *nor needed.* Black labor, therefore, is disposable, and in the event of a Black rebellion the Black body will also become disposable...; the perpetuation of racism, in its own right, combines with economic opportunity to permit the liquidation of Black people. (Original emphasis.)[51]

The possibility that Wilhelm suggests, black genocide, must be admitted. But what, then, is to be done? Wilhelm concludes his book with the following: "Blacks must seek out an entirely new society of justice, one that will destroy racism entirely and institute an economic system predicated upon the technology of production rather than labor and which, consequently, *transcends existing socialist formulations of a classless society*" (my emphasis).[52]

Let us readily agree with Wilhelm that a just social order must eradicate racism (and other socially and personally disabling aspects, including "ageism," patriarchy, and so on). But *who* shall effect and *on what basis* this just new social order? Are blacks, *as a whole and independent of whites,* to be the only citizens of this new society? Are they to declare the independence of Watts, Harlem, Hough, and other ghettos, or perhaps select a state or two from within the United States, or homestead some uninhabited region on some hitherto undiscovered part of the planet? And what kind of economic system based on "production rather than labor" (that such a system can exist even in the imagination strikes me as problematic) does he envision? Despite Wilhelm's correct insistence that racism is not a need of capitalism, he rules out the possibility of the eradication of racism within capitalism. The new society cannot be capitalistic, then, but neither can it be "socialist." All of these questions are begged by Wilhelm's conclusion. He provides neither comfort nor ammunition to blacks and whites who also fear the possibility of black genocide. In the concluding section I shall suggest that mode of production analysis is necessary not only for the analysis of racism, but also because it provides the basis for solidarity by which a more realistic program for social justice can be launched.

The Primacy of the Mode of Production

My discussions of Cox, Reich, and Wilhelm have had two principal aims: (1) to demonstrate the necessity or indispensability of analyzing race relations *within the context of the mode of production (in this case, capitalism) in which they take place,* and (2) showing how such an analysis can be carried out in a way that is neither reductionistic nor "economistic." Put another way, I have argued for the *primacy* of mode of production without reducing racism to epiphenomenal or secondary status. I have also attempted to show, particularly by contrasting Reich's and Wilhelm's analyses, how two theories rooted in Marx's structural analysis of capitalism can nevertheless be quite different, depending on the specific problem selected for analysis. Reich's "problem" concerns the impact of racism as it has affected the general relation between capital and labor in the United States, arguing that both white and black labor, contrary to neoclassical predictions, have suffered economically from racist practices. Wilhelm, on the other hand, stresses the increasing irrelevance of blacks in the labor market of advanced capitalism, owing to changes in the productive forces that make labor of any kind redundant. These quite different analyses, both of which rely on a Marxian framework, indicate the extent to which Marxism, as a theoretical worldview, is "open-ended" with respect to the particular analyses (or subtheories) that can be developed out of it.

Most non-Marxists and not a few Marxists mistakenly view Marxism as a ready-made set of dogmatic principles that can be applied in a recipe-like manner to construct an explanation of any social phenomenon. The critics of Marxism discussed in this chapter make this very mistake by claiming, almost always without argument, that Marxism reduces social phenomena of a noneconomic kind to the economic, or view the economic as *causing* the noneconomic, or treat the noneconomic as "secondary" or epiphenomenal to the economic. These criticisms are rooted in a misunderstanding of Marx's view of causation by implying that the *structures* of capitalism (i.e., private production and accumulation, the capital-wage labor relation, the "law" of capitalistic accumulation, and so on) directly cause (out of some presumed "needs" of the "system") racism, sexism, and the like. In other words, they accuse Marxism of reification. But as Carol Gould has forcefully argued, "on Marx's view *only human agency*, or what Marx calls labor, is properly regarded as causal. The objective conditions [i.e., what I have called structural conditions] for action are precisely that, namely, conditions and not causes. . . . But it should be emphasized that for Marx labor does not create from nothing, but rather presupposes a previously existing world which it works on" (my emphasis).[53]

Marxism, as a theoretical worldview, must be seen as a general, *formal* model in which the forces and relations of production are given ontological primacy. That is, Marx claimed a special role for the economic structure of society insofar as the nature of people depends on the material conditions determining their production: "What they [people] are, therefore, coincides with their production, both with *what* they produce and with *how* they produce" (original emphasis).[54] The "what" and "how" of production are historical processes that Marx defined in terms of the relation between a particular "industrial stage" (the forces of production consisting of tools, machinery, knowledge, that is, the means of production) and its corresponding "social stage" or "mode of cooperation" (the relations of production as between lords and serfs, masters and slaves, capitalists and workers). These social structures, defined in terms of their modes of production, constitute the "existing worlds" within which people produce and reproduce their existence and that thus come to define human existence.

Marxist theories, then, be they of racism or sexism or some other specific social phenomenon, must take the particular economic structure in which the phenomenon occurs as the *primary framework* for analysis. This is because different economic structures produce different effects, given their different organization of productive relations. I illustrated this point in my discussion of ethnic policy in Canada and the People's Republic of China, showing how the same policies lead to different effects on the respective minorities, owing to the differences in capitalist and market socialist modes of production. The economic structure is thus primary to the extent that it is the underlying framework that both unifies the social whole and determines (in a structural sense) how other aspects such as racism will function and be reproduced. If that economic structure is capitalism, then the capital-wage labor relation and the class relations based on this relation constitute the necessary context for interpreting the effects of racism, since class and not race remains the primary mechanism for reproducing the social relations of production.

An example comparing race relations in the United States and South Africa will help to illustrate this point. Both countries are capitalist and, relative to other capitalist countries, racist in the extreme. The history of neither America nor South Africa can even be contemplated, let alone explained, without reference to racial domination. In South Africa racism is even more basic to the institutional structure of society, inasmuch as the state officially sanctions racial separation and uses racial categorizations directly to fill (and deny) various positions within the class structure. The apartheid system is vigorously denounced, and properly so, by the world community as a racist system that must be abolished because it denies human dignity and freedom and causes starvation, disease, and massive loss of life among blacks. Let us suppose that a new regime comes to power and successfully abolishes apartheid by removing all racially discriminatory legislation and institutes, perhaps on the American model, programs of affirmative action, equal opportunity, and so on designed to promote the integration of blacks to all levels of the class structure. Such a change would be fundamental indeed, even revolutionary, relative to the current South African situation. But would racial differences and racism continue as forms of domination, albeit much less severe than currently, under a capitalist system now proclaiming "equality, liberty, and fraternity?" The answer is yes, on the grounds that monopolization by whites of the means of production would not be altered and that most blacks would, even amid the new "equality," be relegated to the least desirable, most dangerous jobs or find themselves with no jobs. Class domination would continue to reproduce racial inequality in a somewhat similar manner to what has occurred in the United States. One of Sidney Wilhelm's most compelling arguments in *Black in a White America* is showing how the new American theme of racial equality has become a sophisticated ideology for continued racial domination by whites:

The socioeconomic disparities between Black and White coexist with tremendous opportunity for equal rights. The impediments of segregation that haunted Blacks for over a century have, especially since the fifties, tumbled. But how is it possible for Blacks, on the one hand, to be granted rights and privileges once the sole prerogative of White people and, on the other, to find their living standards substantially lower than Whites? How can Black people become less like White people now that they are being treated more like Whites? If Blacks are accorded opportunities regardless of color, how is it possible for "two societies" based upon racial distinctions to emerge in an Equal America?[55]

Wilhelm answers that "we must concede that the subordination of Blacks persists *not* in spite of but *because* of Equality" (original emphasis);[56] that "equality only allows a 'common opportunity to achieve unequal status and reward.' "[57] Blacks continue to experience oppression because the effects of racism are reproduced and legitimated by an economic system in which the domination of one class over others remains the central organizing principle in capitalist countries.

Milton Fisk, the noted Marxist philosopher who has best articulated a nonreductionist method that still gives primacy to the economic framework, states the argument that I am making above in the following terms:

My thesis is that in societies with class divisions class represents the primary form of domination. The reason is that class is a form of domination that reproduces the economic relations of production, and that these relations of production are the fundamental framework in explanation. This is not to deny that racial and sexual domination play a role in reproducing the economy. But that they do depends on their facilitating the domination peculiar to class which directly reproduces the economy.

Notice here that I am not suggesting, and may even be taken as discouraging, the functionalist idea that race and gender derive from class since their forms of domination contribute to the success of class domination. I shall assume racial and gender domination to be forms of domination that in some way benefit the racist and the sexist, rather than the financier, the rentier, or the entrepreneur *as such*. That these forms of domination benefit capitalists is from this perspective the good luck of capitalists as third parties. It is thus not necessary to be a reductionist in order to say that class is primary in relation to race and gender. What is necessary is only that class represent the form of domination that is designed to reproduce the fundamental explanatory framework, which is economic.[58]

The recognition that racial oppression and racism continue to be reproduced through a class structure even while society pays lip service to racial "equality" does not mean that calls or movements for the elimination of apartheid or racial discrimination should be subordinated to a socialist movement seeking to abolish capitalist relations of production. Apartheid and racial discrimination need to be abolished even in the absence of a call to socialism on the grounds that they are immoral and unjust social relations. The fact that the elimination of official racial segregation in the United States has not resulted in greater racial equality for most blacks is not an argument for the reinstitution of segregation.

Recognizing the primacy of the economic framework does mean, however, that racism in either the United States or South Africa is *not independent* of the relations of production. On the contrary, it is so deeply imbedded within the relations of production that any call for racial equality must, if it is to be truly effective, be grounded in a program that seeks to transform the relations of production in a nonracist way. It is beyond the scope of this chapter to indicate what system of production this would entail, but in the contemporary United States it is likely to mean some system based on a radical egalitarianism in which all people, regardless of race or sex, are provided with certain necessary economic and political entitlements (meaningful work, decent housing, democratic participation, and control, for example). This implies the abolition of capitalist production relations that provide no such entitlements for the great mass of blacks or the majority of whites.[59] If such a program can be called "socialist," as I think it can, then blacks do have an interest in such a society *as* blacks. Any such socialist program, however, must also recognize the degree to which racism has been a basic institutional feature of American society and that it will not magically wither away with the institution of new relations of production without specific attention paid to its historical role and the legacy of human misery that role has left in its wake. Nevertheless, it seems to me an inescapable conclusion that the remedy for racism and racial inequality requires, from the perspective of a Marxian framework, a radical transformation of capitalist relations of production along socialist lines.

Notes

1. Gabriel Palma, "Dependency and Development: A Critical Overview," in D. Seers, ed., *Dependency Theory: A Critical Overview*. London: Francis Pitner, 1981, pp. 20–78. In this excellent article Palma presents a compelling case concerning Marx's writings on capitalist development in the backward nations. He argues that Marx was rather ambivalent concerning the nature of this development. On the one hand, Marx condemns the "brutalising and dehumanizing" effects of capitalist development in the periphery, but seems to regard such development as "positive" in terms of the worldwide development of capitalism's productive forces, and the necessity of such for the future development of socialism. Marx also shows antipathy for certain precapitalist modes, particularly feudalism and the Asiatic Mode. Thus, Palma says, "for this reason Marx analyses European expansion in India as brutal, but 'a necessary step for Socialism' " (p. 25).

2. The sort of analysis I attempted at the end of Chapter 5 with respect to China is an indication of the rather infantile state of knowledge concerning the structural bases and dynamics of market socialist modes of production, for example. An excellent beginning in analyzing these structures is Allen Buchanan's *Ethics, Efficiency, and the Market*. Totowa, N.J.: Rowman & Allanheld, 1985. As for Marxian analyses of precapitalist modes, useful introductions are found in Maurice Godelier, *Perspectives in Marxist Anthropology*. Trans. by Robert Brain. Cambridge: Cambridge University Press, 1977; and Maurice Bloch, *Marxism and Anthropology*. New York: Oxford University, 1983. Marx's own writings on precapitalist modes are introduced by Eric J. Hobsbawm in Karl Marx, *Pre-Capitalist Economic Formations*. New York: International Publishers, 1965. Important dis-

cussions by Marx of the differences between feudal, capitalist, and future "communist" societies are contained in Karl Marx, *The Grundrisse*. Ed. and trans. by David McClellan. New York: Harper & Row, 1971, chs. 14–22.

3. Brian Fay, *Critical Social Science*. Ithaca, N.Y.: Cornell University Press, 1987, p. 27.

4. Arthur Brittan and Mary Maynard, *Sexism, Racism and Oppression*. Oxford: Basil Blackwell, 1984, pp. 2–3.

5. Ibid., pp. 38–39.

6. Oliver C. Cox, *Caste, Class and Race*. New York: Monthly Review, 1959 [1948], p. 321.

7. Ibid., p. 393.

8. Ibid., pp. 400–401.

9. Ibid., p. 322.

10. Ibid., p. 329.

11. Ibid., p. 335.

12. Ibid., 330.

13. Karl Marx, *Capital: A Critique of Political Economy*, Vol. 1. Trans. by Ben Fowkes. New York: Vintage Press, 1977, pp. 874–875.

14. Ibid., p. 875.

15. Ibid., p. 936.

16. George M. Fredrickson, *The Black Image in the White Mind*. New York: Harper & Row, 1971, pp. 2–3.

17. Cox, *Caste, Class and Race*, esp. chs. 21 and 23.

18. This list is taken from Cox's "restatement" of the relation between capitalism and race relations on pp. 485–488 of *Caste, Class and Race*.

19. Ibid., p. 487.

20. Ibid., p. 583.

21. Michael Reich, *Racial Inequality*. Princeton, N.J.: Princeton University Press, 1981, pp. 7–8.

22. See ibid., p. 80, for a discussion of this.

23. Detailed summaries and critiques of these models are presented in Reich, ch. 3.

24. The discussion and presentation of the econometric analyses are given in Reich, ch. 4.

25. Ibid., pp. 177–178.

26. Ibid., pp. 307, 308.

27. Ibid., p. 269.

28. Ibid., p. 3.

29. In chapter 6, Reich presents excellent historical arguments on the role of racial antagonisms in industry and agriculture between 1865 and 1975. He demonstrates here how racism has produced a weakened labor movement and, with regard to workers' issues, a relatively unresponsive state system.

30. Ibid., p. 267.

31. Ibid., p. 312.

32. Sidney M. Wilhelm, *Who Needs the Negro?* Garden City, N.J.: Doubleday, Anchor Books, 1971; *Black in a White America*. Cambridge, Mass.: Schenkman, 1983.

33. Wilhelm, *Black in a White America*, pp. 132–133.

34. Ibid., pp. 128–129.

35. Ibid., 145.

36. Ibid.

37. Ibid., p. 129.

38. Ibid., p. 135.

39. Ibid., p. 201.

40. Ibid., pp. 231–232, 233.

41. U.S. Bureau of the Census, *Money Income and Poverty Status of Families and Persons in the United States, 1983*. Current Population Reports, Series P–60, No. 145. Washington, D.C.: Government Printing Office, 1983.

42. Daniel Fusfeld and Timothy Bates, *The Political Economy of the Urban Ghetto*. Carbondale: Southern Illinois University Press, 1984, p. 142.

43. Quoted in Wilhelm, *Black in a White America*, p. 231.

44. Marx, *Capital*. Vol. 1, p. 782.

45. Ibid., p. 794.

46. Ibid., p. 797.

47. Ibid.

48. Ibid., p. 792.

49. Ibid., p. 790.

50. Wilhelm, *Black in a White America*, p. 346.

51. Ibid., p. 345.

52. Ibid., p. 352.

53. Carol Gould, *Marx's Social Ontology*. Cambridge, Mass.: MIT Press, 1978, pp. 80–81.

54. Karl Marx, *The German Ideology*, in Robert C. Tucker, ed., *The Marx-Engels Reader*. 2d ed. New York: W. W. Norton, 1978, p. 150.

55. Wilhelm, *Black in a White America*, pp. 318–319.

56. Ibid., p. 319.

57. Ibid., p. 321.

58. Milton Fisk, "Why the Anti-Marxists Are Wrong," *Monthly Review*, March 1987, pp. 14–15.

59. For a detailed argument concerning the necessity of "radical egalitarianism" and its relation to socialism, see Kai Nielsen, *Equality and Liberty: A Defense of Radical Egalitarianism*. Totowa, N.J.: Rowman & Allanheld, 1985.

7

Epilogue

THEORETICAL WORLDVIEWS
AND THEORETICAL CHOICE

> Among the infinity of facts, each science's facts are always selected
> for scrutiny, gathered, and quite literally "seen" or "observed" in
> and through its conceptual framework. The "facts" per se can thus
> never provide any final criterion of truth *between* such different
> frameworks.[1]

This quotation captures well the methodological starting point that has
both informed and provided the framework for the theoretical appraisals
I have presented in the foregoing pages. By treating theories of race
and ethnicity (and the theoretical enterprise in general) as analogues of
cultural worldviews, I have maintained that there are no readily agreed
on criteria or standards against which to judge the adequacy or "superiority" of one theory's truths as against the truths of others. Nor, I
would argue, are there likely to be such standards, insofar as what counts
as the "truth" or "reality" depends centrally on how theories claim to
discover or know the truth (the epistemological issue) and conceive the
very "reality" they seek to know (the ontological issue). Truths about
society are thus embedded into frameworks that differ qualitatively from
other such frameworks at the same time that they might each claim to
be explaining the very same phenomena (in our case racial and ethnic
inequality). The arguments among these theories do not primarily take
place, although they sometimes do, at the level of "facts," but at the level
of assigning significance to and seeking explanations for those facts.

For these reasons the critiques I presented of theories of race and
ethnicity are "internalist" or "relativist" in the sense that I have tried to

evaluate the claims made by the respective theories by reference to the epistemological and ontological standards they have set for themselves. For example, sociobiology conceives "society" (the social whole, or social reality) to be the sum total of individual behaviors that stem from the genetic tendency to maximize fitness. Sociobiology does not "fail" because this ontology is "false," but because it cannot show or has not yet shown, by means of the empiricist epistemology it embraces (discovery or inference of causes through observation, measurement, and manipulation of variables), the extent to which racial and ethnic behaviors have or have not maximized genetic fitness. It has not, then, been able to specify the nature or extent of, or the relation between, its presumed ultimate cause (fitness maximization) and other potential causes of a nongenetic nature. It thus fails on its own terms and not by comparison with assimilationism or Marxism, which, I have argued, would be akin to saying that an apple fails because it is not an avocado or an orange (or that your religion is false because it conflicts with mine, which is true). This is why a cautious sociobiologist can readily agree that sociobiology has "failed" without at the same time conceding either his ontology or epistemology. He can rightfully insist that it might yet succeed if sufficiently careful and detailed studies are carried out, along with perhaps increased technical means for "observing" genes and their behavior. In fact, one of my major criticisms of van den Berghe's sociobiology was his nonrecognition of the kinds of studies required to carry out his own theory.

This same internalist criticism was carried through with respect to the other theories, although the nature of these criticisms varied in accordance with what I consider to be the major deficiencies or strengths of these theories. That is, the nature of my critique was, to an important extent, directed by the nature of the theories themselves. Primordialist theories, for example, provide us with insight concerning the strength of ethnic and racial sentiments and how such sentiments can become important elements of individual and group identification. But they generally fail to analyze the conditions under which such sentiments are created, and how they become activated to the point of serving as the focus, if not the underlying inspiration for, serious ethnic and racial conflicts. Primordialist theories are thus incomplete (and also tend to mistake ethnic "appearances" for nonethnic realities), insofar as they do not address the underlying causes of ethnically and racially based social movements. Assimilationism is similarly "weak" because assimilation theories have been content to *describe* the assimilation process without explaining the social and cultural conditions that lead to assimilation or nonassimilation. This has resulted from the assumption that assimilation by ethnic and racial minorities is, over time, an expected outcome in any industrial society, owing to a kind of "natural selection" by which industrial societies select and recruit their participants on the basis of achieved, universalist criteria rather than on racial, sexual, or ethnic criteria. Such an assumption precludes a critical analysis of the actual operation of industrial societies and leads assimilationists to argue, in cases of nonassimilation, that the "fault" or "blame" for nonassimilation rests with the non-assimilating group. In contradistinction to this view, I provided evidence that industrial society does not operate in the manner assimilationists assume, which at least calls into question their claim that the failure to assimilate rests largely on problems or deficiencies within the minority group. I further argued that the major anomaly for assimilationism, the failure of black assimilation in the United States, led not to a reexamination of assimilationism's assumptions, but to a retreat into a "new ethnicity" that views ethnic identification as a primal attachment.

My critique of world-system theory proceeded along a somewhat different, though still internalist, path. I agree with Wallerstein that the emergence of a capitalist world-economy is a necessary framework within which to analyze racial and ethnic situations, and that the character of racial and ethnic relations is heavily influenced by the relations among the core, semiperiphery, and periphery. Wallerstein's theory enables us, in ways the other theories discussed do not, to explain how racial and ethnic relations are structured differently (as ethnonationalist movements or assimilationist movements or separatist movements, for example), depending on their relational context in the world-economy. Wallerstein also makes a compelling case for viewing race and ethnic relations as intimately connected to the international division of labor and how that division of labor manifests itself in particular regions of the world through proletarianization and the transformation of noncapitalist relations of production into increasingly capitalist relations. What I questioned in Wallerstein's formulation was his conceptualization of the capitalist world-economy and whether this world-economy is the best framework within which to analyze race and ethnic relations. I argued that capitalism, as a mode of production, is certainly dominant in the world economy, but that it is not the *only* mode of production, and that to so argue, as Wallerstein does, can lead to incorrect (or at least grossly oversimplified) analyses of racial and ethnic movements. I thus maintained that a better framework for analysis is a "mode of production" framework in which race and ethnic relations are understood as connected to the contradictory relations between the forces and relations of production or, in other cases, as part and parcel of the struggle between different modes of production.

My critique of Marxian approaches to race and ethnicity was, in some ways, less of a critique and more of a defense in that I attempted to "rescue" a Marxian approach that is not susceptible to the prior criticisms that have been raised against it. This was necessary to the extent that certain varieties of Marxism have been properly criticized for being economistic, reductionistic, and essentialist. I argued that any Marxian or Marx-inspired analysis that reduces race and ethnic relations to economic relations such that the economy is taken to be the "root cause" of race or ethnic relations is an improper application of Marxian theory and method. Although Marxian theory does specify "mode of production" as the proper framework within which to analyze racial and ethnic phenomena, such a framework does not commit one to any claim that "mode of production" (an ontological abstraction that conceives of society as a complex, unified, yet contradictory whole that includes the economic, social, cultural, and political aspects) *causes* race and ethnic relations. I then proceeded to show how it is possible, when analyzing particular instances of ethnic or race relations, that causes of a non-economic kind are not only consistent with, but also demanded by a Marxian approach. Stated another way, I argued for a Marxian approach that is nonessentialist. That is, Marxian theory does not claim as, for example, does sociobiology some root cause or ultimate cause of race or ethnic relations, but specifies a framework within which to search for *mutually determining causes*. Marxian approaches to race and ethnicity must, then, like competing approaches, be evaluated in terms of its own understandings of causation and the nature of society.[2]

Although I have maintained a critical stance of theoretical relativity, I also argued in the Preface that one must nevertheless make a theoretical *choice* in the sense of holding or being partisan to one paradigm over the others. That is, scholars of race and ethnicity should not embrace eclecticism, the stance that the "truth" is at least partially contained in all the competing paradigms. This is because the same set of "facts," when viewed from within each worldview, takes on different significance such that the "truth" itself is variable. It is, therefore, just as difficult to use the notion of "multiple truths," which are often incommensurate with one another, to justify eclecticism, as it is the notion of "truth" per se to choose one theory over others.

How, then, is theoretical choice possible? One basis for choosing is what I call "relative adequacy." By this I mean that one chooses a theory to the extent that it is able to sustain the claims it makes relative to its own epistemological and ontological standards. I regard Marxian theory as superior relative to the others, not because it is "true" and others are "false," but because it is better able to explain racial and ethnic inequality in terms of its dialectical epistemology and its structural or "holist" ontology. Racial inequality and racism are seen as complexly determined *and determining* when viewed in relation to the economic, political, and social structures that characterize advanced capitalism. Sociobiology and assimilationism, on the other hand, both use an individualist or atomist conception of society which requires them to explain social structural aspects as resulting from individual behaviors. This is problematic to the extent that even if people were to engage in those behaviors specified by atomist theories (e.g., blacks achieving an education as a means of alleviating their poverty), the structural "requirements" of capitalism, one of which is the systematic generation of inequality, would nevertheless remain. What would result is a highly educated class of poor people who, to the extent that they remain predominantly black, as they are likely to, given their current disadvantages, would reproduce the very racial inequality that "getting an education" is supposed to alleviate. In this sense, then, Marxism is more adequate than either sociobiology or assimilationism, inasmuch as the practice it specifies—the elimination of capitalist social relations—is consistent with its analysis of race relations as part and parcel of capitalist production relations. Carrying this argument somewhat further, the inability of sociobiology and assimilationism to specify behaviors—behaviors consistent with their ontology— that will alleviate the problems they seek to address casts doubt on the adequacy of that ontology. Despite the existence of theoretical "visions and versions," one can use rational, though still internalist means by which to choose among them.

A second basis for choosing one theory over and against others is normative considerations. By "normative" I simply mean using what are generally called values with respect to theoretical choice. Using value considerations with respect to theories of race and ethnicity is, on one level, quite simple but, on another level, quite complex. It is simple insofar as neither the "truth" nor the "facts" are unambiguous arbiters of theoretical choice, which, by elimination, leaves "values" as the potential arbiter. But even if it is granted that all theories are normative as well as explanatory frameworks, the issue of *which* values are embraced or, as is often the case, *embedded within* theoretical frameworks is a matter of considerable complexity. Moreover, sometimes it appears that different theories embrace the *same* values, which, if that is the case, might seem to eliminate "values" as an arbiter of theoretical choice.

For example, all the theorists I have discussed appear to value racial and ethnic equality over racial and ethnic inequality, regardless of the theory they espouse to explain racial and ethnic inequality. No one argues that racial inequality is a social or personal "good" that we should strive to maintain. Most of the theorists in fact go further, and maintain that racial inequality is a social and personal evil that ought to be eliminated. They share the view that human inequalities, to the extent that they exist at all, should not be based on elements such as skin color, language, cultural differences, and so on unless perhaps the people in possession of ethnic criteria understand how such criteria contribute to inequality and choose that they continue to do so (a rare situation indeed). Furthermore, several of the theories discussed here are considered by their adherents to be *necessary knowledges* by which to eliminate racial and ethnic inequality. Let me again quote Pierre van den Berghe's justification for the knowledge that sociobiology promises with respect to racial and ethnic issues: "Unless we stop behaving naturally—that is, being our selfish, nepotistic, ethnocentric selves—we court collective extinction. . . . It is as an *anti-ethic* that sociobiology holds its greatest promise. We must know the nature of the beast within us to vanquish it. Unless we achieve both—and quickly—we are a doomed species."[3]

Van den Berghe's argument is that knowledge of the genetic basis of race and ethnic relations is basic to the transformation of those relations, that unless we know how we "naturally" are, there is little hope for social and cultural change. Regardless of van den Berghe's inability to explain how we naturally are (i.e., the extent to which presumed natural causes interact with other causes), he has justified his theory in terms of the practice of removing or eliminating racial and ethnic inequality.

Marxist theories are similarly explicit in terms of producing knowledges for the sake of eliminating or ameliorating what they consider to be unjust, immoral, and exploitative social relations. Marxian scholars argue that their theories are explanations directed to the sufferings and unmet needs of exploited classes such that understanding and using these theories might lead to emancipation from the sufferings such classes experience.[4] If racial inequality is intricately tied to class and other forms of inequality rooted in advanced capitalism, then these other inequalities must be addressed alongside racial inequality if racial equality is to be achieved. This is what makes Marxian theories radical and revolutionary—the recognition that racial inequality is bound up with the entire social formation and that piecemeal approaches to racial equality are *not* likely to succeed. Sociobiology might be similarly radical if it could specify, as Marxian theory can, the social practices that are called for by the theory. As yet it cannot do so, nor is it likely to be able to do so.[5] Because of this the emancipatory value it specifies cannot be reasonably acted on by individuals or groups, since they are provided with no adequate theory by which to either understand or change their social conditions.

The other theories addressed are much less explicit concerning the values that underpin their analysis of race and ethnicity. This is due in large part to the degree to which primordialism, assimilationism, and world-system theory are heavily descriptive and less explanatory. Primordial theories generally claim that racial and ethnic identities are "good" in the sense of providing group identities that may be affectively fulfilling, but fail to address those circumstances in which such identities are used as the basis for inequalities and might thus be socially "bad." They do not consider the normative implications of either maintaining or shedding ethnic identities, nor the kinds of social arrangements necessary for them to function in affectively fulfilling ways. The value dimensions of primordialism are as incomplete as the theoretical analyses on which they hinge.

Assimilation theorists decry racial and ethnic inequality *to the extent that such inequality is legitimated by rule of law or is otherwise state-supported.* They thus profess equality before the law and equal opportunity, regardless of racial or ethnic affiliation. However, where such inequalities are the outcome of market competition, they must be accepted as at least lesser evils than any policies designed to enforce racial or ethnic equality, where these policies would affect the functioning of the competitive market. It is their belief that the market will work to eliminate racial and ethnic differentials in wages and occupations, provided minorities accumulate the human capital necessary for competing successfully. Thus, although both Marxists and assimilationists may rightfully claim to be against racial and ethnic inequality, and consequently appear to embrace the same value, they differ fundamentally concerning the practice required to eliminate inequality. Where Marxism is radical, assimilationism is conservative, insofar as it argues that the status quo, the current political-economic structure of American society, is equitable and just, and that minorities must, regardless of historical inequalities, accommodate themselves to the status quo. The same value of racial and ethnic equality as embraced by the assimilationists is, in a very real sense, fundamentally different from that espoused by Marxists, insofar as it specifies a completely different social and political practice for its implementation.

As for world-system theory, Immanuel Wallerstein clearly regards the capitalist world-economy as exploitative and interprets racial and ethnic inequalities as particular forms of economic exploitation, depending on their specific context with regard to core, semiperipheral, and peripheral relations. Insofar as race and ethnic relations are relations of exploitation (and are, for Wallerstein, varieties of class relations), Wallerstein clearly values the elimination of racial and ethnic criteria to the extent that they are used to justify particular forms of labor exploitation. But because the capitalist economy is *the* world-economy that continues to impose its rationale on all states and regions, little is offered by the theory as a means for combating that rationale. What are the racially and ethnically exploited citizens of the world to do? Should they pressure the states in which they live to speed up their trajectory toward the core and, by implication, the process of their own exploitation? Or should they organize social movements against their systematic incorporation into the world-economy (a strategy that appears precluded, given the seeming inevitability of that incorporation)? These are important questions that Wallerstein's theory does not address. Despite his own preference for a socialist system, he considers such a development to be the outcome of a long world-historical struggle in which the contradictions of the capitalist world-economy become transformed into a world-socialist government. Wallerstein's argument is at such a high level of generality that the role to be played by human actors is indeterminate at best or, at worst, minimal. It's as if all people, regardless of their particular circumstances or conditions, are swept along by the dictates of a world-economy that operates by laws independent of human intentions and actions. This extreme generality produces an attitude of resignation that says, in effect, that racial and ethnic equality cannot be achieved or even worked toward until the capitalist world-economy is tottering on the brink of collapse. Even though Wallerstein values racial and ethnic equality, he seems to regard its achievement as beyond the capacities of even knowledgeable and committed actors.

The issue of theoretical choice is much more complex than I have outlined here, and certainly deserves a more sophisticated and lengthy treatment than I can provide in a few pages. What I have tried to argue in general terms, however, is that theories are not selected or embraced by the degree to which their facts correspond to or fit some presumed reality that is "out there" and exists independent of the theory. Nor is theoretical choice based either on what I termed "relative adequacy" or simply on values. Rather, I suggest that there is a *relation between* the adequacy of theory to specify its "causes" or explanations and how such explanations make it possible for the values embedded in the theory—the establishment of racial and ethnic equality—to be brought about by concerted human action. If this is so, then I contend that the kind of Marxian theory I proposed in the last chapter is more adequate than its rivals to accomplish the equality they all espouse.

Notes

1. Stephen A. Resnick and Richard D. Wolff, *Knowledge and Class: A Marxian Critique of Political Economy.* Chicago: University of Chicago, 1987, p. 84 (original emphasis).

2. In Chapter 6 I did not elaborate on the epistemological and ontological foundations of Marxism, preferring instead to focus on applications and misapplications of Marx's thought to race and ethnic relations. The philosophical foundation of the kind of Marxism I advocate in this chapter is similar to and has been influenced by Resnick and Wolff's *Knowledge and Class.* In this important book they formulate a "nonessentialist" view of Marxian epistemology quite similar to the nonreductionist Marxism I argue for in Chapter 6. Readers seeking a detailed exposition of their view should consult this work, especially chs. 1 and 2.

3. Pierre L. van den Berghe, *The Ethnic Phenomenon.* New York: Elsevier, 1981, p. xii (original emphasis).

4. For a detailed explanation of the values embedded in Marxian social science

see Brian Fay, *Social Theory and Political Practice*. Boston: Allen & Unwin, 1975, ch. 5.

5. In order for sociobiology to specify what practices ought to be engaged in to eliminate racial or ethnic inequality, it would at least need to determine the relative strength of presumed genetic causes relative to nongenetic ones. Additionally, it would be necessary to know to what extent the biological bases of race and ethnicity are relatively fixed versus relatively malleable. These are enormously difficult knowledges to produce. Van den Berghe might say, given his argument, that as a kind of overall practice, we should establish social arrangements where "fitness" is maximized by cooperative rather than competitive behaviors. The problem is that we cannot know except in the extreme long term (hundreds, perhaps thousands, of years) what behaviors we chose led to the fitness we attempted to maximize. This does not seem a satisfactory basis on which to engage in social engineering.

Bibliography

Adorno, T. W., Else Frenkel-Brunswick, Daniel J. Levinson II, and R. Nevitt
  Sanford
  1950   *The Authoritarian Personality*. New York: Harper.
Alexander, Richard
  1979   *Darwinism and Human Affairs*. Seattle: University of Washington Press.
Allen, Robert L.
  1970   *Black Awakening in Capitalist America: An Analytic History*. Garden City,
         N.J.: Doubleday, Anchor Books.
Banton, Michael
  1983   *Racial and Ethnic Competition*. Cambridge: Cambridge University Press.
Barker, Martin
  1981   *The New Racism: Conservatives and the Ideology of the Tribe*. Frederick,
         Md: University Publications of America.
Barth, Fredrik
  1969   *Ethnic Groups and Boundaries*. Boston: Little, Brown.
Barton, Josef
  1975   *Peasants and Strangers: Italians, Rumanians and Slovaks in an Industrial
         City, 1890–1950*. Cambridge, Mass.: Harvard University Press.
Becker, Gary
  1971   *The Economics of Discrimination*. 2d. ed. Chicago: University of Chicago
         Press.
Bell, Daniel
  1973   *The Coming of Post-Industrial Society*. New York: Basic Books.
  1975   "Ethnicity and Social Change," in Nathan Glazer and Daniel P. Moy-
         nihan, eds., *Ethnicity: Theory and Experience*. Cambridge, Mass.: Harvard
         University Press, pp. 141–174.
Blauner, Robert
  1972   *Racial Oppression in America*. New York: Harper & Row.

Bloch, Maurice
    1983   *Marxism and Anthropology.* New York: Oxford University Press.
Bonacich, Edna
    1980   "Class Approaches to Ethnicity and Race," *The Insurgent Sociologist,*
           10(2):9–23.
Brenner, Robert
    1977   "The Origins of Capitalist Development: A Critique of Neo-Smithian
           Marxism," *New Left Review,* 104:25–93.
Brittan, Arthur, and Mary Maynard
    1984   *Sexism, Racism and Oppression.* Oxford: Basil Blackwell.
Broom, Leonard, and Robert G. Cushing
    1977   "A Modest Test of an Immodest Theory: The Functional Theory of
           Stratification," *American Sociological Review,* 42:157–169.
Buchanan, Allen
    1983   *Ethics, Efficiency, and the Market.* Totowa, N.J.: Rowman & Allanheld.
Cardoso, F. H.
    1972   "Dependency and Development in Latin America," *New Left Review,*
           74:83–95.
Cardoso, F. H., and E. Faletto
    1979   *Dependency and Development in Latin America.* Trans. by M. Urquidi.
           Berkeley: University of California Press.
Carmichael, Stokely, and Charles V. Hamilton
    1967   *Black Power: The Politics of Liberation in America.* New York: Vintage
           Press.
Carneiro, Robert
    1970   "A Theory of the Origin of the State," *Science,* 69:733–738.
Carson, Clayborne, David J. Garrow, Vincent Harding, and Diane Clark Hine
    1987   *Eyes on the Prize: America's Civil Rights Years.* New York: Penguin.
Chossudovsky, Michel
    1986   *Towards Capitalist Restoration? Chinese Socialism After Mao.* New York: St.
           Martin's Press.
Cox, Oliver C.
    1959   *Caste, Class and Race: A Study in Social Dynamics.* New York: Monthly
           Review (orig. pub., 1948, Doubleday).
Daniels, Norman
    1975   "IQ, Heritability and Human Nature," *Proceedings of the Philosophy of
           Science Association.*
Davis, Kingsley, and W. E. Moore
    1945   "Some Principles of Stratification," *American Sociological Review,*
           10(April):243–249.
Dawkins, R.
    1976   *The Selfish Gene.* Oxford: Oxford University Press.
Di Leonardo, Micaela
    1984   *The Varieties of Ethnic Experience: Kinship, Class and Gender Among Cali-
           fornia Italian-Americans.* Ithaca, N.Y.: Cornell University Press.
Dreyer, June
    1976   *China's Forty Millions.* Cambridge, Mass.: Harvard University Press.
Dupuy, Alex, and Paul V. Fitzgerald
    1977   "Contribution to the Critique of the World-System Perspective," *The
           Insurgent Sociologist,* 7(2):113–124.

Enloe, Cynthia
   1977   "Internal Colonialism, Federalism, and Alternative State Development
          Strategies," *Publius*, 7(4):145–160.
Fay, Brian
   1975   *Social Theory and Political Practice*. Boston: Allen & Unwin.
   1987   *Critical Social Science*. Ithaca, N.Y.: Cornell University Press.
Fisk, Milton
   1978   "The Human-Nature Argument," *Radical Philosopher's Newsjournal*,
          9(Fall):1–17.
   1982   "The State and the Economy," *Midwest Studies in Philosophy*,
          7(February):42–65.
   1987   "Why the Anti-Marxists Are Wrong," *Monthly Review*, 38(March):7–17.
Fredrickson, George M.
   1971   *The Black Image in the White Mind*. New York: Harper & Row.
Fusfeld, Daniel, and Timothy Bates
   1984   *The Political Economy of the Urban Ghetto*. Carbondale: Southern Illinois
          University Press.
Garfinkel, Alan
   1981   *Forms of Explanation: Rethinking the Questions in Social Theory*. New Haven,
          Conn.: Yale University Press.
Geertz, Clifford
   1973   *The Interpretation of Cultures*. New York: Basic Books.
Gellner, Ernest
   1983   *Nations and Nationalism*. Ithaca, N.Y.: Cornell University Press.
Geschwender, James
   1978   *Racial Stratification in America*. Dubuque, Iowa: Wm. C. Brown.
Glazer, Nathan
   1987   *Affirmative Discrimination: Ethnic Inequality and Public Policy*. Cambridge,
          Mass.: Harvard University Press.
Glazer, Nathan, and Daniel P. Moynihan
   1970   *Beyond the Melting Pot: The Negroes, Puerto Ricans, Jews, Italians, and Irish
          of New York City*. 2d ed. Cambridge, Mass.: MIT Press.
   1975   "Introduction," in Nathan Glazer and Daniel P. Moynihan, eds., *Eth-
          nicity: Theory and Experience*. Cambridge, Mass.: Harvard University
          Press, pp. 1–26.
Godelier, Maurice
   1977   *Perspectives in Marxist Anthropology*. Trans. by Robert Brain. Cambridge:
          Cambridge University Press.
Gordon, Milton
   1964   *Assimilation in American Life: The Role of Race, Religion, and National
          Origins*. New York: Oxford University Press.
   1978   *Human Nature, Class, and Ethnicity*. New York: Oxford University Press.
Gould, Carol C.
   1981   *Marx's Social Ontology*. Cambridge, Mass.: MIT Press.
Hamilton, W. D.
   1971   "The Genetical Evolution of Social Behavior I," [1964] and "The Ge-
          netical Evolution of Social Behavior II," [1964], in G. C. Williams, ed.,
          Group Selection. Chicago: Aldine, pp. 23–89.

Harrington, Michael
   1976   *The Twilight of Capitalism*. New York: Simon & Schuster.
Hechter, Michael
   1975   *Internal Colonialism: The Celtic Fringe in British National Development, 1536–1966*. Berkeley: University of California Press.
Hobsbawm, Eric J.
   1965   "Introduction," in Karl Marx, *Pre-Capitalist Economic Formations*. New York: International Publishers, pp. 9–65.
Isaacs, Harold R.
   1975   "Basic Group Identity: The Idols of the Tribe," in Nathan Glazer and Daniel P. Moynihan, eds., *Ethnicity: Theory and Experience*. Cambridge, Mass.: Harvard University Press, pp. 29–52.
Kamin, Leo
   1974   *The Science and Politics of IQ*. New York: Halsted Press.
Kitcher, Philip
   1985   *Vaulting Ambition: Sociobiology and the Quest for Human Nature*. Cambridge, Mass.: MIT Press.
Lefeber, Walter
   1984   *Inevitable Revolutions*. New York: W. W. Norton.
Lewis, Oscar
   1966   "The Culture of Poverty," *Scientific American*, 215(4):19–25.
Lewontin, Richard, Steven Rose, and Leo Kamin
   1982   "Bourgeois Ideology and the Origins of Biological Determinism," *Race & Class*, 24(1):1–16.
Lukacs, Georg
   1967   *History and Class Consciousness*. Cambridge, Mass.: MIT Press.
Lumsden, C., and E. O. Wilson
   1981   *Genes, Mind and Culture*. Cambridge, Mass.: Harvard University Press.
Mandel, Ernest
   1978   *Late Capitalism*. London: Verso.
Marx, Karl
   1971   *The Grundrisse*. Ed. and trans. by David McClellan. New York: Harper & Row.
   1977   *Capital: A Critique of Political Economy. Vol. I*. Trans. by Ben Fowkes with an Introduction by Ernest Mandel. New York: Vintage Press.
   1978   *The German Ideology*. Part I. In Robert C. Tucker, ed., *The Marx-Engels Reader*. New York: W. W. Norton.
Miliband, Ralph
   1977   *Marxism and Politics*. Oxford: Oxford University Press.
Nash, June
   1981   "Ethnographic Aspects of the World Capitalist System," *Annual Review of Anthropology*, 10:393–423.
Nielsen, Kai
   1985   *Equality and Liberty: A Defense of Radical Egalitarianism*. Totowa, NJ: Rowman & Allanheld.
Novak, Michael
   1971   *The Rise of the Unmeltable Ethnics: Politics and Culture in the Seventies*. New York: Macmillan.

O'Connor, James
1973　*The Fiscal Crisis of the State.* New York: St. Martin's Press.
Palma, Gabriel
1981　"Dependency and Development: A Critical Overview," in D. Seers, ed., *Dependency Theory: A Critical Overview.* London: Francis Pitner, pp. 20–78.
Park, Robert E.
1931　"Personality and Cultural Conflict," *Publication of the American Sociological Society,* 25(2):95–110.
Patterson, Orlando
1977　*Ethnic Chauvinism: The Reactionary Impulse.* New York: Stein & Day.
1982　*Slavery and Social Death.* Cambridge, Mass.: Harvard University Press.
Peery, Nelson
1975　*The Negro National Colonial Question.* Chicago: Workers' Press.
Porter, John
1965　*The Vertical Mosaic: An Analysis of Social Class and Power in Canada.* Toronto: University of Toronto Press.
Poulantzas, Nicos
1974　*Classes in Contemporary Capitalism.* Trans. by David Fernbach. London: Verso.
Reich, Michael
1981　*Racial Inequality.* Princeton, N.J.: Princeton University Press.
Renmin Ribao (People's Daily)
1980　"Is the National Question Essentially a Class Question?" July 15.
Resnick, Stephen A., and Richard D. Wolff
1987　*Knowledge and Class: A Marxian Critique of Political Economy.* Chicago: University of Chicago.
Royal Commission on Bilingualism and Biculturalism
1970　*Report of the Royal Commission on Bilingualism and Biculturalism, Book IV: The Other Ethnic Groups.* Ottawa: Queen's Printer.
Royce, Anya Peterson
1982　*Ethnic Identity: Strategies of Diversity.* Bloomington: Indiana University Press.
Sahlins, Marshall
1976　*The Use and Abuse of Biology.* Ann Arbor: University of Michigan Press.
Said, Edward W.
1980　*The Question of Palestine.* New York: Vintage Press.
Shils, Edward
1957　"Primordial, Personal, Sacred and Civil Ties," *British Journal of Sociology,* 8:130–145.
1968　"Color, the Universal Intellectual Community, and the Afro-Asian Intellectual," in John Hope Franklin, ed., *Color and Race.* Boston: Houghton Mifflin.
Smith, J. Maynard
1982　"Introduction," in P. Bateson, ed., *Current Problems in Sociobiology.* Cambridge: Cambridge University Press.
Sowell, Thomas
1975　*Race and Economics.* New York: David McKay Co.

Stein, Howard F., and Robert F. Hill
  1977   *The Ethnic Imperative: Examining the New White Ethnic Movement.* University Park, Pa.: The Pennsylvania State University Press.
Steinberg, Steven
  1981   *The Ethnic Myth: Race, Ethnicity and Class in America.* Boston: Beacon Press.
Tawney, Richard Henry
  1952   *Equality.* 4th rev. ed. London: Allen & Unwin.
Thompson, Richard H.
  1979   "Ethnicity vs. Class: An Analysis of Conflict in a North American Chinese Community," *Ethnicity,* 6:306–326.
  1980   "From Kinship to Class: A New Model of Urban Overseas Chinese Social Organization," *Urban Anthropology,* 9(3):265–292.
Trimberger, K. E.
  1979   "World Systems Analysis: The Problem of Unequal Development," *Theory of Society,* 8:101–106.
Turnbull, Colin
  1962   *The Forest People.* New York: Simon & Schuster.
U.S. Bureau of the Census
  1984   *Money Income and Poverty Status of Families and Persons in the United States: 1983.* Current Population Reports, Series P-60, No. 145. Washington, D.C.: Government Printing Office.
van den Berghe, Pierre L.
  1967   *Race and Racism: A Comparative Perspective.* New York: John Wiley & Sons.
  1979   *Human Family Systems: An Evolutionary View.* New York: Elsevier.
  1981   *The Ethnic Phenomenon.* New York: Elsevier.
van den Berghe, Pierre L., and Peter Frost
  1986   "Skin Color Preference, Sexual Dimorphism and Sexual Selection: A Case of Gene Culture Co-evolution?" *Ethnic and Racial Studies,* 9(1):87–113.
Wallerstein, Immanuel
  1974   *The Modern World-System: Capitalist Agriculture and the Origins of the European World-Economy in the Sixteenth Century.* New York: Academic Press.
  1979   *The Capitalist World-Economy.* Cambridge: Cambridge University Press.
Wenger, Morton G.
  1980   "State Responses to Afro-American Rebellion: Internal Neo-colonialism and the Rise of a New Black Petite Bourgeoisie," *The Insurgent Sociologist,* 10(2):61–72.
Wilhelm, Sidney M.
  1971   *Who Needs the Negro?* Garden City, N.J: Doubleday, Anchor Books.
  1983   *Black in a White America.* Cambridge, Mass.: Schenkman.
Wilson, William Julius
  1978   *The Declining Significance of Race.* 2d ed. Chicago: University of Chicago Press.

Wolf, Eric
  1984   *Europe and the People Without History.* Berkeley: University of California
        Press.
Wright, Erik Olin
  1978   *Class, Crisis and the State.* London: New Left Books.
Wrong, Dennis
  1959   "The Functional Theory of Stratification: Some Neglected Considera-
        tions," *American Sociological Review,* 24(6):772–782.
Yin Ming
  1977   *United and Equal: Progress Among China's Minority Nationalities.* Peking
        (Beijing): Foreign Language Press.
Young, Crawford
  1983   "Comparative Claims to Political Sovereignty: Biafra, Katanga, Eri-
        trea," in Donald Rothchild and Victor A. Olorunsola, eds., *State vs. Ethnic
        Claims: African Policy Dilemmas.* Boulder, Co: Westview Press.

Index

About the Author

RICHARD H. THOMPSON is associate professor of anthropology at James Madison University. He has conducted fieldwork among Chinese immigrants in Toronto, Canada, which resulted in his book, *Toronto's Chinatown: The Changing Social Organization of an Ethnic Community* (1989). He has also done research in the People's Republic of China and among coal miners in southwestern Virginia. He has published articles on topics dealing with race and ethnic relations, ethics in fieldwork, class analysis, and Appalachia in journals such as *Ethnicity, Dialectical Anthropology,* and *Appalachian Journal.* He lives with his wife and two sons in Harrisonburg, Virginia.